POULIN

MAIN STR.

POST OFFICE

Speculator Mine, Butte, Montana

THE GIBRALTAR

Socialism and Labor
in Butte, Montana,
1895-1920

by Jerry W. Calvert

Montana Historical Society Press, Helena • 1988

The Montana Historical Society Press, Helena 59620

Composed by Arrow Graphics and Typography in Janson. Printed by Publishers Press.
Endpaper views are part of a tinted postcard, ca. 1914, MHS Photograph Archives. Cover
and book design by Marianne Keddington.

Library of Congress Cataloging-in-Publication Data

Calvert, Jerry W., 1942-
    The Gibraltar: socialism and labor in Butte, Montana, 1895-1920 / by Jerry W.
Calvert.
        p.   cm.
    Bibliography: p.
    Includes index.
    ISBN 0-917298-14-4
    1. Socialist parties—Montana—Butte—History. 2. Labor and laboring classes—
Montana—Butte—Political activity—History. 3. Trade-unions—Copper miners—
Montana—Butte—History. I. Title.
HX92.B95C36 1988
322′.2′0978668-dc19   88-1629
                                                                              CIP

Contents

Preface

The catalyst for this examination of the working-class insurgency in the mining city of Butte came from a descriptive reference in James Weinstein's *The Decline of Socialism in America*. In his re-examination of the place of the Socialist Party in American political life, Professor Weinstein noted that Butte, Montana, had elected a Socialist mayor in 1911. This was surprising to me, for at the time I knew relatively little of the history of socialism in the United States. I wanted to find out more. My subsequent research revealed an astonishingly rich, dramatic, and largely ignored part of the state's history.

Butte was one of the largest cities ever governed by members of the Socialist Party, and that fact was only one aspect of several attempts by the workers in Butte and in the state to establish themselves as an independent force in Montana politics. This protracted rebellion opposed domination of the state by corporate power and represented a yearning for an alternative cooperative and democratic community. This book attempts to reveal for the first time the richness and power of an indigenous radical heritage which, once understood, may compel a serious re-examination of the American past so that we can better comprehend the present political environment and the limited choices it offers.

In this project, I have had the eager and willing assistance of many others who have given freely of their time and intellect over the past ten years. I want to thank all those who have helped along the way. I hope I don't forget anyone.

With funding provided by a grant from the American Council of Learned Societies, I was able to take time off to write the first draft of the book. In this regard, I would like to acknowledge the support given to my proposal by my three referees—Melvin Dubofsky, Garin Burbank, and the late Herbert Gutman. There can be no doubt that their positive assessment of my project contributed to the Society's response to my grant request. Helpful also was a modest grant from Montana State University, which funded the statistical analysis in the study.

Butte residents Chris Daley, Bill Walker, Brian Shovers, Al Hooper, and the late Terry McGlynn were ready to assist me in finding obscure documents, newspapers, and photographs. Special thanks also to Alice Finnegan of Anaconda, whose commitment and professionalism made visits to the smelter city always a pleasurable experience. Finally, I want to mention the late Fred Thompson, the IWW's "official historian," who told me of his experiences in Butte and gave me the story about the passing of Butte's Wobbly poet Daniel "Dublin Dan" Liston.

Librarians are of enormous help to researchers. First, thanks to Dale Johnson of the University of Montana Special Collections who provided me with perhaps the only surviving copy of *The Truth About Butte*, written by Wobbly George Tompkins in 1917. Montana State University librarians Kay Carey and Minnie Paugh were tireless in assisting me in obtaining the documents I needed, and I am pleased that they will finally be able to see that all the time they put in has paid off. Similarly, I spent many days in the Montana Historical Society Archives and would like to thank Brian Cockhill and the entire staff for their assistance in helping me use effectively their tremendous collection of archival materials.

Documents relevant to the history of labor in Montana are stored throughout the country. I want to take my hat off to all those people in all those places who supplied me with the vital information that made this project possible. The Census History Staff of the U.S. Bureau of the Census, the National Archives and Records Service, the Library of Congress, the Perkins Library at Duke University, the library at California State University-Fullerton, the Western Historical Collections Library at the University of Colorado, and the State Historical Society Library of Wisconsin all contain important material concerning the history of labor radicalism in Montana, and the staff people in all of them were most helpful in assisting me in the quest for information.

In conclusion, I want to applaud my editors, Marianne Keddington and Bill Lang, for their care and consideration, their sensitivity and professionalism in helping to prepare the manuscript. Special thanks and a big hug to people who are close to me for their material assistance and emotional support. Mary Calvert, my stepmother, typed the finished draft of the manuscript that was sent out to publishers. Adele Pittendrigh, my colleague in the MSU Department of English, read the manuscript and provided helpful comments. Barbara R. Honeyman, my partner and best friend, also read the manuscript and gave me continual encouragement and spiritual reinforcement throughout the editing phase. Thank you one and all. Though they are no longer here among us, I would like to dedicate this book to the memory of my parents, Anne Belle Cornelius (1920-1972) and George A. Calvert (1916-1986), to let the healing begin.

THE
GIBRALTAR

In no other state in the union is the tyrannic power of the plutocratic masters of bread more evident or its oppression more evident than in the state of Montana.

— 1912 platform, Socialist Party of Montana

1 ‖ *The City and the Rebels*

Marxists called it the "class struggle," and it was fought in hundreds of cities and towns across the United States at the turn of the century. Butte, Montana, was such a city, and the conflict there was overt, protracted, and sometimes violent. On one side was the economic and political power of concentrated capital embodied in a giant mining corporation. On the other stood a polyglot collection of rebels who fiercely challenged that power, threatening the very foundation of an entrenched socio-economic order.

In 1910, approximately sixty thousand people lived in Butte and Silver Bow County.[1] The largest city in Montana, Butte was the center of commercial and financial power in the state. It had risen to such heights because of one resource — copper. Begun in the 1860s as a typical placer boom camp and rejuvenated during the 1870s as a silver town with an uncertain future, Butte was transformed during the 1880s by the discovery and subsequent exploitation of its vast copper wealth.[2]

Copper made Butte "the richest hill on earth," and by the turn of the century the Butte mining district was the world's leading producer of the red metal. Between 1895 and 1916, the Butte mines produced 5.4 billion pounds of copper, accounting for 31 per cent of all copper mined in the United States during that period.[3] Montana called itself "The Treasure State," and most of the "treasure" was in Butte.

The copper mines attracted large numbers of workers, making Butte a uniquely cosmopolitan city, an enclave of urban culture and ethnic diversity in an essentially rural, agricultural state. In 1910, one-third of the city's population were immigrants; an additional third were first-generation Americans. Dominating the group were those who had emigrated from Ireland or were of Irish descent, but representatives of virtually every nationality could be found in the mining city. Among the most numerous ethnic colonies were emigrants from Cornwall, England, and Germans, Scandinavians, Italians, and South Slavic peoples from the Balkans. There was also a significant number of black Americans and Chinese.[4]

3

Butte was the quintessential worker city. In 1910, approximately 11,400 men worked in manual occupations in the city and county, accounting for slightly less than two-thirds of all employment in Butte. Those engaged in mining were by far the largest working-class element. Two out of every three manual laborers worked in the mining and smelting of the copper ore—and most of them belonged to a union.[5]

Butte called itself the "Gibraltar" of labor unionism in the United States, and for good reason. Virtually every trade was unionized, and all of them had closed shops. There were about fifty different local unions: one for every construction trade, a union for brewers and another for beer wagon drivers, one for blacksmiths and another for horseshoers. There were also a hackmen's union and a teamsters' union, the Musicians' Protective Union, the Theatrical Stage Employees' Union, and the Theatrical Ushers' Union. Dominating the unions in size, prestige, and political clout were the local affiliates of the Western Federation of Miners: the Butte Miners' Union No. 1, the Mill and Smeltermen's Union No. 74, and the Butte Engineers' Union No. 83. Together, these three WFM locals accounted for one-third of all union men in the Butte district. All of the unions were confederated under the umbrella of the Silver Bow Trades and Labor Assembly.[6]

Both a union and a company town, Butte was also a starkly beautiful monument to the industrial age. Set in a high mountain valley nearly six thousand feet above sea level and surrounded by mountains topped with snow for at least half of the year, Butte resembled what one observer called a "miniature Pittsburgh," where

> great shafts of opalescent fire shoot momentarily skyward from slag-heaps that receive the fiery discard of the converters. The hill, just north of the city, out of which has been taken over a billion-and-a-half of actual wealth, is at night like a great dome studded with glittering, electric stars, under whose sharp glare thousands of flitting figures work as under the noonday sun.[7]

The intense energy of the city was applauded by novelist Gertrude Atherton:

> She is alive to her fingertips. Her streets, her fine shops, her hotels, her great office buildings, are always swarming and animated. At no time, not even in the devitalized hours that precede the dawn, does she sink into that peace which even a metropolis welcomes. She has the jubilant expression of one who coins the very air, the thin, sparkling, nervous air, into shining dollars and confident in the inexhaustible riches beneath her feet, knows she shall go on coining them forever.[8]

But lying just beneath the surface, just below the self-satisfied boasting confidence, was the city's dark, grim interior. Local government in Butte was corrupt and inefficient. Workers and working-class families lived in overcrowded, poorly ventilated housing without adequate sanitation. Most of the city's streets were unpaved, and sidewalks were almost nonexistent. One radical trade unionist who visited the city in 1908 reported that Butte was

> just about as dirty and disagreeable a place as the average one-horse mining camp. There are some buildings of skyscraper dimensions, and some of the parasites have quite elaborate residences, but the average wage slave's home

is a miserable, dingy, dirty board shack and the main feature is the numerous boarding and lodging houses, dirty, crowded, and unsanitary. The sky-line is dominated by the gaunt "gallows-frames" and the unsightly change rooms, waste dumps, and railroad tracks of the various mines. The business center for a few blocks each way is paved with rough stone, but the pavement is usually covered one to six inches deep under an accumulation of dust, soot, and garbage. . . . Excepting a half dozen streets in the business center, there are no sewers anywhere and everyone throws their slops, garbage, or waste of any kind out of the front of, or behind the houses.[9]

Sensitive observers were quick to see that Butte was, in fact, two cities. The first was above ground in all its dashing and dirty splendor. The second city, infinitely more dangerous, lay beneath. Every day in three shifts, thousands of men labored in the mines to bring forth copper ore. In this city of darkness, production often proceeded at a breakneck pace with little regard for the miners' health and safety. Death could come suddenly to miners in the fall of rock, a premature blast of dynamite, or a tumble down a shaft. Or it might come slowly and silently in the form of debilitating and ultimately fatal lung disease.

Dozens of men died each year in accidents in Butte's mines. In 1910, for example, fifty miners were killed, an average of 4.2 fatalities per month. In their deaths was an uncommon human solidarity, for miners were killed without regard to race, religion, nationality, or political affiliation. Among the 1910 victims were Shea and Sweeny, Frolio and Toma, Melville and Martin, Belia, Radovich, Kaliva, Maki, and Skari.[10]

Lucky miners might escape serious injury or death, but there was one thing they could not escape—the rock dust generated by blasting and drilling. The dust was a killer. Containing high amounts of silica, the dust scarred the miners' lungs and caused a most frightening lung disease—silicosis, or miners' consumption. The symptoms of damage were a hacking cough, impaired breathing, and general physical weakness. Left untreated—and the only treatment was to leave the mines—miners' consumption often led to pneumonia and tuberculosis.[11]

In addition to the traditional demands for higher wages and shorter hours, the hazards of working in the mines were often the initial incentive for workers to form unions in the West. The Butte Miners' Union, founded in 1878 to press for a raise in miners' wages, also became a way for workers to set up a sick and death benefit fund for themselves and their families. Each member contributed a small amount each month to a benefit fund established by the union, which entitled him to a one hundred dollar accident benefit and a one hundred dollar funeral benefit if he was killed on the job. Given the hazardous nature of mining, the union's financial responsibilities were substantial. Between 1907 and 1913, the Butte Miners' Union paid out $288,018 in accident and sick benefits, a mean outlay of $57,603 per annum; $60,790 was expended for funerals during the same period.[12] Miners could expect at least some help from their union; they could expect nothing from their employers. Mining companies provided no insurance nor did they contribute to the union benefit fund.

The chances were good that victims of mine accidents were employees of one company. Butte was dominated by a single corporation: the Anaconda Copper Mining Company. Founded in the 1880s by pioneering mining man Marcus Daly, the ACM Company acquired smaller companies, until by the turn of the century the Company dominated Montana's economic and political life. In Butte, the Company employed 75 to 80 per cent of the men working in the district's mines and smelters. Through its other operations—a smelter in nearby Anaconda, a refinery in Great Falls, coal mines, and extensive timber holdings—the ACM Company was the largest employer in the state.[13]

The economic power of this corporate behemoth gave it enormous political influence in the city and the state, and the Company's chieftains were not bashful about using it. Forming an interlocking alliance with other large business interests, the ACM Company's role in Montana has been characterized as "a giant faction in a small commonwealth."[14] This "giant faction" and its corporate allies tried to control the state's major parties and courted and corrupted emerging labor leaders. In a word, the Company achieved a well-deserved reputation for ruthlessness. The Company's presumed power defined an essential if not the fundamental division in the body politic between those who acquiesced, accepted, tolerated, or favored the corporation's preeminence in the community's affairs and those who did not.

It was in this milieu—worker city and company-dominated town—that a protracted working-class rebellion was born. The rebellion was fueled in part by the workers' hostility toward industrial capital—particularly as personified by the Anaconda Copper Mining Company—and by a positive, though vaguely drawn, vision of an alternative future. That future, which would be realized when industrial capitalism had run its course, was often called the "Cooperative Commonwealth"—a socialist society.

In the drama of the struggle for a better future and against potential corporate domination, the players ranged from avowed revolutionaries to radical reformers. They may have disagreed about the way the ACM and its allies should be brought to their knees and about the precise nature of the new society they hoped to achieve, but they all agreed on one thing: Present conditions were intolerable. The system was generating great wealth for the unworthy few and increasing poverty and misery for those who did the actual work.

For those who called themselves socialists the case for the alternative was plain enough. It was a bad system that allowed a few to "own" the means of production and amass the wealth that the many had created. It was right that those who worked and produced the wealth should own the means of production. It was right that those who worked should decide economic policy through the instruments of democratic government and manage the means of production for the maximum benefit of the greatest number of people. At the turn of the century, the crusade for revolutionary change was aptly expressed by a locomotive fireman who had become a radical trade unionist and presidential candidate of the Socialist Party of America. Perhaps the most charismatic and popular leader ever produced by the American radical tradition, Eugene V. Debs spoke in Butte many times. In his first presidential campaign in 1900, Debs urged:

> The working class must get rid of the whole brood of masters and exploiters,
> and put themselves in possession and control of the means of production,

that they may have steady employment without consulting a capitalist employer, large or small, and that they may get the wealth that labor produces, all of it, and enjoy with their families the fruits of their industry in comfortable and happy homes, abundant and wholesome food, proper clothing and all the things necessary for "life, liberty and the pursuit of happiness."[15]

A contemporary of Debs, William D. "Big Bill" Haywood, was also well known in the mining city. This former miner and officer in the Western Federation of Miners had been shaped by his experiences in the often bitter and violent conflicts between labor and capital in western metal mining. Pushed to the left by experience and his own personality, Haywood shifted his allegiance in 1908 from the WFM to the revolutionary union, the Industrial Workers of the World, and eventually became its most celebrated and effective leader. Haywood had a vision. In 1914, he told the U.S. Commission on Industrial Relations:

> Do you know the results we are hoping for? We hope to see the day when no child will labor. We hope to see the day when all men will be able to work. . . . We want to see the day when every old man and every old woman will have the assurance of at least dying in peace. Now, you have not got anything like that today. . . . I have an idea that we can have a better society than we have got; and I have another idea that we cannot have a much worse one than it is at present.[16]

Frank Mabie, the state organizer for the Socialist Party of Montana, had similar goals. He recalled a conversation he had had in 1912 with the wife of a coal miner:

> We talked of the future, when the working class shall have come into its own and the child of the coal miner will have as good a chance in life as the child of the mine owner . . . when woman will be economically free and stand beside man, his companion and equal, when science shall have solved the problem of heat and power and grass grows over the mining dump and the skies are blue. And as we talked and pictured the glorious future, the future that her children would enjoy, the look of despair on her face gave place to one of hope that showed a faith in relief this side of the pearly gates.[17]

This optimism gave birth to a multifaceted movement for fundamental social change. The revolutionaries were found in both the Socialist Party and the IWW, working-class organizations whose ultimate goals were the destruction of the capitalist system and the creation of a cooperative society that would be managed by the workers. But the two groups differed about the appropriate means for achieving those ends. The Socialists advocated working-class "political action" to achieve emancipation; the Wobblies, as IWW members were called, believed that only "direct action" by the workers would bring on the destruction of capitalism and create the cooperative commonwealth. The distinctions between "political action" and "direct action" generated the most heated debates among radical opponents of the social order and deeply colored the evolution of the working-class insurgency that developed in Butte.

Founded as the Social Democratic Party in 1898, the Socialist Party of America saw itself as the builder of a majority coalition of all exploited groups, a coalition in which workers would be the leading element and constitute the largest bloc. This emerging coalition would use its collective "power of the ballot" to overthrow capitalism by peaceful means and begin to construct a socialist society.[18]

Most Socialists counseled that achieving a cooperative commonwealth would take time. It might take years, even decades, before the party was politically strong enough to win control of the national government and bring forth socialism through legislative action. Two distinct but interrelated elements comprised the Socialist Party program: a statement of the party's ultimate revolutionary goals and a list of the reforms that the party was prepared to support and work for in the present.[19] The former appealed to the committed and idealistic; the latter attracted a larger constituency that was seeking immediate improvement in the quality of life. Typical of the Socialist Party's enunciation of its ultimate revolutionary aims was the appeal made in the 1902 state platform of the Socialist Party of Montana, which urged workers

> to vote with the party of their class at all elections until they control the machinery of government, abolish industrial classes in society, terminate forever the class struggle, and inaugurate the cooperative commonwealth based upon this fundamental principle of justice: to each worker the full produce of his labor.[20]

But Socialists in Montana and elsewhere were also willing to support and work for simple reform. These "immediate demands" were almost always appended to national, state, and local party platforms, following the general statement of the party's revolutionary goals. The reforms included proposals designed to improve workers' lives, the public ownership of utilities, and support for the expansion of democratic majority rule. The 1908 platform of Montana's Socialists, for example, called for public works jobs for the unemployed, strict enforcement of the state's eight-hour-day law, and enactment of a workmen's compensation law. Montana's Socialists also demanded a progressive tax on all "capitalist property"; the creation of public hospitals in every county, which would be open to everyone regardless of ability to pay; and the expansion of free public educational opportunity for both children and adults. The 1908 platform also supported the direct election of U.S. senators; the initiative, the referendum, and the recall election; and the abolition of all laws that denied women "economic and political equality."[21]

The Socialist Party believed that some measure of relief, some substantive improvement in the conditions of working-class life could be achieved within the existing capitalist system. To get relief, the party urged workers to vote for the Socialist ticket. The party reasoned that if Socialists were elected they would invariably "make good" in public office, and their performance as the political representatives of the working class would serve as a catalyst for further expansion of the party's base of support.[22] Consequently, the Socialists in Butte and elsewhere eagerly entered local election campaigns. For the Socialists, "political action" meant using the electoral process as the primary means for achieving the liberation of the workers by gradually gaining control of the instrumentalities of government.

In the Socialist scenario for radical social change, the party had to have the active support of labor unions. Socialists who were union members were urged to seek office in their local unions and to use their influence in persuading the rank and file to vote the Socialist ticket.[23] But the Socialist Party also operated in an environment in which labor unions effectively represented only a small minority of the labor force, primarily skilled craftworkers. The majority of workers in semiskilled and unskilled occupations remained unorganized and outside the international unions of the American Federation of Labor.

Since its founding in 1886, the AFL had evolved into the only significant national labor union federation in the country. Under the dynamic leadership of Samuel Gompers, the AFL had survived and prospered in an era of intense business hostility toward labor unionism. The union had carved out a niche, and Gompers and his lieutenants were not about to engage in any activity that might threaten its tenuous legitimacy. As a result, the AFL kept its distance from the Socialist Party and made no serious efforts to organize the unorganized, as the Socialists had repeatedly urged it to do.[24]

The Socialists also asked the AFL to consider a more "effective" form of labor union organization—industrial unionism. The Socialists argued that organizing the workers according to craft skill, as the AFL did, unnecessarily divided the workers and often produced conflict between unions in the same industry and even within the same plant. This was especially the case during a strike. One union might strike, but others within the same industry and plant might not follow. This was one way, the Socialists argued, that strikes were often lost. The Socialists believed that it was imperative that workers be represented by all-inclusive industrial unions, with every worker belonging to one industrial union and all the unions in the same industry joined in one confederation. This was the only way workers could present a united front to managers and employers.[25]

The Socialists also supported the industrial union idea, because they believed that the industrial form of union organization would tend to facilitate the development of working-class consciousness. Debs predicted in 1904: "The workers once united in one great industrial union will vote a united working class ticket."[26] In short, the expansion of labor unionism, especially industrial unionism, into unorganized industries was critically important in preparing the way for the Socialist political advance. But the AFL ignored the advice of the Socialist industrial union advocates; with the exception of the United Mine Workers of America, there were no large industrial union affiliates within the AFL.

The Socialists often talked about the "two-armed" working-class movement: the party expressed the class interests of workers in the political arena; the labor unions defended the economic interests of workers in their battles with employers. But at the national level, Gompers's opposition prevented any such alliance between the party and the AFL unions.[27]

Many Socialists were not enamored with the party's attempts to influence the AFL. This was especially the case in the Rocky Mountain West, where the AFL had a relatively weak organizational presence and where the tradition of militant and politically active industrial unionism was particularly strong. These westerners loathed the AFL's conservatism and doubted that it could be reformed from within.[28] This impatience and frustration helped form the Industrial Workers of the World as a revolutionary alternative. Founded in Chicago in 1905 by a disparate collection of Socialists and radical trade unionists, the IWW was to be the industrial union that was committed to the overthrow of the capitalist system by a working-class revolution.[29]

Socialists like Eugene Debs hoped that the infant revolutionary union would grow and forge a close alliance with the Socialist Party. Weak and debilitated by serious factionalism and under constant attack from the AFL, however, the IWW almost ceased to exist within a year of its founding. Emerging from that traumatic beginning, the IWW began to articulate a revolutionary philosophy that was uniquely its own. The union was committed to organizing the unorganized, but many of those whom it sought to represent—immigrants, women, blacks, children—could not vote. For them, only a militant industrial unionism could improve the quality of their lives. Therefore, the Wobblies reasoned, the emancipation of the working class required more than working-class political action; it also required "direct action."

"Direct action" encompassed any activity that workers used to better their condition in the workplace, including organizing a local union, strikes, boycotts, and sabotage. The AFL also engaged in direct action, but it had no intention of overthrowing the capitalist system. The Wobblies fully intended to do so. The IWW argued that when workers used direct action to advance their own interests, they were educating themselves in the class struggle. Equally important, the use of direct action would make the workers fully conscious of their power and strength and would psychologically prepare them for the eventual seizure of the means of production.[30]

The IWW's scenario for revolutionary change became something that was dramatically different from that designed by the Socialist Party. Many Wobblies acknowledged that workers should participate in the electoral process, because the local election of pro-working-class officials would at least minimize the use of police force to break strikes.[31] But the Wobblies also viewed government as merely an instrument of capitalist power. Capitalists were the ruling class because they owned and controlled the means of production. Without that power they were nothing. Therefore, argued the IWW, why should the workers take control of the government to gain the means of production? The direct route, the union suggested, was for the workers to simply seize the means of production through a revolutionary general strike.[32]

The IWW's alternative to government—even Socialist government—was a decentralized, cooperative society in which the industrial unions would be the principal administrative components. The structure of the IWW, a decentralized confederation of industrial unions, was the microcosm of a workers' republic. As the IWW was fond of saying, a "new society" was being formed "within the shell of the old."[33]

It was the IWW and the Socialist Party that represented the revolutionary wing of Butte's working-class movement. The mining city was the center of Socialist Party strength in Montana. Local Butte, with approximately five hundred members organized in two branches in 1912-1913, comprised approximately one-quarter of the party's state-wide membership. It was in Butte in 1911 that the people elected Socialist Mayor Louis Duncan, making Butte one of the largest American cities ever governed by Socialists. In Butte, the Socialists' faith in political action was tried, sorely tested, and ultimately found wanting.

The Socialists' faith would also be questioned and tested by the IWW, for the Wobblies were a troublesome presence in the mining city. Uncompromisingly and vocally hostile to capitalist enterprise and all its works, the Wobblies were also antagonistic toward political reform—even Socialist-leaning reforms—and any form of labor unionism save their own. The Wobblies' critique of political action and "pure and simple" trade unionism was incisive and telling. But most importantly, they believed that Butte's reputation as a union "Gibraltar" was more myth than reality. The reputation of the huge Butte Miners' Union was the rock upon which that image was built, and the BMU was reportedly corrupt and certainly impotent as a representative of the miners' interests.

Fueled by the revolutionary industrial union idea, the IWW and those sympathetic to its philosophy attempted to create a new and avowedly militant form of miners' unionism, which through sheer militancy and class solidarity would force employers to meet the miners' demands for better wages and working conditions. The IWW would try again and again in Butte to create that kind of unionism. They would also fail, crushed by employer hostility and government repression.

The working-class insurgency that dominated the city from 1895 to 1920 was more than the work of self-acknowledged revolutionaries. There were also radical reformers who articulated many of the immediate demands that the Socialists championed. Like both the Socialists and the Wobblies, they were vocally hostile to corporate capital, especially the Anaconda Copper Mining Company and its business allies. They also were committed to making a better world for the working class. But these activists were reformers, not revolutionaries. They had no well-defined and clearly articulated idea of an alternative future. For them, winning immediate demands for the working class was not a step toward something else. The demands were an end in themselves.

One radical reform organization was the People's Party, the Populists. Explicitly pro-working class in its political program, the People's Party of Montana was the first important involvement of workers in third-party politics. The Populists, who advocated expanding the money supply through the "free coinage" of silver, were more than a one-issue party offering a simplistic panacea for the economic benefit of certain classes. In Montana, Populists also stood for extensive public ownership of the means of production, immediate improvements in working conditions, and the expansion of democracy through such electoral devices as the initiative and the referendum.[34] When the Populist Party faded, many of its supporters found a home in the Socialist Party.

The Nonpartisan League also contributed to the mining city's working-class insurgency. Founded in North Dakota in 1915 to represent the interests of the state's farmers against bankers, elevator operators, and railroads, the NPL found its way into Montana and Butte just as the Socialist Party was dying after years of political frustration, no closer to the cooperative commonwealth than when it began.

The NPL idea was simple and compelling. Ideologically, the League self-consciously avoided articulating misty images of a noncapitalist society. The NPL's goal was to win the immediate economic demands of the exploited and to expand the political power of farmers and workers. In rural Montana, the NPL stood for tax reform and easy credit for farmers; in the cities, it carried the demands of organized labor.

Unlike the Socialists and the Populists, the Nonpartisan League was not a third party; it was a self-conscious ideological faction that worked within the parameters of the two-party system. Rather than field its own slate of candidates, the NPL sought to capture one of the major parties by running its own candidates in the party primary. By 1912, the party primary election, championed by moderate reformers such as

Senator Robert LaFollette of Wisconsin, had replaced the party caucus and convention as the means used to nominate major party candidates in almost all of the states. Rather than having to attend a party meeting in which voters publicly made their preferences known, citizens could cast secret ballots for the candidates of their choice. The adoption of the direct primary opened up the process so that a self-conscious group like the NPL could capture a major party simply by having its candidates win the party's nominations.

Taking full advantage of the direct primary, the NPL captured control of the North Dakota Republican Party in the 1916 primary election and then saw its candidates elected in the November general election.[35] Having elected their man as governor and won majority control of the lower house of the state legislature, the NPL was in a solid position to begin to legislate into being its immediate demands.

Radicals in Montana quickly identified the methods of the infant Nonpartisan League as the way to break out of the political marginality to which third parties are traditionally assigned. In Butte, many former Socialists and radical trade unionists formed a Nonpartisan group and effectively captured control of the local Democratic Party in 1919-1920. Under the dynamic leadership of William F. Dunne, the forces of organized labor joined with the more militant farmers to create a state-wide farmer-labor coalition in 1920. Formed out of an alliance of the rural-based Nonpartisan League of Montana and the Montana Labor League, the coalition won control of the state Democratic Party in the June 1920 primary. With a reform-minded Butte attorney, Burton K. Wheeler, as their gubernatorial candidate, the coalition's slate of farmer-labor candidates almost captured control of the state government in the general election, posing the most serious threat to Montana's established economic and political order during the insurgent period.

Historians of this period have focused on the titanic fights among Montana's copper kings for economic and political mastery, the corrupting influence of corporate money in the state's politics, and the rise of the Anaconda Copper Mining Company. In all of these dramas that so colored and shaped Butte's politics and its idea of itself, the workers and their leaders have often been cast as bit players. Consequently, the lives and the actions of the men and women associated with the Populists, Socialists, Wobblies, and Nonpartisan League have remained largely a part of the hidden history of Montana. But these were the people who offered the most determined resistance and articulated the most sophisticated critique of the emerging corporate order that was forging a copper collar around Butte and the state of Montana. They speak to us through the words of struggling and short-lived labor newspapers; they argue and dream in the surviving records of labor unions and political organizations; they tell us about their lives in investigations and statistical records; and they become fully human in the poems and songs they wrote.

To look at the lives and actions of Butte's insurgents is to come to appreciate their idealism, their dedication, and their self-sacrifice. They faced not only the predictable hostility of the powerful few but also the ignorance and the doubting of those they desperately tried to convert. Again and again, they found that the solidarity of labor in economics and politics was a wonderful slogan but that it was hard to achieve and sustain in political organizing. They also discovered that Socialist Party platforms did not easily translate into a practical guide for governing.

Finally, the lives and actions of Butte's insurgents demonstrate that the labels "revolutionary" and "radical reformer" are constructions of intellectual convenience, a shorthand that allows us to bring order and understanding to a complex reality. But the labels do not identify mutually exclusive ways of acting and thinking, for individuals moved from one extreme to the other depending on the time, the circumstances, and the issues and opportunities confronting them. Socialists and Wobblies preached revolution, but they also wanted to get things done, so they would often temporarily let go of the revolutionary dream to work for immediate improvements in the awful present. Radical reformers might only talk about immediate improvements, but some dreamed about the possibilities of a radically different future. This story is not about the conflict of political ideas as much as it is about people who had ideas and who acted to bring those ideas into effect.

The [Butte] city government during those troublous times was first in the hands of one corporation magnate and then in the hands of the other. Much money was spent to gain control.

—*Montana News*,
March 21, 1907

2 ‖ *The Birth of the Insurgent Era*

In the decade and a half after Montana was granted statehood in 1889, state politics was largely defined by the men who waged the "War of the Copper Kings." Butte's copper kings, whose deeds and exploits have long occupied center stage in Montana historiography, were a handful of enterprising men who had the wit to see the vast potential for accumulating personal wealth from Butte's rich copper resource and who took full advantage of the opportunity. These men also acquired a penchant for heavy-handed intervention in state and local politics as a way to either advance their social status or protect themselves from the regulation of business and labor.

The war of the copper capitalists took place in three phases.[1] In all three phases the Anaconda Copper Mining Company was under attack. In the first phase, the assault was led by copper tycoon William A. Clark. In his second battle with the "Copper Trust," Clark acquired an ally, Frederick A. Heinze, in the continuing warfare. The war ended with the third round, in which Clark made peace with the Company and Heinze was left to fight on alone.

The first battle pitted pioneer owners-entrepreneurs William Andrews Clark and Marcus Daly in fierce combat over who would rule the roost in Montana. Throughout the 1890s, the so-called Clark-Daly feud was a raw and open fight between two wealthy and ambitious men. Clark wanted to become a United States senator, but Daly used his influence to block Clark's bid for the seat during the 1893 legislative session. Clark got his revenge the next year. Daly wanted Anaconda, the smelter city he had built to service his mines in nearby Butte, to become Montana's permanent capital. In the November 1894 general election, the choice between Anaconda and Helena (the temporary state capital) fell to the people in a referendum. Clark championed the Helena cause, and he and Daly spent enormous sums of money to influence the outcome; one estimate placed the total at $2.9 million, or $56 for each vote cast. Helena won by a narrow margin in that corrupt and nasty plebiscite.

In 1899, the Montana legislature was once more obliged to elect a U.S. senator. By all accounts, Clark was ready, money in hand, eager to persuade a majority of legislators to vote for him. Clark bribed freely and well, and the state legislators gave him the seat he had purchased. But Daly would not let go; he used what influence he had to successfully persuade the U.S. Senate that it should refuse to seat Clark. The spectacle of a successfully bought state legislature earned Montana a national reputation as a playground of political corruption.

Almost lost sight of in the war of the titans was the growth of the Montana labor movement as an independent political force—a growth helped along in part by Clark and Daly. In seeking their political goals, both capitalists had courted the labor vote by being friendly toward labor unions and by paying their employees relatively good wages. Further, the immediate economic interests of the workers and their employers temporarily coincided in the early 1890s. The enterprise wanted maximum profit, and the workers wanted jobs with good pay. Thus, both groups avidly supported the free coinage of silver, which meant greater federal government purchases of the metal and a subsidy to maintain corporate profit and wage levels in metal mining.[2]

The primary political vehicle in the state for the "free silver" cause was the People's Party of Montana. As a national movement, Populism was essentially a broad-based agrarian protest; but in Montana, Populism was primarily an urban, working-class phenomenon. Because of its constituency, the People's Party of Montana advocated such reforms as a state law guaranteeing an eight-hour day, the abolition of child labor, and laws to protect the health and safety of workers.[3]

As an electoral force, however, Populism was short-lived. Founded in Butte in 1892, the People's Party elected only a small number of their candidates to the state legislature in that year and in the following two general elections. The Populists enjoyed their greatest success in the 1896 election. But the success was a dubious one, for it had been fostered by fusion with the Democrats to support the presidential candidacy of William Jennings Bryan, the champion of free silver. Bryan lost to Republican William McKinley, and with his defeat Populism as an independent political force went into a steep decline.

Short as it was, the Populist interlude signaled the entry of the working class into Montana politics as an independent political force. It was also during this period that the labor movement was consolidated and labor unionism spread. Union activists closely allied with the People's Party pushed for a state federation of labor unions to advance the workers' economic and political interests, with the *Butte Bystander*, a labor weekly, beating the drum. The party was joined in 1894 by the Populist-inspired Butte Industrial Conference and in the following year by the State Trades and Labor Assembly, which union activists had formed in Helena.[4] Because the Butte Industrial Conference and the Helena organization stood for similar principles, they agreed to merge into one organization. In November 1895, the deed was done at a convention in Anaconda, and the Montana Federation of Labor was born.[5]

Initially calling itself the Montana State Trades and Labor Council (it became the Montana Federation of Labor in 1903), the MSTLC evinced its close ties with the People's Party by adopting virtually the entire party platform in its statement of principles. The federation went even further by endorsing planks that were explicitly socialist in nature, calling for public ownership of municipal utilities, mines, mills, smelters, and all means of transportation and communication.[6]

Another indication of the federation's radicalism was its hostility toward the American Federation of Labor. To these Montana union men, the AFL was politically conservative and narrowly protectionist in its policy of only organizing and representing skilled craftworkers. The Montana federation turned its back on the AFL and in 1898 joined hands with the Western Federation of Miners in founding a new federation, the Western Labor Union. The WLU pledged that its affiliated unions would be committed to organizing all workers regardless of craft skill, race, gender, or ethnic origin. Dan McDonald, a Butte iron molder and vice-president of the MSTLC, led the new union, which was the organizational precursor of the IWW in the state.[7]

Montana labor unionists who wanted workers to be an independent force in state politics faced a dilemma at the turn of the century. The People's Party no longer had any power or influence, and some organization was needed to carry the workers' banner. The MSTLC responded by voting in its August 1900 convention to establish the Labor Party. The party's platform echoed the planks previously carried by the Populists, but the Labor Party broke ranks by immediately leaping into fusion with the Democrats in the November election, subverting its image as an independent party.[8]

Other labor unionists had already gone further. In May 1899, a dozen men met in a cafe on East Park Street in Butte and founded the state's first local chapter of the Social Democratic Party of America. Most of the founding members of what would become the Socialist Party of Montana in 1902 were former Populists. Among the twelve were three former Populist state representatives—Martin Elliott, Paddy McMahon, and Malcolm G. O'Malley—who would play important roles in the formative years of the Socialist movement in Montana. Also present were Frank Curran and Henry J. Davis, both of whom would be elected to the Butte city council in 1911.[9]

The Socialist movement began with few supporters; in 1900, it could claim only about one hundred members in five local branches across the state. Despite its small membership and near invisibility in Montana, the Social Democratic Party resolved to enter state politics, and in September 1900 the party held its first convention in Butte with about two dozen delegates attending. In his opening address, Martin Elliott predicted that the "socialistic" party would grow and prosper in the coming years. The delegates nominated a slate of presidential electors and state and congressional candidates and adopted a lengthy platform. The platform announced:

> We declare that independent political action and the trade union movement
> are the chief emancipation factors of the working class, the one representing
> its political and the other its economic wing, and both must cooperate to
> abolish the capitalist system.

The party's immediate demands called for public ownership of utilities, equal rights for women, unemployment and old-age insurance, a shorter workday, the initiative and referendum, and the "abolition of war" as a means for settling international disputes. The first convention of this small political party went virtually unnoticed, and when the votes were counted in November the party polled just 2 per cent of the vote state-wide.[10]

The public's attention was riveted elsewhere during the 1900 election, because by then the second phase of the copper king war was well underway. The year before, in 1899, Marcus Daly had merged his Anaconda Copper Mining Company with the Amalgamated Copper Company, a holding company controlled by men associated with John D. Rockefeller's Standard Oil Company. Butte's mining industry was dominated by two powerful interests. On one side was the Amalgamated, which was angling to become the dominant enterprise in world copper; on the other were two "independent" operators, William A. Clark and the young and brilliant mining engineer-turned-capitalist Frederick Augustus Heinze. Under Daly, the Anaconda Copper Mining Company had boldly made its political presence felt; the Amalgamated kept the tradition alive and ruthlessly expanded upon it. Clark and Heinze, who had been lively competitors, united in the fight only because the Company was their common enemy. For Clark, the goal was the same as it had been during the early 1890s. He wanted a legislature in place that would appoint him to the U.S. Senate, this time without splashing him with the stain of bribery. Heinze's goal was more complex.

"Fritz" Heinze had arrived in Butte in 1889 just as the city's copper industry was beginning to boom. Trained as a mining engineer, Heinze proved himself to be a bold, aggressive capitalist. In 1895, he purchased the Rarus Mine. With his talent for finding profitable ore bodies and his instinct for the main chance, he used the Rarus as a base from which to raid veins of ore in adjacent properties, claiming that the plundered ore bodies really belonged to him. Heinze's raids brought him into direct conflict with the Anaconda Copper Mining Company.

To prevail in lawsuits against the Company, which owned the ore, Heinze realized that he could advance his cause by helping to elect a judge who might be sympathetic to his side. Heinze found such a man in District Judge William Clancy, who had already demonstrated a record of ruling in Heinze's favor in contested mining claims.[11] Clancy had been elected on the Populist ticket in 1896 and was up for re-election in 1900. Heinze's economic self-interest dictated that he do everything he could to ensure that Clancy remained on the bench, so he turned his considerable organizational talents and oratorical skills to politics. It was while pursuing this goal that Heinze and Clark fashioned their political coalition against the Company.

Clark and Heinze, each for his own reasons, entered into a temporary *entente cordiale* against the Amalgamated Copper Company in Montana. To win the votes of the working class, the Clark-owned daily, the *Butte Miner*, and Heinze's little weekly, the *Reveille*, printed lurid tales of the alleged anti-labor practices of the Standard Oil Company. The *Reveille* told its readers that the ACM Company, directed by the Amalgamated, was secretly planning to import what the paper called "coolie" labor to replace men working in the mines. The *Reveille* asked: "Are you ready to sacrifice the interests of the working people of Montana to this great moneyed power, which will compel you to compete with Japanese laborers who work for $1.15 a day?"[12] Such stories were no doubt fabricated, but the Company management was so clumsy in its response that the tales carried an aura of verisimilitude. For example, organized labor had long demanded an eight-hour day with no reduction in pay. Clark and Heinze gave the reduced hours to their miners and invited the Company to do the same. The Company refused, injudiciously calling the action a "bribe."[13]

Having carefully prepared the social terrain, Clark and Heinze fashioned an *ad hoc* political coalition against the ACM Company using as their major theme opposition to "monopolists" and the "Trust." The Clark-Heinze forces began their campaign by capturing the state Democratic Party convention and then linking that party's organization in Silver Bow County with the Populists and the newly created Labor Party. This fusion ticket then divided up the nominations for county and state legislative races. The combination proved to be unbeatable when put up against the Republicans and the "independent" Democrats, which was a rump formation composed of those who had remained loyal to the ACM Company.[14] Heinze's rhetorical skills helped push the cause forward. In a brilliant stump speech, he had a "heart-to-heart" talk with the "workingmen of Butte" at the county courthouse on the eve of the election. Aligning himself with labor, Heinze told the crowd:

> My fight against the Standard Oil is your fight. In this glorious battle to save the State from the minions of the Rockefellers and the piracy of the Standard Oil you and I are partners. We stand or fall together. . . . If they crush me to-morrow they will crush you the day following. They will cut your wages and raise the tariff in the company store on every bite you eat and every rag you wear. They will force you to dwell in Standard Oil houses while you live and you must be buried in Standard Oil coffins when you die. . . . Those people are my enemies, fierce, bitter, implacable, but they are your enemies too. Let them win to-morrow and they will inaugurate conditions in Montana that will blast its fairest prospect and make its very name hateful to those who love liberty. In this fight you and I, my friends, are partners and allies. If you stand by me I will stand by you.[15]

The next day an avalanche of working-class votes swept the Clark-Heinze fusion party to victory. Silver Bow County sent five Laborites, five Clark-Heinze Democrats, and two Populists to the state legislature. Clark got a legislative majority that would send him to the U.S. Senate in 1901, Heinze saw Judge Clancy easily returned to the bench, and organized labor got a legislature that would mandate an eight-hour day in metal mining.[16] The Company had been soundly beaten. The second phase of the copper king war was at an end.

For ten years, Montana had been a market where votes were bought and where the corruption of governmental authority by economic power was brazen and public. In this den of thieves, alliances between players were often temporary, and in the wake of their smashing victory Clark and Heinze went their separate ways. Clark made his peace with the giant corporation, allegedly in return for the Company's promise not to oppose his confirmation in the Senate. Heinze was left to continue the struggle alone in the third and final phase of the copper king war (1901-1906). But this "champion" of the workers was not without resources. He had forged a seemingly unbeatable political coalition in Butte and in Silver Bow County, and he had retained a small army of lawyers to represent his interests in the courts.

In Heinze's protracted legal combat with the "octopus" of the Amalgamated, one set of cases was particularly important. John MacGinniss, vice-president of Heinze's Montana Ore Purchasing Company, and two attorneys employed by that company had quietly purchased small blocks of stock in smaller mining companies that had subsequently been absorbed by the ACM. In their capacity as minority stockholders, MacGinniss and the others filed a lawsuit in 1901 in which they argued that the Company's acquisitions had violated state law, which required the consent of minority stockholders as a prerequisite for such takeovers. The plaintiffs argued in district court that the Company's takeover was illegal and asked Judge William Clancy to enjoin the corporation from paying dividends on the income generated by the companies it had acquired. Should Clancy rule in their favor, the monopoly that had been so carefully patched together under the umbrella of the Amalgamated Copper Company would be placed in serious legal jeopardy. Clancy procrastinated and did not hand down a decision until October 1903.[17]

Meanwhile, as Clancy was slowly formulating a decision in the MacGinniss case, the Socialist movement was quietly gaining strength. The first signs of growth were manifested by increasing Socialist influence in the state labor movement. In the 1901 annual convention of the Montana State Trades and Labor Council, a majority of delegates, apparently in sympathy with the Socialists' analysis of society, readily resolved that "the nature of economic development" had spawned "two antagonistic classes," the capitalist class and the working class. Therefore, the delegates resolved, "we urge upon the workingmen of Montana to study the question of ownership of the means of production."[18] To advance the process of "educating" the workers, convention delegates appointed and charged a committee with finding and distributing literature to all affiliated unions that would "clearly and concisely" address these subjects:

1. The nature of the capitalist system of production.
2. The development of the capitalist class.
3. The functions of the capitalist class in modern society.
4. The development of the wage earning class.
5. The functions of the wage earning class in modern society.
6. The class struggle.
7. The nature of the cooperative commonwealth.[19]

Frank Ives, a carpenter and avowed Socialist from Missoula, was elected president of the federation for the coming year; selected as secretary was Oscar M. Partelow, a charter member of the Butte branch of the Socialist Party.

In August 1902, the MSTLC met in convention in the railroad town of Livingston. The Council went even further in openly supporting the Socialist Party of Montana, signifying the federation's official separation from the largely stillborn Labor Party, which had been created just two years earlier. President Ives established the tone of the convention when he told the assembled delegates: "In my judgement there is but one way out of the conditions that confront us; namely collective ownership of the means of production and distribution through independent political action."[20] Socialists and their supporters then drafted a resolution worded so that it won the almost unanimous approval of the delegates. The resolution announced that the MSTLC "approved" and "concurred" in the July 1902 endorsement of the Socialist Party by the American Labor Union and the Western Federation of Miners. It requested that all MSTLC-affiliated unions "adopt on the economic as well as the political field a clear and distinct policy in harmony with the spirit and the letter of the Denver organizations, and make them effective by a vigorous policy of education along the lines of political economy."[21] In a subsequent resolution adopted on the eve of the 1902 general election, the WFM's executive board openly declared: "We . . . call upon laboring men everywhere to study the platform of the Socialist Party and the program of Socialism and vote for that party alone."[22]

Not surprisingly, the Socialists were confident that some of their candidates would win, especially in Butte and in Silver Bow County. Clarence Smith, secretary-treasurer of the American Labor Union and candidate for the state senate, headed the county Socialist ticket.[23] Also in the field were Democrats, Republicans, and members of Heinze's fusion party, which the Company-owned *Anaconda Standard* jocularly labeled the "Heinzeantitrustboltingdemocratic-laborpopulist" party.[24]

During the election campaign, the Socialist Party was endorsed by the *American Labor Union Journal* and the *Labor World*, the new independent labor weekly owned and operated by J. W. Gilbert. The *Labor World* averred that the Socialist Party was the only "real labor party" in the election. Clarence Smith agreed, arguing that the fight between Heinze and the ACM Company was a "sham" designed to distract the workers. Smith counseled:

> Every Socialist is a workingman, and almost every Socialist is a union man. Out of the twenty-seven Socialist candidates in Silver Bow County, twenty-four have union cards in their pockets. . . . Let the capitalists fight their own battles. *Vote for your own interests.*[25]

The entry of the Socialist Party into the political field clearly worried Heinze's fusion forces. Heinze feared that the Socialists might draw enough working-class support away from the fusion party to throw the election to either the Democrats or the Republicans, both of which, he claimed, were "controlled" by the ACM Company. Heinze's *Reveille*, therefore, counterattacked, charging that the Socialist Party was an "Amalgamated trick" that had been set up to divide the workers. The *Labor World*, *Reveille* editor P. A. O'Farrell charged, was really a "Standard Oil newspaper."[26] O'Farrell offered no evidence to support either allegation. The irony, of course, was that Heinze's antitrust stance had helped create the very atmosphere of opinion that could ultimately redound to the benefit of the upstart Socialists.

The Heinzeites need not have worried. When the ballots were counted the fusion party swept the county races for a second time, while the Socialists elected none of their candidates. Even so, the Socialists were pleased with the results. Although the Socialist Party had received only 6 per cent of the state-wide vote, in Silver Bow County it had garnered 10 per cent of the vote in county races. It was a beginning, and the Socialists announced that they were "mightily encouraged."[27]

The real breakthrough for the Socialists occurred elsewhere, in Deer Lodge County and in the Company-created smelter town of Anaconda. There the county's local Labor Party, whose supporters were openly socialistic in their opinions, won most of the county races. After their stunning election triumph, the Labor Party announced that it had been chartered as a new local branch of the Socialist Party of Montana.[28] The Anaconda Copper Mining Company had once more taken a drubbing at the polls; the corporation's political ordeal was not yet over.

As the April 1903 municipal elections approached, Socialists in Butte and Anaconda confidently predicted victory. In Butte, the Socialists nominated P. A. Leamy, the principal of Butte High School, as their candidate for mayor. Leamy was joined on the ballot by schoolteacher J. W. Dale for city treasurer, former Butte Miners' Union president Mike McCormick for police judge, and a full slate of aldermanic candidates.[29]

The Heinze forces were second to place a slate of candidates in the race, and it was here that the Labor Party ran into trouble. For mayor, the party had nominated Larry Duggan, an undertaker and state legislator. But Duggan had earlier earned Heinze's enmity by voting for a bill that the ACM Company supported and Heinze opposed, so he could not bear the standard for the fusion forces. The Heinzeites quickly shoved the Labor Party vehicle aside and fielded a third ticket headed by Pat Mullins, the candidate of the "anti-trust" Democrats.[30] Rounding out the field was an entirely new group, the "citizens'" party, with Henry Mueller, a prominent Butte businessman, at the head of its ticket. With the *Anaconda Standard* applauding wildly, Mueller was clearly the Company's choice.[31]

In nearby Anaconda, Democrats, Republicans, and Socialists were in a three-way race. The Socialists had placed on the ballot cigarmaker John Frinke for mayor, smelterman Mike Tobin for city treasurer, blacksmith's helper Con McHugh for city police judge, and six aldermanic candidates. The Socialists championed the public ownership of municipal utilities (owned by the ACM Company), public works projects for the unemployed, "sufficient kindergartens for all children," the teaching of useful vocational skills, political economy, the rights of children in the public schools, free textbooks and medical care for children, a free city employment office, and a municipal labor temple for the educational and cultural enjoyment of working people. It was an ambitious program, and the Socialists readily admitted that the city did not have the legal authority to effect many of the reforms. Nevertheless, they pledged that if elected they would push as far as the law would allow in the direction of "full economic freedom."[32] The *Anaconda Standard* was surprisingly tolerant of this rhetoric, perhaps because its editors believed that the Socialists could not win.[33]

In April, Frinke, Tobin, and McHugh easily won their races, and three of the six Socialist aldermanic candidates also won. It was the Socialist Party of America's first municipal electoral success west of the Mississippi River—a "splendid victory," wired Socialist Party National Secretary William Mailly.[34]

In Butte, the Socialists met defeat. Predictably, the Heinze forces revived their accusation that the Socialist Party and its ally, the *Labor World*, were Amalgamated trojan horses set up to divide the anti-monopolist working-class vote that Heinze had so carefully nurtured. The *Reveille* editorialized: "The Amalgamated Copper Company is the financial backbone of the Socialist movement in Montana. The wiseacres that run the Rockefeller show in Montana are cultivating the movement in order to deceive the ranks of the toilers."[35]

But the Heinzeites were running scared, and the close election justified their fears. Fusion candidate Pat Mullins won, but just barely, polling 3,063 votes compared to 3,006 for Mueller; Leamy ran third with a respectable 2,621 votes. Had the Socialists not been in the race, the votes Leamy had received probably would have gone to the fusion party, and Mullins would have had a landslide.[36] But the Butte Socialists did not come away from the election empty-handed. George Ambrose, a barber by trade, was elected alderman in the Seventh Ward.

The Socialists could not rest easy, however; even after the election the *Reveille* pelted them with accusations that they were dupes in the service of the Amalgamated's interests.[37] On the surface, the *Reveille's* reports were implausible, given the paper's reputation for sensationalism and intense partisanship. But there is some evidence that

"The Double-Headed Octopus"
Montana News, May 3, 1905

the *Reveille's* charges had some substance. Six years later, the Socialist Party's outgoing state secretary, James D. Graham, recalled in an article in the *Montana News* that everyone, including the Amalgamated, was surprised by the Socialists' strong showing in the 1902 general election. The Amalgamated, Graham recalled, had realized that the more votes polled by the Socialists (who posed no electoral threat of their own), the fewer votes Heinze's party would get in the 1903 municipal election. Graham claimed that after the 1902 election Amalgamated men joined the Socialist Party in droves and implied that the Company used intermediaries to deliver doses of financial assistance to the party. In any case, Graham concluded, the Amalgamated experiment had proven to be a bust. Heinze had won, and the Company had decided for the moment that it had more important things to do than flex its muscles in the arena of Butte politics.[38]

The *Reveille's* charges were also supported by an April 1911 letter written to Socialist Mayor-elect Louis Duncan by Percival Cooney, who had been SPM state secretary in 1903. According to Graham, Cooney was so upset by Amalgamated's infiltration into the party that he had successfully lobbied to move the Socialist state party headquarters from Butte to Helena. In the 1911 letter, Cooney supplied this enigmatic postscript: "I cannot help recalling the organization of the first local. . . . Hard indeed was it for the infant party in those days to steer a course clear between the Scylla and Charydis of Heinze and the Amalgamated, but thank heaven the Crisis passed and the party emerged, if not stronger at least wiser."[39]

The final piece of evidence is the sudden demise of the *Labor World* shortly after the 1903 election. Lavishly printed and apparently adequately financed (even though it carried little advertising and was not connected to either the Socialist Party or the Butte unions), this champion of the Socialist cause suddenly ceased publication in September 1903 without preamble or protest. Its quiet passing was unusual; typically, struggling labor weeklies warned their readers that the end was near unless they saved it with voluntary contributions. But there is no evidence that either readers or the Socialist Party was bothered by the passing of the *Labor World.* The party had never endorsed the paper and had, in fact, started its own weekly, the *Montana Socialist Advocate.*[40] For its part, the *Reveille* opined that the *Labor World* had died because the mining corporation had withdrawn its covert financial support. When that decision was made, the paper "dropped out of existence as if the ground had opened up and swallowed it."[41]

In the fractured political landscape created by the copper kings' political war, the ACM Company was as covertly manipulative or openly ruthless as the need dictated. In Anaconda, the corporation now showed its hard face and destroyed the local Socialist Party.

In May 1903, the management of the Company's Washoe Smelter in Anaconda began a mass firing aimed at every Socialist and suspected Socialist in ACM's employ. The Anaconda Mill and Smeltermen's Union No. 117 of the WFM wired frantic appeals for help to the Federation's headquarters in Denver, but the national union was tied up in a protracted and violent struggle with the Colorado mining companies and could offer no tangible support.[42] A smeltermen's committee met with ACM Company President William Scallon, but the workers got no satisfaction from that quarter. Scallon told the group that the corporation was perfectly within its rights in dismissing men who evinced hostility toward it: "Some of them, and probably all of them, those I have in mind, are men who are rabid enemies . . . men who are going around preaching bitterness and hatred toward the company." A union committeeman asked: "Then you mean to say that a man can't vote as he pleases and use his own judgement politically and continue to retain his position in the company?" Scallon answered with another question: "He can do as he pleases, but can the man compel me to employ him?"[43]

To help ensure political orthodoxy in its workers, the Anaconda management instituted what became known as the "blue ticket" system. Employees' activities were monitored, and if an employee's behavior was found wanting—for example, if he was a member or supporter of the Socialist Party—he got a blue ticket at the end of his shift, signaling his summary discharge. It is impossible to say how many workers lost their jobs and were blacklisted in this way, but contemporary estimates placed the figure as high as several hundred.[44]

In the summer of 1903, the Socialists attempted to deliver a counterpunch of their own by levying higher taxes on the corporation's property in Deer Lodge County. The Company had escaped paying its share of local taxes because the county assessor had valued the property considerably below its realistic market price. Even Governor Joseph Toole felt compelled to complain about the county's assessment of Company property in his biennial address to the state legislature in January 1903: ". . . the burdens of taxation are most unequally distributed now. Millions of dollars of money and property escape taxation in this state year after year."[45]

County Assessor Newton Levengood, who had been elected on the Labor-Socialist ticket in 1902, attempted to apply the remedy by hiking the assessed valuation of the Washoe Smelter from $795,440 to $1,315,000. He also made proportionate increases in the assessment of other ACM Company properties. Overall, Levengood increased the assessed valuation of all property in the county from $7,579,021 to $15,881,178, three-quarters of the increase to be borne by the corporation.[46]

It was a good show while it lasted. Especially touching were the piteous cries of the *Anaconda Standard* in its editorial criticism of the heartless Levengood, who had also raised the assessed valuation of the local Catholic school and the Hearst Free Public Library.[47] The *Standard* remained judiciously silent on Levengood's assessment of Company property, however, trusting no doubt that the county commissioners, who also served as the reviewing Board of Equalization, would never go along with the reappraisal.

The *Standard*'s confidence was well placed. When the county commissioners met (all were Democrats), they rejected Levengood's assessments and shaved his figures back to the absurdly small valuations of past years.[48] Levengood's sally against the Company was the Socialists' last hurrah in Anaconda.

By the time of the 1904 aldermanic elections, Local Anaconda of the Socialist Party had been reduced to a handful of stalwarts. They bravely went forth to do battle and adopted a platform condemning the Company's blacklist.[49] The Socialists were soundly whipped in the aldermanic election, their share of the popular vote having declined by 75 per cent since the previous year. The *Standard* gave the last rites:

> In all likelihood nothing more will ever be heard of the Socialist Party in Anaconda. Its fate suggests the epitaph on the tombstone over the grave of a three-year-old child in Cheltenham churchyard: "It is so soon that I am done for, I wonder what I was begun for."[50]

The story of the destruction of the Socialist Party in Anaconda, however, was overshadowed by the Amalgamated's brutal reaction to the long-delayed decision of Judge Clancy in the minority stockholders lawsuit. On October 22, 1903, Clancy finally ruled that the acquisition of the two mining companies had violated the rights of the plaintiffs, and he enjoined the Amalgamated from paying dividends on the income from those companies. In a word, Clancy ruled that the Company's carefully pieced together mining empire was illegal.[51] Within hours of the decision, the Company's local officers had wired its headquarters in New York and received their marching orders. All of the Company's operations in Montana were immediately shut down, throwing an estimated fifteen thousand wage earners out of work. The Amalgamated explained that it could not possibly continue to do business in the state as long as the legality of its operations was in doubt.[52]

In the wake of the "great shutdown," the Amalgamated specified the conditions that would have to be met before it would consider reopening its operations. First, the Company demanded that minority stockholders sell their stock. Second, the governor must call the state legislature into special session to pass the "fair trial" bill, which would allow a litigant to challenge the authority of a judge to try a case and have him removed if it could be shown that the judge was biased. The passage of the bill would almost guarantee that the Amalgamated could have Judge Clancy removed from any case, thus stripping Heinze of his major weapon in his legal combat with the Company.

Heinze once more employed his oratory to rally the workers to his cause, but the game was up. Winter was fast approaching, and the men needed their jobs back. The Amalgamated had played its hole card—economic power—and it gave every sign that it would willingly drive the state's economy to ruin to get what it wanted.[53]

Governor Toole naturally hesitated to call the legislature back into session under such conditions; he must have realized that to do so compromised the very sovereignty of the state. But he was under enormous pressure, as demands for a special session came at him from most of Montana's newspapers (many Company-owned or influenced by the Company), the state's leading citizens, and many labor unions. Toole finally succumbed and issued a call for the session in early December. As soon as the governor acted, the Amalgamated, no doubt confident of the result, resumed operations. The legislature duly met and quickly passed the bill over the protests of the Labor Party and Labor-Socialist state representatives, who characterized the legislature's action as an "outrage" and an "ignominious surrender."[54] And so it was, but the Amalgamated had a point and the end it sought—a fair and impartial judiciary—was a worthy one. The Amalgamated may have brutally "squeezed the state into submission" and "burned the consciousness of a generation," but the directors of the corporation no doubt reasoned that the end justified the means.[55]

By the spring of 1904 Heinze must have realized that the struggle was over, and he began to carefully prepare to leave the state on the best possible terms. By early 1906, he had divested himself of most of his property for a sum reputed to be between $10.5 and $12 million. The buyer was the Butte Coalition Mining Company, a newly created Amalgamated subsidiary.[56] In the interim, the workers had stood with Heinze (the fusion party once more swept the Silver Bow County elections in 1904), but he did not stand with them. By 1907 the fusion party was defunct. "The big fish has swallowed the little fish," editorialized the Socialist *Montana News*. "Individualism in copper mining has received its death blow." Now, the newspaper predicted, the "class struggle" would begin in earnest.[57] The Socialist Party looked to the future with confidence.

Still the fact remains that the American working class
are in the most abject and degrading slavery because of
their ignorance. They have no conception of how to use
the ballot box. They vote in the form of government
that makes them paupers.

—editorial, *Montana News*,
April 9, 1908

3 ‖ *A Time of Frustration*

In the aftermath of the ACM Company's great shutdown in October 1903, Montana
Socialists were confident that they would inherit a good chunk of the anti-monopoly
sentiment that had hitherto gone to the Heinze coalition. They were mistaken. While
Heinze, that "friend" of the working class, was secretly preparing the ground for a
profitable departure, he kept his options open by publicly declaring that the war
against Amalgamated would continue. The fusion party remained in the field,
faithfully soldiered on behalf of the good cause, and continued to draw support from
the working-class constituency that the Socialists believed rightly belonged to them.

On February 4, 1904, the Butte Socialists nominated their aldermanic candidates
for the April election. They drew a distinction between themselves and the Heinzeites: "We point to the city council of Butte as a flagrant example of corporation government—government by corporations and of corporations—and denounce the present mayor [Pat Mullins] and his administration as the representatives of the two con-
tending corporations in the county." They argued:

> We warn the working class of this county not to allow their attention to be
> distracted from the worldwide class struggle by this corporation fight, in
> which they have no interest as workers, and point out that in all struggles
> between the capitalists and the workers all the capitalists will be found on
> one side and that is not our side.

The Socialists concluded their platform by charging that the fight between the
Amalgamated Copper Company and Heinze's men in the city council was a
meaningless "vaudeville" show and advised the city treasurer to charge admission for
the performances.[1]

When the votes were counted in April, the vaudeville show had prevailed. In a
four-way field of Democrats, "Anti-Trust" Democrats, Republicans, and Socialists,
the Socialists came in last. Only in the Seventh Ward did they record a victory with

the election of Silas Wainscott to the city council. The "corporation fight" had fractured Butte politics, and the new city council would consist of five Heinze ("Anti-Trust") Democrats, one Laborite, five regular Democrats, three Republicans, and two Socialists.[2]

In 1904, the major Socialist gains in the state were recorded in the coal-mining town of Red Lodge (population 2,112) in Carbon County. The previous year, Red Lodge Socialists had elected two aldermanic candidates to the six-man council; in 1904 they added a third alderman, creating a three-three partisan split. Socialist mayoral candidate T. R. Austin tied with his opponent in the popular vote, each receiving 205 votes. Under the law, the city council had to pick one of the candidates to be mayor, but the council deadlocked three to three. Retiring Mayor C. C. Bowlen broke the deadlock by casting the deciding vote for Austin's opponent, prompting local Socialists to predict an outright victory the next time around.[3]

By the end of 1904, the Socialist Party of Montana had 450 members organized in 25 local branches. The movement also had a weekly newspaper to champion its cause, the *Montana News*. Founded as the *Judith Basin News* in 1903, the paper began as a typical rural weekly dominated by local news, social events, and gossip. It differed from other weeklies only in that editor-owner J. H. Walsh preached the Socialist message in its pages. In hopes that he could reach the widest possible audience, Walsh changed the paper's name to the *Montana News* in 1904 and moved the operation from Lewistown to Helena. During the next year, Walsh donated the printing plant and the newspaper to the Socialist Party of Montana in return for the party's agreement to assume the paper's outstanding debts.[4] Walsh then left Montana to pursue the working-class revolution as a general organizer for the Industrial Workers of the World in the Pacific Northwest and to lead that organization's famous 1909 fight for "free speech" in Spokane.[5]

During 1904 and 1905, the Socialist Party of Montana also elected a new state secretary to replace Percival Cooney, who had been fired from his position as schoolteacher in Butte, presumably because of his Socialist political activities. Cooney's replacement to head a new state headquarters in Helena was James D. Graham of Livingston. Born in Scotland, Graham was a machinist by trade with strong ties to the labor movement.[6]

Party leaders were also obliged to appoint a new editor of the *Montana News*. They selected Ida Crouch Hazlett, who had recently come to Montana as part of the national party's traveling corps of Socialist orators. Hazlett had been raised in Illinois, where she attended college before moving to Colorado around the turn of the century. Active in the woman suffrage movement and the Socialist Party, Hazlett had considerable skill as an orator and a writer. But at the *News* she proved to be a most indifferent administrator, preferring to play the role of roving reporter and leaving Graham to do double duty as the newspaper's business manager. Eventually, the party's strongest local, at Butte, would grow increasingly critical of both workers' performance, and both would be expelled from the state party's ranks.[7]

For the moment, however, things seemed to be looking up for the Socialists in Montana. In the 1904 general elections, the party fielded tickets in thirteen of Montana's twenty-six counties. In November, Eugene Debs polled 5,676 votes (8.9 per cent) in Montana, making the Treasure State one of the strongest in the Socialist column that year. In populous Silver Bow County, Debs's share of the vote (14 per cent) accounted for one-third of his total state-wide vote.[8]

Locally, the party once more drew a blank. Socialist candidates in Silver Bow County received only about 10 per cent of the popular vote. In Red Lodge, party candidates were elected to the minor posts of justice of the peace and constable. And in Anaconda, its mauling by the Amalgamated had all but ended the party as a political organization. Labor-Socialist J. H. Schwend, a state representative from Deer Lodge County, received just 240 votes out of a total of 3,251 cast in his race for the state senate. Other Socialists in the county fared as poorly.[9]

This pattern of electoral futility was repeated in the spring 1905 municipal elections. In Butte's contest for mayor, Heinze's lieutenant, John MacGinniss, won easily. The Socialist mayoral candidate, C. M. Parr, came in fourth with 11 per cent of the vote in a six-sided race between an "Anti-Trust" Democrat, a regular Democrat, a Republican, a Socialist, an "Anti-Trust" Republican, and an independent. George Ambrose was elected to a second term on the city council, salvaging something for the Socialists on that dismal day.[10] In Red Lodge, the Socialists elected two aldermen; but in Anaconda, Mayor John Frinke and the other Socialist officeholders were retired from office. Many surviving Anaconda Socialists subsequently left the city or stayed out of politics altogether. Former city judge Con McHugh moved to Butte, where he stayed active in the movement. John Frinke moved out of state and out of the Socialist Party. He later returned to Anaconda and ran unsuccessfully for mayor as an independent in 1907.[11] Anaconda became known in radical circles as the "City of Whispers," a place where political heterodoxy and militant labor unionism were not allowed.

The Socialists made no headway over the next four electoral campaigns in Butte. In the 1906 Butte aldermanic elections, the Socialists elected no one, although their candidate in the Seventh Ward, Jerome Savage, lost by only fourteen votes.[12] In November 1906, Silver Bow County Socialists again played out their role as also-rans. Malcolm O'Malley did the best of the lot, polling 996 votes (11 per cent) in his race for the state senate.[13] The only significant outcome of the election was the re-emergence of the Democrats as the dominant party in the county.

In the 1907 Butte municipal campaign, the fusion party disappeared along with its patron, and voters were presented with a three-cornered race of Democrats, Republicans, and Socialists. The Socialists trailed the field with only 19 per cent of the vote, suggesting that the anti-monopoly sentiment that Heinze had mobilized did not transfer readily to the Socialist column. Ambrose was elected to a third term. In the following year, however, the Socialists elected no aldermen, leaving Ambrose in the unenviable position of being the token Socialist on the city council.[14]

But in Red Lodge, the Socialists won the victory denied them two years earlier. T. R. Austin won easily against his lone opponent, and the Socialist candidate for city judge was also elected. The new city council would be composed of two Socialists and four non-Socialists.[15] In the November 1906 general election, Carbon County Socialists made no additional gains, electing only two justices of the peace to office.[16] The Socialists dragged their feet in nominating a ticket in the 1907 Red Lodge aldermanic elections and drafted no platform for the contest. Turnout was light and the Socialists elected no one, leaving the Austin administration without a majority in the city council. Lacking a majority and publicly committed to only the mildest of municipal reforms, Austin's Socialist government accomplished nothing of substance during its two years in office. In 1908, it was turned out of office, never to return.[17]

The futility of Socialist electoral efforts from 1904 to 1908 was matched by the erosion and eventual elimination of Socialist influence in the Montana Federation of Labor. Since 1902, when the Federation came very close to officially endorsing the party, the Socialists' performance in state and municipal elections had lagged behind its expectations. Some trade unionists were beginning to have second thoughts about the MFL's close connection with a losing political cause. To be effective, labor had to work with and lobby those who could get elected; for the most part, the electoral victors were Democrats and Republicans. In addition, many Federation members were not Socialists and never would be, so they were uneasy with the MFL's quasi-endorsement of the party in 1902.

When the Montana Federation of Labor met in its annual convention in Missoula in August 1903, the tide began to run against the Socialists. In his keynote speech, President William Erler, a Butte barber who was not a Socialist, addressed the issue of organized labor making alliances with political parties. He advised delegates that it would be in the Federation's best interests to remain neutral toward all political parties. In subsequent debate, Socialist-leaning delegates tried and failed three times to get the MFL to go on record as favoring the Socialist Party. One such resolution failed by just one vote, 47 to 48. The convention then adopted a resolution declaring the Federation's neutrality in politics, with a vote of 48 to 47.

The Montana Federation of Labor, however, was not yet ready to abandon the ideas that the Socialist Party advocated. Convention delegates in Missoula adopted a new constitution recognizing that society was "divided into classes." An attached statement of principles included a demand for "the collective ownership by the people of all means of production and distribution." In the election of the MFL's officers for the coming year, convention delegates elected as president Alex Fairgrieve, a Red Lodge Socialist and coal miner. The Missoula convention thus ended as a standoff between Socialist and non-Socialist elements in the Federation.[18] The Socialists considered the outcome a victory. If it was, it was short-lived.

When the MFL convened in Hamilton in 1904, the proportion of delegates who were sympathetic to the Socialists had declined dramatically. Delegates reaffirmed the Federation's policy of political neutrality by a lopsided vote of 76 to 17. Equally symptomatic of the shift away from the party was the convention's decision to drop its affiliation with the American Labor Union, which had failed to become a serious alternative to the AFL. President Fairgrieve recommended that the convention consider a new national congress of autonomous state labor federations. He envisioned granting charter rights to state federations, which could then organize the workers that the AFL could not or would not organize. Convention delegates endorsed the plan.[19]

Independent of the MFL's action, the Western Federation of Miners took the initiative in creating a new national industrial union. Called together by the WFM, a select group of radicals met in Chicago in January 1905 and issued their "Industrial Union Manifesto," calling on all trade unionists to meet in Chicago in June to establish a new labor organization, the Industrial Workers of the World.[20]

Fairgrieve attended the IWW's founding convention as the representative of the Montana Federation of Labor. His plan for a state federation-based national union was rejected in committee and never reached the floor for a vote.[21] Instead, the delegates created a system of national industrial unions that had no place for state federations. Arguing that the MFL could not support such a plan, Fairgrieve returned home determined to fight the IWW. At its August convention in Great Falls, delegates heard Fairgrieve's report and on his urging amended the organization's constitution to authorize the MFL to charter unions that were "without a home," that is, those that were outside either the AFL or the IWW. The Butte Mill and Smeltermen's Union No. 74, which had a strong Socialist element that supported the IWW, vigorously opposed Fairgrieve's plan. The Butte smeltermen also fought to retain the public ownership plan in the Federation's statement of principles, but the plan was dropped by a vote of 53 to 47.[22]

The MFL's decision to charter unions necessarily brought it into conflict with the Western Federation of Miners. The WFM responded to the constitutional change by implying that Fairgrieve had a "personal interest" in state autonomy. Such autonomy, the WFM reasoned, would ensure a nice salary for people like Fairgrieve. In protest, the 1906 convention of the WFM ordered its twenty-six Montana affiliates to withdraw from the Montana Federation of Labor and directed its Helena union to expel Fairgrieve from its membership.[23]

Shortly thereafter the Butte Socialists pressed their own indictment against the wayward MFL president. They offered a motion in a meeting of the state committee that Fairgrieve be expelled from the party for being a "scheming labor fakir," among other things. They need not have bothered; by that time Fairgrieve had dropped out of the party.[24]

Under Fairgrieve's leadership, the Montana Federation of Labor became a bastion of conservatism. It fought with the IWW over which union would organize the lumber workers in the western part of the state, and it lost interest in fighting for political reform, including woman suffrage.[25] The transformation was completed in 1908, when the Montana Federation of Labor asked for and received a charter from the once-despised AFL. For all that, the chief architect was not rewarded with regular employment. In 1909, the Federation elected conservative trade unionist Mortimer M. Donoghue of Butte over the unfortunate Fairgrieve.[26]

By the middle of 1908, the Socialist Party of Montana was without influence in politics or the state's labor federation. The question was increasingly being asked: "What's the matter with the Socialist Party?" Butte's Socialists thought they had the answer.

The party's problem, the Butte comrades charged, stemmed from mismanagement of the party and its newspaper by state secretary Graham and editor Hazlett.[27] In the party's state convention, Butte insisted that a committee be appointed to audit the books. Louis Duncan of Butte, who was named committee chairman, subsequently reported that he and the committee could not perform the audit because the party's financial records were in "wretched condition."[28] In alliance with some other branches, Local Butte demanded that Graham and Hazlett resign. Graham eventually gave in, but Hazlett refused to step down. In the spring of 1909, the Socialist Party of Montana responded by formally severing its ties to the *Montana News* and expelling Graham and Hazlett from its ranks.[29]

Mismanagement was not the only area of conflict in the state party. The personal rancor on both sides seemed to emanate primarily from ideological differences of opinion over the IWW. Local Butte of the SPM enthusiastically supported the IWW and warmly endorsed "industrial unionism"; it even formally endorsed IWW general organizer William D. Haywood as its choice for Socialist candidate for president of the United States in 1908.[30] Graham and Hazlett pointedly refused to endorse anyone. Hazlett argued that the *Montana News* would adhere to the national party policy of "neutrality" on questions of labor union organization and tactics; that is, it would not take sides officially in the bitter fight between the AFL and the IWW.[31]

In this atmosphere of internal bickering, the Socialist Party of Montana could only suffer.[32] Between 1908 and 1909, party membership declined by 45 per cent. By the spring of 1909, no Socialist held an elective political office in the state, and a succession of temporary state secretaries came and went during the remainder of the year.[33] Finally, in the spring of 1910, the party reached stable ground. State headquarters was back in Butte, Louis Duncan was elected state secretary, and Frank Mabie became the traveling state organizer. Duncan and Mabie proceeded to rebuild the party from the ground up.

Louis Duncan had joined the party in 1902. He had studied to be a lawyer in his native Illinois, but he tired of the practice of law rather quickly and subsequently held a series of clerical jobs. While clerking, Duncan earned a certificate as a minister in the Unitarian church, and he came to Butte to be pastor of the church there. By his own account, Duncan's Socialist Party activity prompted the church to fire him in 1909. His unemployment nicely coincided with the party's need for a "live" state secretary, and he had a place to put to use his considerable administrative ability, drive, and intellectual power.[34]

While Duncan was the prototypical middle-class "intellectual," Frank Mabie was the essential proletarian. A lather by trade, Mabie had been a union member since 1890. After reading Edward Bellamy's utopian novel of a socialist future, *Looking Backward*, he later wrote that he "discovered myself and from that time called myself a socialist." Mabie was one of twelve charter members of the first Social Democratic local in Butte, and he organized the next two locals in the mining camps of Chico and Fridley in Park County. In his new capacity as state organizer, Mabie traveled throughout the state, setting up new locals and pumping up those that had survived the 1909 debacle.[35] He approached his task with good humor, patience, and optimism.

By August 1910, the Socialist Party of Montana had climbed back from the abyss with a state membership of 500 organized in 22 locals. Considering where it had been, the party made a respectable showing in the fall election. Heading the state ticket as the party's candidate for Congress, Mabie received 9 per cent of the vote. He did much better in Silver Bow County, where he gathered 18 per cent.[36]

The party was on the move in Silver Bow County. Local Butte had approximately 125 members organized in two branches, one English-speaking and the other Finnish-speaking. On September 29, the Socialists held their county convention at Finlander Hall on North Wyoming Street and, according to an *Anaconda Standard* press report, with "harmony and dispatch" approved a platform and nominated candidates. The platform called on workers "to cast a class-conscious ballot" and unite "on the political field" under the Socialist banner. The party's list of "immediate demands" emphasized its commitment to enact laws that would protect workers' health and safety. If elected, the Socialist legislative candidates promised to introduce and support legislation that would establish a shorter workday in "hot, gaseous and unhealthful underground working places," require better ventilation in mines, mandate "better and more scientific inspection of the mines," and provide for a workmen's compensation law.

In what was already a firmly established pattern, the Socialists emphasized the proletarian character of their movement by nominating a slate of candidates, mostly from the working class. The legislative ticket included Duncan for the state senate and eleven working-class men and one salesman for the house of representatives. The fourteen-member Socialist slate for county offices was made up of twelve working-class men, a civil engineer, and a homemaker.[37]

When the votes were counted in November, the Socialist candidates for the state legislature and the county offices received an average of slightly less than two thousand votes, or 19 per cent of the total votes cast. No Socialist candidate came close to winning, but the percentage of the vote going to the Socialists was higher than it had been in 1908 and considerably better than the Socialist totals received in the previous two municipal elections.[38]

Local morale also received a boost from outside Butte. For the first time since its founding in 1901, the Socialist Party of America was receiving nation-wide attention. In 1910, Socialists were elected to local offices in fifty-seven communities in twenty-four states. Most notably, Socialists captured control of Milwaukee, and in the fall Wisconsin voters elected Socialist leader Victor Berger to the U.S. Congress.[39] Inspired by the Wisconsin success, the Butte Socialists began their campaign for the upcoming municipal elections by consciously emulating the Milwaukee effort. They relied heavily on door-to-door canvassing to spread the Socialist message. In December 1910, they founded a biweekly campaign newspaper, the *Butte Socialist*, for free distribution to every household. The time had come, said the Socialists, to "Milwaukeeize" Butte.[40] This time they would win.

Not all at once does the Socialist Party expect to achieve the full measure of emancipation from the power of the capitalist class, which is its aim; but it does expect, gradually by political successes in municipalities, in state legislatures, and in the national congress, to secure for the working class certain advantages of benefit in their struggle for economic freedom.

—state platform, Socialist Party
of Montana, 1910

4 | *A Socialist Government*

Buoyed by the party's success in Milwaukee, Butte's Socialists approached the 1911 city election with confidence. By March, the *Butte Socialist* had a press run of 12,000, and volunteers were distributing the paper door-to-door every other Sunday.[1] In formulating its municipal program, Butte's local party had borrowed heavily from their Milwaukee comrades. Stressing their party's "immediate demands," Milwaukee's Socialists had guaranteed honest and efficient government—an important promise to make and keep in an era marked by machine politics, official corruption, government ineptitude, and indifference toward municipal problems such as housing and sanitation. Second, the Milwaukee party had promised to institute public ownership of city utilities, a step toward the realization of full socialism along with less expensive rates and more efficient service. Third, the party had pledged to establish a municipal fuel yard, which would sell coal and wood to consumers at cost. Finally, Milwaukee's Socialists had advocated a series of reforms to improve the urban quality of life for the working class, promising to build more public parks, playgrounds, recreational facilities, and "comfort stations."[2]

With Milwaukee's successful bid as ballast, Butte's Socialists criticized the way in which both Democrats and Republicans had governed the city. They cited as evidence Butte's poor sanitary conditions, the cheating of consumers by dishonest merchants, the spread of vice, and an increase in the municipal debt with no concomitant increase in either the quality or quantity of public services or public works. Butte's Socialists also pointed to the city's gerrymandered and malapportioned wards, which they believed helped perpetuate old party rule, especially by the dominant Democrats. Gross population disparities skewed representation of the city's eight wards. For example, 40 per cent of Butte's registered voters lived in The Flats, the heavily working-class Seventh and Eighth wards south of uptown; yet, only four aldermen on the sixteen-member city council represented this area. The malapportionment, the Socialists charged, also shortchanged those wards by giving them fewer city services, especially sewers, streets, and sidewalks. The Socialists also wanted to annex those areas that had developed substantially beyond the city's boundaries, primarily to the south and east. They also advocated the consolidation of city and county governments, which the Socialists claimed would lead to more efficiency and economy. Consolidation would also increase the political representation of working-class neighborhoods in the unannexed portions of the county.

The Socialists were also strong supporters of municipal "home rule," which would give city governments a greater measure of legislative and fiscal authority in dealing with the problems of the urban community. The Socialists wanted state law changed to give cities greater leeway in their taxing and spending authority and to allow them to engage in enterprise, that is, to provide light, power, water, urban transportation, and fuel.

Butte's Socialists promised only those things that they believed they could deliver. Their platform declared:

> We realize that to elect our candidates in this municipal election will not bring Socialism. But we also realize that all hope of betterment of local conditions for the working class depends solely upon the application of Socialist principles and methods to municipal affairs.[3]

Socialist "principles" and "methods" suggested honesty and efficiency, the application of modern management techniques, professional expertise, and planning, all of which non-Socialist progressive reformers also supported to some extent. But the Socialists in Butte and elsewhere were more than reformers. For them, achieving their "immediate demands" was only "the starting point." As one student of the Milwaukee experiment noted:

> The distinguishing mark between Socialists and reformers in public office was that the Socialists always had a further demand. Unlike middle-class reformers whose platform was circumscribed, Socialists sought further changes leading to the alteration of the system, and this goal was shared by Socialists both in and out of office.[4]

The Socialists also differed from middle-class reformers in their explicit class bias. They openly and frankly declared that if elected they intended to primarily advance the interests of the working class.[5] Nevertheless, the Socialist municipal program in Butte and in other cities was designed to be potentially attractive to reform-minded middle-class voters as well. Louis Duncan argued: "There is not one item in those demands that would not be of benefit to every honest, high-minded and public-spirited citizen in Butte." "There are thousands of Republicans and Democrats," the Socialists claimed, "who are disgusted with old party rule."[6]

The party nominated Louis Duncan to head the Socialist ticket as its mayoral candidate. Miner Dan Shovlin was the Socialist candidate for city treasurer, and miner Thomas Booher was running for city police judge. The Socialist aldermanic slate was composed of four miners, two stationary engineers, a shoemaker, and the business agent of the Butte Workingmen's Union.[7]

During the campaign, Butte's Socialists tried to capitalize on the miserable conditions under which many workers and their families lived. A state health department inspector described two working-class neighborhoods this way:

> North Wyoming, 700 block. This is one of the dirtiest and most insanitary places inspected. Houses built throughout the block with little regard for alleys. Small and dirty. Slops thrown into street from nearly all places. Houses are so thick there is scarcely room for toilets, and from the odor think toilets are not cleaned regularly. . . .
>
> Ohio, Hopkins, New, and Mahoney Streets. This section is what is known as the Cabbage Patch and is too filthy to describe. Found but one garbage can covered. . . . Houses small, poorly ventilated; alleys filthy. Dead dog found in alley and, judging from odor, believe had been dead three or four days. Understand many miners live in this section on account of the cheap rent.[8]

State health inspectors had examined 438 houses in 1911 and had found 97 of them to be "substandard," with overcrowding, poor ventilation, and no indoor plumbing.[9] The report concluded:

> Conditions on the surface are all remediable. There is no excuse for permitting the renting of rooms or houses that are not provided with proper air space and adequate ventilation.
>
> There is no excuse for permitting the existence of insanitary conditions found to exist in many of the houses, yards, and streets inspected.[10]

In this environment it was not surprising to find that the incidence of tuberculosis and other contagious diseases was high. For the decade ending in 1910, state health department statistics showed that a disproportionate share of deaths attributed to pneumonia and tuberculosis occurred in Butte and in Silver Bow County, a finding that the department found "interesting."[11]

These living conditions could only assist the Socialist cause, but it would be simplistic to suggest that they alone could have tipped the electoral scales toward the radicals. But conditions did serve as important evidence in the Socialist Party's indictment of city government under the old parties. In a vigorous and well-organized grassroots campaign, the Socialists increased their distribution of the *Butte Socialist*, held frequent rallies in different neighborhoods, and distributed thousands of one-page "extras" on the eve of the election, printing a different one for each ward in the city.[12]

Acting as if they had little to fear from the upstart Socialists, the Democrats and the Republicans waged lackluster campaigns. Both parties had alternately governed the city since the demise of Heinze's fusion party, and both had accomplished so little that even the three daily newspapers (two Democratic, one Republican) stayed on the sidelines, giving only indifferent and obligatory support to their partisan preferences.

Also fatal to the old parties' chances for success were the shocking results reported in an audit of the city's finances. Thousands of dollars had been lost, misappropriated, or stolen by the incumbent Democratic administration. The city was also one million dollars in excess of its statutory debt ceiling. The release of the audit results two days before the election added a vital and perhaps decisive increment of votes to the Socialist column and turned what might have been a close election into a Socialist landslide. [13]

On April 3, 1911, Duncan, Shovlin, and Booher coasted to victory, each capturing an absolute majority of the votes cast. Five out of eight Socialist aldermanic candidates were elected: miner Frank Curran in the First Ward; shoemaker Hugh McManus in the Third; miner Andrew Rissell in the Fifth; miner Arthur Cox in the Seventh; and the Workingmen's Union business agent Henry Davis in the Eighth. [14]

In the wake of the stunning Socialist victory, the daily press claimed and the Socialists readily admitted that one-quarter of their support may have come from disgruntled middle-class voters. Clarence Smith told his celebrating comrades:

"House-Cleaning Time"
Anaconda Standard, April 4, 1911

We should take a cool and calm view of the situation, and freely and frankly recognize the fact that it was not so much a Socialist Party victory as a victory due to the protest from the whole people; the voters of all parties.[15]

But the Socialists also knew that the hard core of their support had come from the working-class neighborhoods east of Main Street and in The Flats.[16] It was from this constituency that the party expected to draw support in the future. In a letter to a friend shortly after the election, Louis Duncan argued:

For the first time, the Socialists have the opportunity to demonstrate their methods and efficiency before the people of Montana. The demonstration will be in the strongest organized labor town in the state, where, if we make good, we shall be able to get the practical support of industrial organizations in our political efforts. It was the labor vote that carried us into power this time and it can do so every time if we can retain the confidence of the workers. This situation is going to result in a clear class alignment in future political fights—organized labor with the Socialists on one side and the Amalgamated with the old party machines on the other.

"Should we prove convincing in city affairs," Duncan predicted, "we shall be able to get the county in the next election and send representatives to the legislature."[17]

Duncan had perfectly summarized the view of social change held by most Socialists in the United States. Enhanced by a strong labor movement, the ballot was the instrument of proletarian liberation. Once elected, Socialists' performance in office was the key to further political advance, and they would certainly "make good." It was only a matter of time. In 1911, the party's scenario for social change was ready to be tested in Butte.

On May 1, Mayor Duncan delivered his first annual state-of-the-city address to the city council. Announcing that his Socialist administration would devote its attention to fulfilling the promises made in the party's platform, Duncan delivered a speech that was moderate in tone. The daily press responded with a tolerant "wait-and-see" attitude. The *Anaconda Standard* editorialized: "There is nothing of the anarchistic tone in the message, nothing perhaps in the entire document to which every good citizen cannot subscribe and be ready to lend a hand to assist the new mayor in bringing about its accomplishment."[18] Simple arithmetic dictated that Duncan be moderate and conciliatory. He faced a sixteen-member city council, eleven of whom were non-Socialists. If his government was going to achieve any of the party's goals, it would need the votes of at least three non-Socialist aldermen.

In the end, the aldermanic majority confirmed most of Duncan's appointments to city patronage jobs. Except for a few posts that required professional qualifications, the mayor's nominees were Socialist Party stalwarts, including H. L. Maury as city attorney, Clarence Smith as assistant city treasurer, Harvey Smith as street commissioner, and Frank Mabie as sanitation inspector.[19]

Persuading the non-Socialist aldermen to support a Socialist program for the city was quite another matter. In June, when the Socialists proposed an ordinance to levy a new city license tax on corporations and banks, the council split along party lines to reject the proposal. In August, Alderman Rissell sponsored a bill to add more health inspectors to the city health department; that bill was also rejected on a straight party-line vote. In December, Alderman Davis introduced the promised municipal fuel-yard ordinance, which the council rejected in the same fashion.[20] The Duncan administration did have some successes, however. The council voted to hire two new assistants for Dr. Carl Horst, the city health officer, and it approved street paving and sidewalk construction projects in working-class neighborhoods.[21]

The Duncan administration had the most success in its determined enforcement of existing laws. Municipal graft ceased; the vice laws were strictly enforced; and dishonest merchants were investigated, hauled into court, and fined for cheating customers or for selling goods that were in violation of the health code. Streets and alleys were cleaner, the health inspections of homes and food establishments increased dramatically, and street maintenance work was done by the city's expanded street department at presumably lower costs than had been paid to private contractors.[22]

As the April 1912 aldermanic elections approached, the Socialists began to campaign hard to persuade the voters to give Duncan a Socialist majority in the city council. Pointing with pride to their record in improving public health, the Socialists averred that under the Duncan administration the incidence of contagious diseases had been reduced from 745 cases in 1910 to only 78 in 1911. The number of deaths attributed to contagious disease had been reduced by 17 per cent, and the mortality rate among children under twelve years old had dropped by a dramatic 60 per cent. These improvements, the Socialists explained, were the result of "purer milk, cleaner streets and alleys, and fewer cesspools and houseflies." The gains not only benefited public health, the Socialists claimed, but they also had direct economic benefits for the workers: "For the common people, the effect of these policies has been to decrease the cost of their living and to increase the purchasing power of their dollars; which is to say that the Socialist administration has practically raised the wages of the working class of Butte."[23] The party asserted:

> We believe that, regardless of what big business and cringing politicians say or do, the common people of this city know their interests are safe in the hands of the Socialists, and that by their votes this spring they will relegate the outgoing aldermen to private life and will send to the support of the administration eight Socialist aldermen, to give us a majority to control the city council.[24]

Electing eight Socialist aldermen, however, would not be easy. This time, the opposition took off their gloves and waged a vicious campaign using the most outrageous exaggeration and falsehood. The daily press claimed that the Duncan administration had achieved nothing and charged that the Socialists were motivated by a "spirit of fanaticism" and "hatred of American institutions." They cried that Socialism had proven to be "impractical," "unwise," and "un-American," that most Socialists were foreigners, and that Socialism was a foreign ideology imported from "southern Europe."[25]

In fact, the Socialist "menace" was mostly imagined. The city council had turned down *all* of the Duncan administration's "radical" proposals, and no matter how hard they campaigned the Socialists were not likely to achieve a majority given the city's malapportioned wards. But there was still the possibility that the Socialists would gain a majority on the city council, which would pass ordinances challenging the prerogatives of business enterprises. Fearing such an outcome, the mining operators decided to take preemptive action. The day after the Socialists held their city convention, Butte's mining companies fired what some estimated to be five hundred "socialists." The Socialist Party protested loudly, as did the officers of the Butte Miners' Union; and Alderman McManus introduced a resolution condemning the companies' "cowardly and dastardly act." The city council rejected the resolution on a straight party-line vote.[26]

When the polls closed on April 1, it was clear that the Socialists had fallen far short of their goal. Only one Socialist candidate had been elected—Edmund Landendorff in the Seventh Ward.[27] It is impossible to say with certainty whether or not the mass firing was responsible for the disappointing results.[28] What is certain is that the mining companies had sent workers a clear message that it was risky to openly support the Socialist Party.

When Mayor Duncan delivered his second annual address to the city council on May 6, 1912, he faced a hardened opposition majority. He made no new proposals and did not introduce the bills that had been rejected during his first year in office. The one exception was ward malapportionment. Duncan appointed a council committee to draft a plan to redistrict the city's eight wards based on the principle of population parity. In January 1913, the committee reported that under the current system the population difference between the largest and the smallest ward was 1,464 voters. Under the new plan, the difference would be reduced to 85 voters. The city council rejected the new plan by a vote of 7 to 9, with the Republican committee chairman joining the six Socialist aldermen in voting "aye."[29]

Checkmated by the council majority, the Socialists turned their energies away from local reform and toward the November general election. In July 1912 the party held its state convention in Butte, drafting a state platform and nominating candidates for state offices and Congress. The convention delegates also passed a resolution establishing a new state-wide Socialist Party newspaper, the *Montana Socialist*, which began publication in September 1912.[30]

Shortly after the convention adjourned, Eugene Debs came to Butte in late August in his fourth campaign for president of the United States. He spoke before a packed audience of twenty-five hundred people at the Broadway Theatre, while an equal number stood outside. The *Anaconda Standard* reported: "The reception given Debs was in the nature of an ovation. He spoke entirely without notes. With little exception, his talk was a plea for the workers to unite as a class."[31]

Debs was the most gifted stump speaker the American Socialist movement ever produced, and his appearance in the mining city energized the local campaign. Shortly after Debs left the city, the Butte Socialists held their county nominating convention. The local party platform condemned the Democrats' "lawless, corrupt, and extravagant administration" of the county government. Nominated to head the ticket as candidate for county attorney was city attorney Maury; for sheriff, the convention nominated Dan D. Sullivan, former president of the Butte Miners' Union. Delegates also nominated a twelve-man slate of candidates for the state house of representatives.[32]

The Socialist legislative candidates would be running for the twelve seats in the Silver Bow County delegation under an at-large electoral arrangement. Unlike members of the Butte city council who were elected from single-member districts (wards), legislators were elected out of a county multi-member district of twelve seats. This meant that each voter could vote for up to twelve legislative candidates, and those candidates who finished first through twelfth in the popular vote totals would be declared elected. Under this system, if voters support a straight ticket, the party that claims the largest share of the vote could win all of the at-large seats in the contest even though its total share of the vote might be less than a majority of votes cast. Given that the Democrats typically won the largest bloc of votes in Silver Bow County, the at-large election worked to their advantage and gave them a disproportionate share of legislative seats in relation to their actual share of the popular vote. If legislative candidates had been elected from single-member districts (as Butte's aldermen were), the Socialists would have been assured of electing at least some of their candidates from those parts of the county where Socialist support was high. Because this was not the case, the Socialists had to persuade enough Democratic or Republican voters to vote the straight Socialist ticket or to split their tickets and vote for those Socialists who were running for county and legislative offices. If neither of those things happened, the Socialists could poll a large number of votes and still end up electing none of their candidates.

A more immediate problem for the Socialists, however, was ensuring that the votes they did receive were honestly counted. Democrats controlled the county election machinery, and the Socialists worried that they might be "counted out" unless their own election judges and clerks could observe the voting. Normally, the county commission appointed a clerk and a judge from each party for each precinct; but the commissioners claimed that the party's list of nominees had come too late to be considered, and they refused to appoint any Socialists. Confronted by formal protests from the Socialist Party and the labor unions, the commission relented somewhat and said it would appoint Socialist clerks and judges in half of the county's forty-six precincts. The Socialists were not satisfied. "It will be apparent to every citizen," they thundered, "that the purpose is to steal the election."[33] The commission explained that it could not appoint more Socialists because the taxpayers would then have to pay an additional three hundred dollars in election costs. The Socialist Party responded by sending the commission a certified check for three hundred dollars with the demand that more Socialists be appointed. The commission refused, now claiming that the law did not permit it to appoint additional clerks and judges. Because the commission had already appointed two Democratic clerks and judges in each precinct, the Socialists demanded that the commission dismiss half of the Democrats. The commissioners refused.[34]

As election day approached the Socialists faced another problem. The county clerk failed to print and post the precinct voting lists eight days before the election, as was required by law. How could they challenge the eligibility of those on the lists, the Socialists asked, if they could not see the lists? When party leaders demanded to see the main registration rolls at the county courthouse, access was denied. Exasperated, the Socialists filed suit in district court demanding that the county clerk obey the law. The judge issued the order, and the precinct lists were immediately posted. The actions of the county commission and the county clerk clearly gave the impression that the Democrats were contemplating some election-day shenanigans.[35]

The election campaign reached a new level of nastiness as the daily press trundled out the usual anti-Socialist charges. Once more the Socialists were accused of sedition, irreligion, and disloyalty.[36] On the morning of the election, the *Butte Miner* made its position clear in bold, black letters across its front page:

THE ISSUE

SOCIALISM	DEMOCRACY
STRIKE	PEACE
STRIFE	PLENTY
STAGNATION	PROSPERITY[37]

The daily press, the old parties, and the interests they represented were frightened—and for good reason. When the votes were counted, the Socialist Party had come close to winning it all (see Table 1 for an accounting of each party's share of the vote). In the county and legislative races, Socialist candidates trailed the Democrats by margins of only 200 to 400 votes out of 12,000 cast. The closest call was in the county attorney's race, where H. L. Maury lost to the Democrat by just thirty-eight votes. In the state legislative races, the pernicious at-large system denied the Socialists any seats. The Socialist legislative candidates had polled between 3,875 and 3,965 votes (34 per cent of the total), but the twelve Democrats did slightly better, polling between 4,024 and 4,233 votes (36 per cent of the total). Twelve

TABLE 1: *Popular Vote in the Silver Bow County General Election, November 1912*

	Democrat	Socialist	Republican	Progressive
President	38.2%	27.9%	18.8%	15.1%
Governor	38.4	32.2	20.3	9.1
County attorney	37.0	36.7	20.6	5.7
Sheriff	36.8	33.7	22.5	7.0
State House of Representatives	36.1	34.2	22.3	7.4

Source: Official Canvass of the Election Returns, published in the *Butter Miner*, November 13, 1912.

Democrats would go to the state legislature, even though the majority of votes cast had gone to the candidates of other parties. Except for electing two justices of the peace and two constables, the Socialists came away empty-handed.[38] Even so, the *Butte Miner* readily admitted that the election had been a "close call" and only "luck" had saved the day for the Democrats.[39]

But the Democrats' razor-thin victory was more than luck. The bias in the at-large electoral system had worked to their advantage. In addition, the Democrats controlled Butte's election machinery, and the actions of Democratic officeholders gave credence to the Socialists' charges that they would "count out" the Socialists if they had to in order to carry the day. On December 2, some defeated Socialist candidates filed suit in district court alleging that the Socialist vote had been undercounted in four precincts and that votes had been switched from Socialist to Democratic candidates in thirteen others. The case was eventually moved to district court in Billings. There the Socialists' lawsuit was dismissed because they had failed to file their suit within twenty days after the election, as required by law.[40] The Socialists did not appeal the ruling, and there the matter came to rest.

Even though they may have been counted out in some races in 1912, the Socialists' rise from near oblivion in 1908-1909 to second place in the county election was impressive. The Socialists' upsurge can be attributed to at least four factors. First, the public's antipathy toward corrupt and inefficient government had brought many votes their way, including the votes of some of the middle class. Second, the Socialists received substantial electoral support from Butte's working-class voters. Third, the party had become a well-organized and zealous practitioner of campaign tactics in which there was a strong and necessary emphasis on appealing to the grass-roots. Finally, the Socialists had demonstrated that they could govern competently and imaginatively.

In spite of their efforts, however, the political payoff for the Socialists had been meager. They had failed to gain a supportive majority in the city council, which was a prerequisite for legislative enactment of the party's immediate demands. They had been thwarted not only by the skewed ward boundaries but also by their opponents' apparent application of economic coercion. These factors had combined to significantly reduce the Duncan administration's capacity to "make good" in office. It is perhaps this, along with the threat of economic sanctions and the bias in the electoral rules and election administration, that contributed most to the Socialists' failure to win control of the county and the legislative delegation in the 1912 general election.

In spite of such limited rewards for such mighty efforts, most Butte Socialists remained confident that victory was inevitable. Local Socialist confidence was no doubt buoyed further by a modest Socialist electoral surge throughout the country in 1911-1912. The Socialists had elected thirty-nine state legislators, mayors in seventy cities and towns, and hundreds of lesser local officials.[41] To American Socialists, such victories were surely evidence of a growing working-class consciousness favoring independent political action.

More dispassionate observers were not so sure. In two analyses of the Socialists' efforts nationally, Robert Hoxie argued that Socialist electoral successes were most often the result of a strong public sentiment that favored municipal reform. The Socialist Party at the local level, he said,

> stands for greater local autonomy; for direct control of officials; for clean, honest, and efficient administration of affairs; for the equalization of tax burdens; the curbing of corporations; the improvement of housing, education, and amusements of the people.[42]

Many of the reforms that the Socialists advocated were attractive to non-Socialist and reform-minded middle-class voters. And it was this aspect of Butte's Socialist government that the *National Municipal Review* found particularly laudatory:

> Butte, like many other American cities, suffered from misgovernment and graft until the hope of betterment under the old parties was lost and the citizens elected the Socialist administration under Mayor Duncan. It is said that the new administration has made the city clean morally and physically. For the first time in the history of the city, the streets and alleys are clean and sani-

tary, and it has been shown that the infant mortality due to unclean conditions has been almost eliminated. Streets have been graded, traffic regulated, adequate police protection provided, city employees compelled to be efficient, and as a result of good, honest management all around, the city lifted itself out of bankruptcy to a position of good credit.[43]

There was still the question of whether or not Socialist "reform" would be enough to retain the allegiance of middle-class voters. More importantly, would it be enough to satisfy both Butte's working class and those who had been attracted by the party's larger goal of proletarian power and the overthrow of capitalism? Some radical spirits were growing impatient with Socialist municipal reform. For them, the slow pace of change and the promise of gradual movement toward the cooperative commonwealth was not enough. Some were now doubting the efficacy of the party's electoral strategy. The opposition had stolen the last election. Would they try again? And how could workers vote their preferences with the threat of being fired and blacklisted hanging over their heads?

Some of the doubters were members of the Industrial Workers of the World and belonged to a local chapter of the IWW's Propaganda League. Many of these IWW men also held cards in the Butte local chapter of the Socialist Party. The Wobblies and their sympathizers had always coexisted in harmony with the party, with one group helping the other. IWW men voted the Socialist ticket, and the Socialist party in Butte staunchly supported the industrial union idea.[44] Together, they had fought against what they saw as the corruption and conservatism of the Butte Miners' Union (see Chapter 7). But as Butte's Socialist Party began to prepare for what would certainly be a hard fight to stay in office, growing antagonism between the party and the IWW was fermenting just below the surface.

Every citizen who is on speaking terms with the truth is compelled to admit that the Socialists have MADE GOOD in every particular affecting the welfare of the municipality and its people.

—*Montana Socialist*, April 6, 1913

5 | *A Parting of the Ways*

Not only did liberal reformers praise the Socialist performance in Butte, but Socialists throughout the country were proud of the accomplishments of the Duncan administration. Frank Bohn, a writer for the monthly *International Socialist Review*, observed: "In every matter which comes before the government of the city of Butte this question is asked: 'Will it benefit the working class?' And their party policy is outlined and pursued with that alone in view." Bohn opined that the Socialist government seemed to have achieved a "maximum of results" under "the backward form of government now obtaining everywhere in America."[1] In a sense, the 1913 municipal election was a referendum on the Socialist experiment in city government.

Butte Socialists began their campaign by pointing to their efforts since the 1911 election. They had tried to establish a municipal fuel yard, levy a new license tax on corporations, and redistrict the city's malapportioned wards; but all of these reforms had been rejected by the non-Socialist aldermanic majority. Despite opposition, however, the Duncan administration had made a difference in public works, public health, control of vice, and public management. The Socialists averred that the city administration had protected consumers from "commercial exploitation" by dishonest merchants; that the streets and alleys, especially those in working-class neighborhoods, were cleaner and that the incidence of contagious disease had been sharply reduced; that laws regulating prostitution and the sale of alcohol were "strictly enforced" and that policemen found guilty of corruption had been dismissed; and that city government was more efficient and financially sound because of Socialist management. The Socialists then promised that if they were re-elected they would create more public playgrounds and parks when the budget would allow and they would push for the public ownership of utilities.[2]

The Democrats and Republicans tried to counter the Socialists' popularity by using a tactic that had worked elsewhere to keep Socialists out of office—a fusion of the old parties. Realizing that their combined vote had been greater than the Socialists' in the 1912 election, the two parties put together a united "citizens" ticket for 1913. At the head of the fusion ticket was Republican Sam Barker, who announced: "There is only one issue—socialism."[3] The *Butte Miner* advised its presumably Democratic readership: "If Butte is to be redeemed this spring from the menace of Socialism, it will be necessary for patriotic citizens of the community to forget their partisanship."[4] The Socialists commended "the frankness of the fusionists and welcome the issue thus submitted to the voters of Butte."[5] Butte's Socialists wanted the election to be a referendum on Socialist governance; the opposition ensured that it would be.

But the fusion tactic did not work as the old parties had expected. When the votes were counted, Duncan, Shovlin, and Booher had won easily. The new city council would be composed of five Democrats, four Republicans, and seven Socialists—the six newly elected aldermen plus one holdover, Landendorff.[6]

The party had come close to achieving a clean sweep, and the Socialists' morale soared. The *Montana Socialist* enthused that theirs was "the most significant victory that the Socialists have yet won in the United States; the first Socialist administration to succeed itself; the first that has been able to triumph against the old party fusion."[7] In Milwaukee, where a fusion party had beaten the Socialists in 1912, the *Milwaukee Leader* predicted: "It is only a question of time when the Butte achievement will be repeated in every industrial center in the country. The awakening intelligence of the workers cannot be halted. The very atmosphere is charged with enlightenment."[8] But the "very atmosphere" in Butte was charged with something else—factionalism. The catalyst was the IWW.

Since its inception, the Socialist Party of America had been committed to using the ballot as the primary means of emancipating the working class. A minority of party members, many of them affiliated with or sympathetic to the IWW, did not completely share that view. While never denying that electoral politics had a proper and legitimate function in overthrowing capitalism, the Wobblies emphasized the liberating potential of revolutionary industrial unionism and preached direct action and sabotage. The IWW believed that the social revolution would come all at once in the form of a general strike of all workers, not one step at a time, as the Socialist Party believed.

Despite such philosophical and tactical differences, the IWW and the Socialist Party had fairly amicable relations until 1912, especially in the West. In Butte, the differences had been subsumed by a common commitment to industrial unionism and the memory of earlier bitter and bloody fights between miners and employers. But by 1911, the Socialist Party was breaking into the political mainstream, and some Socialists believed that the IWW's informal ties to the party might undermine its electoral appeal and its internal cohesion. The Wobblies denigrated elections and the achievements of Socialist governments. They hated the AFL and had nothing but contempt for those Socialists who said that the AFL could be reformed. Bill Haywood, the best known of the IWW leaders, was a strident critic of Socialist tactics, but he had also been elected to the party's National Executive Committee. Haywood's election no doubt reflected his celebrity status and the respect he enjoyed from many party members, especially in the West. But the "reform" or "constructive" wing of the national party believed that Haywood's presence on the party's national council undermined the Socialists' political respectability. Because of that, these "reform"

Socialists were determined to rid the party of Haywood and the Wobblies. In May 1912, they made their move.

The site was the party's national convention in Indianapolis. With the express purpose of driving the IWW and its sympathizers out of the party, the reformist wing offered an amendment to Article 11, Section 6, of the party's constitution:[9]

> Any member of the party who opposes political action or advocates sabotage or other methods of violence as a weapon of the working class to aid in its emancipation shall be expelled from the party. Political action shall be construed to mean participation in elections for public office and practical legislative and administrative work along lines of the Socialist Party platform.[10]

After a long and occasionally acrimonious debate, the delegates adopted the amendment by a vote of 191 to 90. The party membership subsequently ratified the amendment by a vote of 13,215 to 4,196.[11]

The issue could have been left at that if the opponents of the IWW had not used the amended article to recall Haywood from the National Executive Committee. They accused him of violating the article's anti-sabotage clause in public utterances made in New York City in December 1912. Haywood had advocated sabotage in "so many words," but he had also endorsed political action, a fact that was conveniently ignored in the rush to get rid of the controversial labor agitator.[12] Haywood was recalled from the party's National Executive Committee in a membership referendum in March 1913 by a vote of 22,495 to 10,944, with Montana's party voting against the recall.[13] Local Butte formally protested the "arbitrary methods" used against Haywood and claimed that his only crime had been to organize "the workers on the industrial field in the only form that will properly express itself on the political field."[14] But the membership had spoken on the question, and party members who "opposed" political action or who advocated "violence" were put on notice. Now, in the wake of the April 1913 election, the issue came to Butte.

The catalyst was a difference of opinion between Mayor Duncan and the party's central committee over the mayor's choices for two city jobs. In line with Socialist Party practice, which required its elected officials to accept advice and instructions from the party, the mayor had submitted his list of nominations for the committee's review and routine approval. The committee majority, however, refused to endorse H. L. Maury for city attorney and Harvey Smith for street commissioner. Maury was turned down because he served as legal counsel for a local private utility, supposedly making his commitment to public ownership suspect. Smith's particular fault was his alleged failure to put more active party members on the street department payroll, especially those connected with the IWW.

Duncan was inclined to accept the committee's recommendations, but his friends persuaded him to resist and submit the issue to the membership in a referendum vote. Much to the chagrin of Duncan's supporters, the party membership not only endorsed the central committee's recommendations, but it also "instructed" the mayor to nominate to the post of street commissioner William G. Sullivan, a Wobbly and an irritating critic of the local Socialist government. The vote had been close and had revealed an interesting ethnic split. The Finnish branch of the local party had voted overwhelmingly against the mayor, while the English-speaking branch had voted in favor of Duncan's nominees.[15] The Finns' vote may have been an expression of resentment toward their English-speaking comrades. During the 1912 general election campaign, the Finns had requested proportional representation on the slate of candidates and on the party central committee. Their demand had been turned down on the grounds that most of them were not citizens and could not vote. In taking this action, the Butte party's English-speaking branch had implicitly defined two classes of party members: those who were citizens and those who were not.[16] In voting for Sullivan and against Mayor Duncan, the Finns now demonstrated their clout in Local Butte while also showing their strong support for the IWW.[17]

The mayor reacted to the referendum vote by labeling it merely advisory, not mandatory. He announced that he was not going to nominate Sullivan and rather intemperately said that elected Socialist officials were not the "automatons of the Socialist mob."[18] The real issue, of course, was not the mayor's authority to make appointments, but the presence of a divisive IWW faction in the Socialist local (especially among the Finns), whose criticism of party policy had blossomed after passage of the revised Article 11, Section 6, and Haywood's recall. According to Duncan's report to the national party, a local chapter of the IWW Propaganda League had been established in Butte in the summer of 1912. Some party members joined the league, and others supported it because of their industrial union sympathies. But the league did not agitate much among the labor unions, deciding to devote most of its attention to infiltrating the Socialist Party. Party meetings became heated, with the mayor, the city attorney, and the street commissioner becoming "special targets." Duncan recalled:

> I cannot begin to detail the various forms of "heckling" that developed or the way in which these tactics changed our local meetings into wranglings, and the central committee meetings into convocations for criticism, crimination, recrimination and the breeding of discord, suspicion and factionalism.[19]

It was clear that the Wobblies had become a disruptive element in the meetings of the local party, but it is unlikely that the IWW plotted to capture the Socialist local and transform it into an adjunct of the IWW. Party leaders who remained neutral in the growing factionalism doubted the existence of an IWW plot. Further, many of the neutrals, including City Treasurer Shovlin, were particularly upset with Duncan's refusal to follow the clear instructions of the party membership.[20]

By the middle of May, the conflict between Duncan's "yellow" faction and the IWW's "red" faction had become almost irreconcilable. Each group now moved to have the other expelled from the party. Duncan's forces moved first and accused Sullivan and two other Wobblies of violating Article 11, Section 6. The "reds" responded by calling the mayor and the Socialist aldermen to task for refusing to accept Sullivan's nomination as street commissioner.[21]

Hearing the charges against the three "reds" first, the local's grievance committee ruled that there was insufficient evidence to justify their expulsion from the party. The committee next turned its attention to the charges against the mayor and the aldermen. But rather than risk the committee's indictment and possible expulsion, the Duncan forces petitioned the state central committee to revoke Local Butte's charter and to grant a new one to Duncan and his supporters.[22]

On June 15, 1913, the state central committee heard testimony on the petition in Butte. Speaking for his group, Duncan told the committee that the IWW element had grown so large that revoking the charter was the only way to "eliminate the direct actionists." The Socialist Party had become afflicted by a debilitating disease, Duncan complained, and only radical surgery would cure it. He advised the committee: "You must act with scientific and ruthless accuracy on this regardless of friendship and other considerations. . . . If this is condoned here," he concluded, "it may be condoned in Billings, Livingston, Missoula, Phillipsburg, or Conrad. First thing we know the party will be shot through with this thing. . . ."[23] Speaking for the accused, Sullivan said that the real issue was not the IWW, but the "bossism" of the mayor in his studied refusal to follow the party's instructions. If any party rules had been broken, Sullivan averred, it was the mayor who had broken them.

After hearing the testimony, the majority of the state central committee accepted Duncan's explanation and voted to revoke the charter: "We would advise locals in the state to ascertain more carefully the loyalty to party principles and tactics of all applicants for party membership before admitting them into the organization."[24] In one fell swoop, the local party's membership was reduced from more than five hundred to fewer than the one hundred who had signed the request for a new charter.[25] For their part, the "reds" established headquarters in Finlander Hall and called themselves the "real" Socialists.[26]

It had been a nasty internal fight in which neither faction could claim a monopoly on virtue. The IWW faction had forced the question of tactics into the local's meeting in an apparently belligerent and divisive manner. The behavior of this group before and after the charter was revoked conformed to the critical observations made by writer Frank Bohn, a strong supporter of the revolutionary union:

> They [members of the IWW propaganda leagues] make their main purpose in life to attack the Socialist Party. Conceiving themselves to be gifted with the power to set the whole Socialist movement right, they are usually found, not in the shops organizing and educating the workers, but in the Socialist Party headquarters or meetings, expounding theory and sneering at the ignorance of "politicians," meanwhile describing how they were "once upon a time just as ignorant," etc., etc.[27]

Eugene Debs, whose commitment to industrial unionism was well known, was also critical:

> The I.W.W. has treated the Socialist Party most indecently, to put it very mildly. When it gets into trouble it frantically appeals to the Socialist Party for aid, which has always been freely rendered, and after it is all over the I.W.W. kicks the Socialist Party in the face. That is the case put in plain words, and the Socialist Party has had enough of that sort of business, and I don't blame them a bit [for Article 11, Section 6]. There are I.W.W. anarchists who are in the Socialist Party for no other purpose than to disrupt it, and the Socialist Party is right in taking a decided stand against them.[28]

This appeared to have been the case in Butte, but it was not the whole of the matter.

The Socialists had boasted that their party was different because its officeholders were obliged to follow the platform and party advice.[29] If they failed to do so, the party could "recall" them by simply submitting their signed, undated resignations to the local government in which they served. By holding the letters of resignation, the party could "instruct" its officeholders.[30] Duncan had been "instructed" and had refused to fall in line. He had initiated a process that led to the revocation of the local charter, resulting in a reconstituted Socialist Party that was clearly subordinate to its office-holders, the opposite of what the Socialist Party expected.[31] The problems between local parties and their officeholders were not specific to Butte. Locals elsewhere that had also presumed to instruct their officeholders had met resistance that had led to the expulsion of elected officials from the party or their resignation from it, accompanied by a disavowal of the resignation letters.[32] Had the Duncan forces not won their fight, their expulsion or resignation from the party would have been almost certain. Duncan's victory had prevented such an outcome, but at what cost?

The Socialist Party in Butte had rid itself of the IWW, but it had also lost four hundred members, including the entire Finnish group, City Treasurer Shovlin, Alderman McManus, and most of those who had been active in the local union movement. Some among this last group, which included several former officers in the Butte Miners' Union and the Butte Engineers' Union, would devote their attention to labor union activity.[33] Some were already in the IWW, and others would drift into its orbit to join those who had never had anything to do with the Socialist Party.

Butte's Socialist Party responded to the schism by rebuilding. By the end of 1913 it had 205 members in good standing, and by April 1914 membership once more reached approximately five hundred when the Finns were readmitted after agreeing to accept party rules.[34] Ideologically, the reconstructed Socialist Party sought to demonstrate that "political action" got results. The *Montana Socialist* chastised "impatient comrades" by offering the following example:

> Even the much despised [*sic*] and condemned "garbage can," which many of the impractical comrades delight to ridicule when they criticize what they are pleased to call the ineffectiveness and bourgeois tendencies of Socialist politicians, is an important factor in the revolution, and the city employees who faithfully perform that social service, are doing as fully a revolutionary service as are the orators and paragraph writers who see nothing but a joke in political action.[35]

Improvement in public health was no joke either. The *Montana Socialist* asked: "If a Socialist city administration can cut down your doctor bills, save the lives of your children, and improve your health, isn't that INCREASING YOUR PAY? Isn't that direct action? Isn't that getting something now?"[36]

The Duncan administration's 1913-1914 term *had* accomplished a great deal. The Socialists sponsored a bill to give city street maintenance workers a two-week paid vacation. The ordinance was approved by a vote of 10 to 5, with three Democrats joining the seven Socialists.[37] The Butte Workingmen's Union asked for a wage increase of fifty cents a day for city street laborers, and the Socialists won the wage increase with the votes of some Democratic aldermen.[38] The Socialists also improved the city's finances. Mayor Duncan explained its importance for workers:

> Some of you thought that a city government could not raise wages. When we took hold in Butte the city was bonded for $400,000 in excess of the legal limit, and warrants, in which all city employees were paid, sold on the market for 20 to 30 percent discount. Thus, a working man who was nominally getting $3.50 for a day's work, actually received about $2.75. . . . In less than a year we brought warrants to par, thus increasing the real pay of city employees by an average of 25 percent. How's that for raising wages by political action?[39]

Finally, Duncan's administration implemented the ward reapportionment that it had sought for so long. On December 13, 1913, by a vote of 10 to 6, the city council adopted a reapportionment plan that made the population of the city's eight wards more equal in size.[40]

In two other important initiatives, however, the Socialists were defeated. First, the city council rejected the administration's proposal that the city annex the Race Track Addition, a Socialist stronghold that bordered the Seventh Ward on the east.[41] Second, the Socialists had proposed creating the office of city assessor. Under the existing system, the county government determined property tax assessments. The Socialists claimed that the county assessor was valuing corporate and business property below its real market value. The result was an inequitable distribution of the tax burden. Opponents of the proposal tried to distort the issue by charging that the ordinance was just a scheme to provide more patronage jobs for the Socialist Party "machine." The ordinance went down to defeat on a straight party-line vote.[42]

Butte's Socialists would be the first to admit that what they had achieved was not Socialism. What they did achieve was a reform government with a decidedly pro-working-class bent. As they prepared for the 1914 aldermanic elections, their rhetoric shifted ever so slightly. Reaffirming that Butte's Socialist government was committed to representing "the interests of the enslaved and exploited workers" and "the overthrow of economic privilege and class rule of all sorts," the new platform laid out the party's list of reforms for the coming year and then pointed out the larger significance of Socialist political action:

> Working men of Butte: In the struggle for greater economic and political freedom, the working class of America finds its first and greatest opportunity in the industrial centers. Securing control of the government of these cities, we shall not only gain a great strategical advantage, politically speaking, but the opportunity to demonstrate our ability to govern wisely and well, to exercise this power for the interests of our class, to train and educate members of our class in the arts of government, and to fit ourselves for the larger fields of civic duty and responsibility which before long will devolve to us, as the cause of industrial emancipation gains strength.[43]

While the Socialists tried once more to rally the workers to their cause, the daily press and the old parties ran their usual negative campaign. The party clearly had significant electoral support in the working-class wards. What could the opposition do this time?

The answer came on Sunday, April 5, the day before the city elections. The mining companies suddenly announced a "full shift" on Monday, violating a long-established practice of giving miners election day off. "Fully Two Thousand Miners Were Disenfranchised Monday," screamed the *Montana Socialist*.[44] The action of the mining companies had drastically reduced turnout. Only 54 per cent of those registered cast ballots, compared to 77 per cent in 1913 and 83 per cent in 1912.[45] The problem was time. The day shift ended at five o'clock in the afternoon and the polls closed an hour later. In that one hour a miner would have to be hoisted to the surface, shower and change, and then rush to his polling place, which might be two or more miles away. The plain fact of the matter is that many of them did not make it and, the Socialists charged, that was exactly what the mining companies had intended.

For all that, 1914 was not a repeat of the miserable showing of 1912. The Socialists elected three of their aldermanic candidates: Landendorff won a second term in the Seventh Ward; Mike Allen, a blacksmith, was elected in the Fifth Ward; and Anton Obermeyer, a brewer, was victorious in the Eighth Ward. The new city council would be composed of eight Socialists, seven Democrats, and one ex-Socialist (McManus).[46] The administration had a clear majority. Now it was possible to push through the city council some of the party's long-sought legislative goals, such as the municipal fuel-yard bill, public ownership of utilities, and a corporate license tax.

The "reds" who had led the charge against Duncan had presumed that they better reflected the attitudes of the working class than the Socialist "politicians" did. They presumed too much. Support for the Socialist ticket remained steady among the city's working-class voters. In the April 1914 aldermanic election, Socialist candidates polled 42 per cent of the votes cast compared to 44 per cent in 1911, 35 per cent in 1912, and 54 per cent in 1913. But many working-class voters refused to support the Socialist Party. Butte's workers might have had a common economic interest against the employing class, but for many the ties of neighborhood, ethnicity, and religion were more powerful. These more compelling and immediate bonds of human solidarity often pitted workers against each other, militating against the party's determined efforts to create and sustain a solid base of support among Butte's working class.

Looking at the Butte Hill from Meaderville in 1904, residents could see the MOP smelter (in the foreground) and (from left) the Rarus, Mountain View, High Ore, Diamond, and Speculator mines.

At the turn of the century, Butte's downtown (shown here at the intersection of Main Street and Park Street) was dynamic and prosperous.

From "Investigation of Sanitary Conditions in Mines," MHS Photograph Archives

Between 1908 and 1912, a survey of living conditions in Butte documented poor sanitation, as seen in this photograph of an open sewer in the back of the 1100 block on East Broadway.

From "Investigation of Sanitary Conditions in Mines," MHS Photograph Archives

The county Health Department's Report on Sanitary Conditions pointed out many unhealthy areas, such as this hole on West Daily Street in Walkerville that contained green-colored, stagnant water.

By the first years of the century, Butte was an industrial city with tenements, boarding houses, commercial blocks, and a range of problems that were common to the nation's urban areas.

Poor sanitation conditions were evident to investigators who visited this newer residential area at 1600 2nd Avenue in the Flats.

The mines and mills in Walkerville (1. Moulton Mill, 2. Moulton Mine, 3. Alice Mill, 4. Alice Mine) were some of the oldest in Butte.

The Rarus Mine, shown here in about 1900, was one of the principal mines in the F. A. Heinze-Amalgamated copper war.

Butte's industrial landscape included the tracks of the Butte, Anaconda & Pacific Railroad, which cut through residential neighborhoods.

Shift bosses posed for an informal picture in the offices of the Mountain View mine in north-central Butte.

A photographer for the Report on Sanitary Conditions (1908-1912) took this candid view of shift bosses at noon hour in one of the mines.

This group of miners was photographed at the 2,500-foot level of one of Butte's deep mines, where heat and humidity often produced extreme work conditions.

These miners at the Neversweat were gathered at the mouth of the mine's upcast shaft, which ventilated "bad air" from the mine.

From "Investigation of Sanitary Conditions in Mines," MHS Photograph Archives

These miners, shown here at the 1,900-foot level and some 500 feet from the nearest ventilation, worked in 90 per cent humidity and at 92 degrees fahrenheit.

In a free country like ours, in which the richest man has
exactly the same voting power as the poorest, there does
not seem to be the slightest excuse for the Socialist Party.
— editorial, *Butte Miner*,
March 26, 1913

6 | *Class and Community*

In Butte and in hundreds of other cities and towns across the United States, the Socialist Party was a potentially potent revolutionary alternative to the status quo during the
decade preceding the country's entry into World War I.[1] Capitalism in Butte was not
an abstraction. It was personified in the powerful and ruthless Anaconda Copper
Mining Company, and it was visible in the fine homes of the rich and well-to-do and
in the shacks and boarding houses where the workers lived. It was also implicit in the
sacrificial offerings made to capitalism by the numbers of miners killed and injured in
the frenzied drive to produce wealth for the chosen few.

Into this setting the Socialist Party brought ideology and organization. The
Socialists were convinced that a proletarian majority organized into a solid voting bloc
was an inevitable outcome in the ongoing evolution of the capitalist state. For them,
politics was basically a conflict between the "haves" and the "have nots" — between
employers and employees, masters and servants, the buyers and sellers of labor. The
antagonism between these separate and competing interests was the "class struggle."
Morris Hillquit, a leading theorist of the Socialist Party of America, defined the class
struggle as follows:

> The inhabitants of every state . . . may always be divided into several
> groups of persons with reference to their source of income or mode of ac-
> quiring the material means of their existence. Within each group the single
> individuals may strive for the largest possible share of the common income,
> but against all the other elements of society, each of such groups is interested
> in the maintenance and increase of its special revenue and material wealth.
> Each of such social groups constitutes a separate "class" of society, and the
> characteristic features of every class are these: its individual members are
> united in their general economic interest with each other, and as a whole
> they are opposed to all other classes contending with them for their share of
> national wealth.

The existence of classes thus creates the instincts of class solidarity and class antagonism, and the socialists contend that the efforts of each class to maintain or improve its position, and the resultant conflicts between them, constitute the politics of nations and makes their histories.[2]

Butte's Socialists believed that the workers' common economic interests and their desire for higher wages and safer and healthier working conditions would induce them to make common cause with each other against their employers. The catalyst would be the mobilization of the "instincts of class solidarity," which were already assumed to be present in the workers' minds. But Butte's workers were not united as a class. They were divided by the pull of traditional party attachments, ethnic affiliation, and religious persuasion, which dampened their inchoate sense of themselves as a class distinct from all others.

For example, the ties of ethnicity might divide individuals of different nationalities even though they shared a common economic interest; at the same time, those ties might unite individuals of the same ethnic community who occupied different positions in the class structure. Mine superintendents often had an antagonistic relationship with working miners, but they might be strongly and positively linked by a common ethnic identification, expressed in fraternal and political affiliations and religious belief. An Irish immigrant foreman might have been at loggerheads with the Irish immigrants who dug the ore, but they shared a membership in the Knights of Columbus and the Ancient Order of Hibernians, their Catholicism, and their unwavering support of the Democratic Party.[3] Consequently, while common social class interests might push workers toward a conscious sense of class solidarity and support for the Socialist Party, other factors might keep them apart and fighting among themselves. The Socialists would have to overcome those divisions to succeed.

When Mayor Louis Duncan assumed office in 1911, forty thousand people lived in Butte. A workers' city, Butte was a wonderful stew of nationalities brought together by the district's immense mining enterprise. In his autobiographical novel, *Mile High, Mile Deep*, Richard K. O'Malley described growing up in Butte during the 1920s and captured the pull of the mines and Butte's diverse social environment:

> The town grew upon the side of the Hill, perched on its flanks and the shacks sprouted like weeds around the mines. There were families that followed and it was Butte all at once, out of the copper womb.
>
> Finntown, Hungry Hill, Dublin Gulch, Stringtown, Butchertown, Dogtown, Centerville, Meaderville, Walkerville, The Flat, The Cabbage Patch.
>
> Talk English at school. Talk Czech, Italian, Yugoslav, Serb, Finn, Swede, Norwegian at home. The old folks don't talk English so good, grandma don't know a word ain't it funny I wish grandpa would talk something besides Gaelic he's been here five years now.[4]

The Irish were by far the largest ethnic group in Butte. In 1910, one in four immigrants in the mining city was from Ireland, and almost one-third of the registered electorate in the county were Irish by birth or lineage. Members in the next largest bloc were from England, most of them from the southwestern mining area of Cornwall.

Next in number were the Canadians, many of whom were also of Cornish or Irish descent. There were also significant German, Scandinavian, and Finnish communities. There were many Italians and south Slavic peoples—Serbs, Croatians, Slovenians, and Montenegrins—and a Jewish community, a "China Town," and a small contingent of black Americans (Table 2).[5]

TABLE 2: *The Distribution of Butte's Foreign-Born Residents, 1890-1920*

	1890[a]	1900	1910	1920
Irish	21.7%	24.2%	24.3%	20.7%
British[b]	26.5	19.4	20.5	20.9
Canadian[c]	16.6	20.3	15.4	12.9
German	7.7	8.8	6.5	5.3
Scandinavian[d]	6.2	8.7	8.0	9.5
Slavic[e]	3.6	4.0	7.2	9.6
Italian	3.2	1.3	1.2	1.7
Finnish	n.a.	4.0	7.7	8.8
Other	14.5	9.3	9.2	10.6
	100%	100%	100%	100%
	$n = 4,047$	$n = 10,209$	$n = 13,128$	$n = 11,454$

Sources: *11th Census of the United States (1890), Vol. 1: Population,* 641; *12th Census of the United States (1900), Vol. 1: Population,* 796-799; *13th Census of the United States (1910), Vol. 1: Population,* 179; *14th Census of the United States (1920), Vol. 2: Population,* 577.

[a]Data for entire county; Butte was not presented separately.

[b]Small numbers of Welsh, Scots, and Manx (from the Isle of Man) were included; most were Cornish.

[c]The majority were of British or Irish lineage rather than French Canadian.

[d]Danes, Norwegians, and Swedes.

[e]Primarily Serbs and other Slavic peoples now incorporated in the state of Yugoslavia; few Russians, Poles, or Ukrainians settled in Butte.

In 1910, the *Anaconda Standard* noticed "a tendency of the peoples who come from far-off lands to flock together" in their own neighborhoods.[6] Less kindly, the *Butte Evening News* reported the same tendency in a racist attack directed at the town's Slavic immigrants:

> There are bohunk saloons and tobacco stores where the invaders buy their drinks and smoking tobacco. Doctors and druggists get little or no patronage from these people. For light in their dingy cabins, candles stolen from the mines are used. These people shave themselves and cut each other's hair. They rarely ride street cars; they attend no theatres except perhaps in a wild splurge of extravagance they go to a moving picture show. It will readily be seen that there is not a commercial interest in Butte that profits from the invasion of this class of foreigners.[7]

What the *Standard* and the *News* had observed and interpreted in their own peculiar way was a national phenomenon that was not confined to Butte. One byproduct of the country's industrialization was what the U.S. Immigration Commission called "chain migration." The process began when members of a particular immigrant group found employment in a town or city and wrote home to tell others. Family and friends soon arrived looking for work, and an ethnic neighborhood began to take shape. The U.S. Immigration Commission described the process:

> Immigration to the United States was not an indefinite movement westward on the part of the people studied. They came to a particular street in a particular city because relatives or acquaintances who had come earlier were living in that locality; or lacking personal connections they came to the city of their residence because it was a place to which the migration from sections of the home country had been directed. They had no choice in location. They came to the only spot in America with which they were familiar by report.[8]

The chain migration process produced distinct ethnic enclaves within the larger Butte community. The result and its causes were neatly and sympathetically recalled by Jacob Ostberg, an old-time resident of Butte:

> Cosmopolitan old Butte had the racial segments of its population almost as neatly divided as the parts of an orange. Entire residential areas were often occupied by those of one nationality, of immigrants and their American-born families. It was both a convenience and a necessity for the newly arrived future citizens to seek those of their kind, not alone for aid in getting established in the strange surroundings of the new country, but as a step-by-step means of acquiring a new language with a tongue often rooted in a culture not their own. In a friendly atmosphere of familiar customs and speech, those little everyday aids rapidly gained for them common experiences and bits of knowledge necessary to conduct the affairs of home-life and the work-a-day world. . . . An interpreter, a guide, or a dependable witness was usually quite readily found in a community wherein those of like racial origin predominated. Thus, did such communities grow, as much or more through necessity than from any special desire to maintain exclusiveness.[9]

This is the way Butte's ethnic neighborhoods developed. The city's Irish and the older immigrant Cornish, nicknamed "Cousin Jacks," settled near the mines in north Butte in the First, Second, and Third wards and in the suburban villages of Walkerville, Centerville, and Dublin Gulch. Italians established an enclave to the east of Butte in Meaderville, where many found employment in the Leonard and Tramway mines. The Finns formed a tight community along East Granite and Park streets in the Third Ward in what came to be called Finntown. The Slavs settled in Dublin Gulch northeast of Butte, bounded on the east by Division and Chicago streets, and in the Boulevard Addition. Most native-born residents, especially the middle class, lived in the neighborhoods west of Main Street, which ran from north to south, forming the major boundary between the "Americans" and the "foreigners." Finally, to the south of uptown Butte was the newer residential area called The Flats, where many Germans and Scandinavians and native-born manual workers lived (Table 3).[10]

Not only did the chain migration process produce distinct national enclaves, but it also led to the concentration of particular ethnic groups in industries and occupations. Two-thirds of those employed in copper mining in the United States were immigrants in 1910. In 1913, only one-third of the workers in the Butte mines were

TABLE 3: *The Distribution of Foreign-Born Registrants in Butte by Ward, 1913*

	Ward							
	1	2	3	4	5	6	7	8
Irish	59.5%	42.9%	44.5%	19.9%	18.8%	18.4%	14.9%	15.1%
British	10.9	28.9	12.5	18.2	21.4	24.7	25.5	22.6
Canadian	7.2	13.9	8.1	29.7	14.6	26.6	19.2	23.7
German	3.0	4.8	3.1	11.9	7.2	11.4	10.0	11.7
Scandinavian	3.0	5.8	3.5	9.1	9.5	8.2	11.0	11.9
Slavic	13.2	1.9	5.5	4.2	14.9	1.9	11.8	4.7
Finnish	1.6	0.3	18.9	0.4	4.6	0.0	3.4	0.3
Other	1.6	1.5	3.9	6.6	9.0	8.8	4.2	10.0
	100%	100%	100%	100%	100%	100%	100%	100%
	$n = 304$	$n = 585$	$n = 544$	$n = 286$	$n = 431$	$n = 158$	$n = 698$	$n = 729$
Total proportion of foreign-born	50.8%	40.3%	49.1%	28.2%	47.7%	16.6%	39.3%	33.3%

Source: Great Register of Butte City – 1913.

native-born: 19 per cent were Irish, 15 per cent were Cornish, 9 per cent were Slavs, 5 per cent were Finns, 5 per cent were Canadians, 3 per cent were Scandinavians, and 3 per cent were Italians.[11]

This particular mixture of nationalities often led to tension in the mines over the competition for jobs. The competition, which was sometimes encouraged by Company employment practices, generated resentment. Butte miners vented some of their frustration in songs, such as "Jimmy Gleason's Rustling Song":

> Molly dear, and did ya hear
> The news that's goin' round?
> They're cannin' all the shovelers
> A-working underground.
>
> I rustled at the Diamond
> I rustled at the Con
> The dagoes are the only ones
> That they are putting on.[12]

The competition also found a voice in local newspapers, as in this bigoted account that appeared in the July 24, 1910, *Butte Evening News*:

> Since the bohunk influx to Butte began it has never ceased. Day after day, and night after night, as the trains pull into Butte, the bohunks step off at the station. Once landed they are met by one or two old-time bohunks, who immediately take them on a long hike to "Cork-town" or the "Gulch." . . . Every train that dumps these foreigners off as it pulls in takes just as many old-timers aboard as it pulls out.[13]

The stratification of jobs also fueled the intra-class ethnic conflict in the mines. The hardest, dirtiest, most unhealthy, and most dangerous jobs went to the newest immigrants, while the more comfortable and better-paying jobs tended to be the province of native-born Americans and immigrants from northern Europe. Seven out of ten stationary engineers and machinists employed in copper mining in the United States were native-born, while two-thirds of the unskilled jobs were held by immigrants. The same was true for supervisory positions in the mines. In Butte, two-thirds of the shift bosses were native-born; of the remainder, most were Cornish, English, and Canadian immigrants.[14]

What was true for mining in Butte was also true for other manual occupations. Recent immigrants tended to dwell at the bottom of the occupational and wage ladder, with the native-born and the older immigrants standing above them in job status and income. Native-born Americans, for example, constituted two-thirds of those employed in skilled trades, such as blacksmiths and carpenters.

Non-manual work was also the special territory of native-born Americans. In Butte, they comprised 83 per cent of professionals (doctors, lawyers, accountants, and the like), 83 per cent of clerical and sales personnel, and 60 per cent of those engaged in business either as managers or as independent proprietors.[15]

Because immigrant workers in Butte faced limited occupational opportunities, it is not surprising that ethnic origin closely paralleled social class. The heaviest concentrations of native-born Americans were in the neighborhoods west of Main Street in

TABLE 4: *Distribution of Occupational Groups in Butte by Ward Residence, 1913*

	Ward							
	1	2	3	4	5	6	7	8
Middle Class								
Professional	2.1%	5.7%	1.7%	9.1%	0.2%	9.6%	1.5%	2.9%
Business	5.1	9.5	7.9	21.3	9.8	16.5	8.6	11.1
Clerical/Sales	4.4	11.2	6.2	16.7	3.7	14.5	7.0	14.4
Subtotal	11.6	26.4	15.8	47.2	13.7	40.6	17.1	28.4
Working Class								
Skilled	7.5	9.3	5.3	12.6	9.2	16.9	16.0	19.6
Semiskilled	2.6	2.6	2.6	2.3	4.6	4.0	11.8	10.5
Laborers	3.4	3.3	2.8	3.0	5.6	3.0	6.9	7.4
Miners	66.9	45.5	63.6	23.9	53.5	22.3	34.4	21.8
Other mine*	5.3	9.7	6.1	6.5	6.5	6.7	9.9	8.0
Service	2.7	3.2	3.8	4.6	6.9	6.5	3.9	4.3
Subtotal	88.4	73.6	84.2	52.8	86.3	59.4	82.9	71.6
	100%	100%	100%	100%	100%	100%	100%	100%
	n=586	n=1409	n=1092	n=967	n=888	n=1068	n=1699	n=2098

Source: *Great Register of Butte City—1913.*

*For example, mill and smelter workers, hoisting engineers, timbermen, and other non-supervisory mine employees.

the Fourth and Sixth wards, those parts of the city with the heaviest concentrations of workers engaged in non-manual occupations. In those wards with the highest concentrations of foreign-born residents, miners were the majority occupational group (Table 4). During the Socialist era, Butte was a social landscape characterized by a significant degree of class, ethnic, and occupational stratification. Butte was also an environment in which ethnicity was clearly reflected in partisan political attachments.

The Democratic and Republican parties were largely cross-class coalitions based on Irish-Catholic and English-Protestant identifications. One-third of the Democratic precinct delegates and alternates in the 1912 Silver Bow County nominating convention were Irish immigrants; a great many more were of Irish descent. Among Republican precinct delegates and alternates, slightly less than one in five had been born in England. In contrast, only one in eight Butte voters were Irish immigrants and one in eight were English. Of the two old parties, the Democrats were decidedly more proletarian. Sixty per cent of the Democratic delegates and alternates were manual workers compared to 48 per cent of the Republicans.

In both Democratic and Republican parties, the middle class—Butte's doctors, lawyers, and businessmen, for example—played the leadership role. If we look at the leaders of the major parties (those elected to the county central committee or nominated for county and state legislative office), we find that 62 per cent of the Democratic and 69 per cent of the Republican leadership group worked at occupations that can be considered middle class. In a word, the Democratic and Republican parties in 1912 were bifurcated cross-class coalitions of middle-class and working-class elements in which the former, by virtue of their higher social status and economic position, took the leading part.[16]

The Socialist Party was more diverse in ethnic composition and was, not surprisingly, decidedly working class. The membership roll for Local Butte Branch No. 1 (English-speaking) for about 1913-1915 shows the Irish to be the largest immigrant contingent, but they constituted less than 10 per cent of the whole. Those born in Canada followed with 9 per cent, the English 8 per cent, and Germans and Scandinavians each accounted for 4 per cent of the party members. There were also a small number of Slavs and Finns in the English-speaking branch. Local Butte No. 1 also had a decidedly proletarian tilt. Almost three-quarters of the members were manual workers. Miners made up the largest group, followed by skilled craftsmen and laborers.

The Socialist leadership group (county central committeemen and county and legislative candidates) was also working class. In 1912, 71 per cent of this group were manual workers. To be sure, there were also influential "bourgeois" individuals in the party, such as Louis Duncan and H. L. Maury, but Socialism in Butte was fundamentally a working-class movement, as it claimed to be. As such, the Socialist Party stood in sharp contrast to the middle-class-dominated parties that opposed it.[17]

The Socialists were attempting to build a majority working-class movement, a decidedly difficult task given the divisions within the ranks of the workers and the traditional ties that bound many of them to the old parties. Seeking to prevent the Socialists from achieving their goal, the enemies of Socialism unleashed a steady stream of propaganda to persuade voters that a vote for the Socialists was unwise, unpatriotic, and un-Christian.

The Socialists responded with their own campaign, poking fun at their journalistic detractors. They took special delight in awarding *Butte Miner* editor Larry Dobell the sobriquet "Comrade Larry" for his unintentional and untiring efforts on behalf of the Socialist Party. Responding to Dobell's allegation that establishing an office of city assessor was motivated by the Socialists' desire to increase the number of political patronage jobs, the *Montana Socialist* crowed: "We are almost never disappointed in anticipating that the editor of the *Miner* will make a consummate political ass of himself in his editorial attacks upon the Socialist Party of Butte."[18]

One line of attack required a more serious and measured response. Church leaders and the Socialists' detractors routinely accused the party of being against religion, particularly the Catholic church. The daily press willingly reported these accusations, most of them made by parish priests, just before elections in which Socialists were candidates. In a heavily Catholic community like Butte, the attacks could not go unanswered.

The Catholic church's opposition to the Socialists was based primarily on the encyclical *Rerum Novarum*, issued by Pope Leo XIII in 1891. Pope Leo had used the encyclical to condemn the capitalists for their greed and to commend the workers' efforts to organize trade unions for their economic and social self-defense. But he had condemned the Socialists for their advocacy of the class struggle, their opposition to the institution of private property, and their egalitarianism.[19] In America, the Catholic church tended to place the most emphasis on the anti-Socialist portion of the papal encyclical.

The effects of the Catholic church's anti-Socialist propaganda in America remain the subject of historical controversy; but in Butte, Catholics who read the local newspaper, attended mass, or simply commingled with their fellow church members knew the church's opinion of the Socialist Party.[20] The Catholic church in Butte indicted the Socialists as "immoral, irreligious, un-Christian and specifically anti-Catholic." One parish priest thundered: "No man who professes socialism as it is preached and written by its exponents can still honestly profess the Catholic faith."[21]

Church spokesmen also delivered sermons heavily laden with economic theory. Helena Bishop John P. Carroll announced that Socialism was economically "unsound." Carroll asked:

> Who would work in the field, in the factory and the mine if his surplus earnings were confiscated by the state? Where would be the incentive to toil if one were not permitted to accumulate capital and make it productive?

On another occasion, Carroll told Montana workers to beware of "unscrupulous agitators" who falsely assert that "labor is the source of all wealth." Poverty, like wealth, Carroll urged, was evidence of the personal qualities of individuals and not blind economic forces. Those who were poor had obviously led intemperate lives, the Bishop believed, and diligent workers should expect a "living wage" and nothing more.[22] The church advised the poor and oppressed to have patience and offered the promise of a better "future state" in the afterlife where "full compensation shall be made for every inequality submissively borne."[23] Father Adalbert of Butte took another approach:

> If we are asked what are the remedies to the wrongs under which the working classes groan, we should reply: a virtuous Christian life, education, frugality, temperance, the organization of the forces of the working classes, and attainment of their lawful and just demands by those just and peaceful methods which bring to their aid the sympathy of the community.[24]

The Socialists responded to this ecclesiastical criticism by repeatedly stating that the party was neutral toward religion and that it had no interest in whether or not party members professed a religious faith.[25] Louis Duncan replied specifically to Bishop Carroll's attack:

Socialism is not an enemy to the church or to religion. It leaves that subject alone—prefers to do so believing it to be a matter of individual determination. But when the church in the name of religion gets out of that field and into our chosen field of economic and political science, and begins to misrepresent the teachings of Socialism, and to hand out to the working class economic and political teachings that are false and have a tendency to keep the workers in ignorance and thus hinder the day of their emancipation, then indeed, the Socialists will and do fight back. . . . But this is not fighting religion or the church. It is fighting political error and falsehood. If the church will foster such teachings—well, so much the worse for the church.[26]

The *Montana Socialist* expressed a similar hope:

Laboring men and women in Montana will scarcely relish the pasture to which this well-fed shepherd [Carroll] leads them. They will recognize at once the old, dry husks of admonition and counsel which the church has fed its sheep for generations. It is only the modern version of "be content with the condition in which it pleases providence to place you."

The *Socialist* urged workers to ignore the "quietistic teachings" of the Catholic church and to vote for the Socialist Party.[27]

Who did vote for the Socialists? The answer can be found in the composition of Butte's neighborhoods.[28] The city was composed of three distinct social communities (see Table 5). *Northeast Butte* was the city's working-class core. Bounded on the west by Main Street and on the south by First Street, Northeast Butte comprised the First, Third, and Fifth wards; three precincts in the Seventh Ward north of the Northern Pacific tracks; and two precincts in the Second Ward that were abutted on the east by North Main Street, on the south by West Granite, and on the west by Washington Street (see map). The highest concentrations of working-class and foreign-born voters lived in this section of the city. Most of the workingmen were employed as miners. Finntown was located here, as was the notorious Cabbage Patch. Immediately north of the city limits was Centerville; farther up the hill was the village of Walkerville. To the northeast of the city line was Dublin Gulch. Northeast Butte was a world of miners' cottages, cheap boarding houses, and saloons.

The *Middle-Class Enclave* began west of Main Street and encompassed all of the Fourth and Sixth wards, the two western precincts in the Second Ward, and one precinct in the northwest corner of the Eighth Ward. The highest concentrations of middle-class voters lived in this part of the city. The Middle-Class Enclave also had the lowest percentage of foreign-born voters in the city. Butte's business and professional elites called this part of town home.

The Flats was composed of five precincts in the Seventh and Eighth wards. Slightly more than two-thirds of the voters in the community were native-born, and three-

WALKERVILLE

🭲 BADGER STATE

🭲 LEXINGTON

CENTERVILLE

🭲 BELL · SPECULATOR
🭲 DIAMOND

🭲 MTN CON

🭲 HIGH ORE
MEADERVILLE
🭲 LEONARD

DUBLIN GULCH
🭲 W.COLUSA
🭲 MTN. VIEW
🭲 RARUS
🭲 TRAMWAY

🭲 STEWARD
ORIGINAL
🭲 ANACONDA
🭲 ST. LAWRENCE
🭲 BERKLEY

2
NEVER SWEAT

1
WASHINGTON
N. MAIN

Finlander Hall
Miners Union Hall
County Courthouse

W. GRANITE
E. GRANITE
3
City Hall
E. PARK
🭲 PENNSYLVANIA

4
W. PARK
🭲 SILVER BOW

6
W. SILVER
5
CURTIS
DIVISION

S. MAIN
7

8

MIDDLE CLASS ENCLAVE
NORTHEAST BUTTE

S. WYOMING

CITY LIMITS

LEGEND
ooooooo SOCIAL COMMUNITIES
••••••• CITY COUNCIL WARDS

Northern Pacific R.R.

Socialist Hall

THE FLATS

CITY LIMITS

8   7
CITY LIMITS

Map by Cecilia Vaniman

City Council Wards and Social Communities,
Butte, Montana, 1912

quarters of the residents were employed in manual occupations. Here there were fewer miners and a relatively large number of workers employed in skilled and semi-skilled occupations. Most of the housing was single-family dwellings.

In the 1912 election, Woodrow Wilson comfortably carried the city precincts with 38.3 per cent of the vote; Eugene Debs trailed with 29.3 per cent. Debs carried The Flats in that election with 33.7 per cent of the vote, placed second in Northeast Butte with 34 per cent, and finished almost 20 percentage points behind Wilson in the Middle-Class Enclave (see Table 6). The Socialists' state and local candidates did much better, especially county attorney candidate Maury, but the pattern was the same. The Socialists won in The Flats, placed a strong second to the Democrats in the Northeast, and fared rather poorly in the middle-class community west of Main.

Typical of the local election returns were those in the sheriff's contest, which pitted Socialist Dan Sullivan against Democrat Tim Driscoll. Sullivan was a first-generation Irish-American born in Michigan, a miner, and a former president of the Butte Miners' Union. Driscoll, an Irish immigrant, was a working miner who had risen to the position of shift boss. When the ballots were counted in Butte, Driscoll had edged Sullivan by a thin 37 to 35 per cent. Driscoll was the victor in sixteen of the

TABLE 5: *Distribution of Ethnic and Occupational Groups in Butte's Social Communities, 1913*

	Middle-Class Enclave	The Flats	Northeast Butte
Middle Class			
Professional	8.8%	1.9%	1.4%
Business	16.1	12.3	7.8
Clerical/Sales	16.1	11.2	5.5
Subtotal	41.0	25.4	14.7
Working Class			
Skilled	14.6	20.1	8.3
Semiskilled	4.0	12.2	4.7
Laborers	3.5	7.3	4.6
Miners	25.2	22.5	56.8
Other mine	7.7	8.3	6.6
Service	4.0	4.2	4.3
Subtotal	59.0	74.6	85.3
	100%	100%	100%
	$n=3,228$	$n=2,385$	$n=4,225$
Ethnic Origin			
Native-born	69.9	65.7	53.0
Irish	6.5	5.0	17.3
British	7.3	8.2	9.1
Canadian	7.2	8.9	5.1
German	3.5	3.5	1.9
Scandinavian	2.5	3.7	3.2
Slavic	1.1	1.7	4.9
Finnish	0.2	0.5	3.3
Other	1.8	2.8	2.2
	100%	100%	100%
	$n=3,395$	$n=2,440$	$n=4,288$

Source: From *Great Register of Butte City—1913.*

TABLE 6: *Butte's Social Communities in the 1912 Election*

	Middle-Class Enclave	The Flats	Northeast Butte
President			
Wilson (D)	39.0%	30.1%	42.1%
Debs (S)	20.7	33.7	34.0
Taft (R)	20.1	19.3	13.9
Roosevelt (P)	20.2	16.9	10.0
Governor			
Stewart (D)	38.1%	32.3%	43.0%
Duncan (S)	25.6	37.6	38.0
Wilson (R)	22.8	19.8	14.1
Edwards (P)	13.5	10.3	4.9
County Attorney			
McCaffery (D)	38.1%	30.4%	40.8%
Maury (S)	32.5	43.4	40.9
Smith (R)	23.1	19.0	14.4
Barta (P)	6.3	7.2	3.9
Sheriff			
Driscoll (D)	37.5%	29.2%	41.6%
Sullivan (S)	28.8	39.5	38.7
Stewart (R)	24.7	23.2	15.2
Carns (P)	9.0	8.1	4.5

Source: Butte Miner, November 13, 1912.

Note: D = Democrat; R = Republican; S = Socialist; P = Progressive

city's twenty-seven precincts and carried the First, Second, Third, Fourth, and Sixth wards. Sullivan carried the majority in the remaining precincts and won a majority in the Seventh and Eighth wards. Sullivan received slightly less than 29 per cent of the vote in the Middle-Class Enclave, was edged by Driscoll by fewer than three percentage points in Northeast Butte, and coasted to a comfortable victory in The Flats.

Sullivan and the other Socialists should have won the day in the heart of working-class Butte. They did not. The key to their defeat lies in the ethnic composition of Northeast Butte precincts. The highest concentrations of immigrant Irish voters in the city were in eight of those precincts (where the mean percentage of Irish voters was 24.3). Driscoll won in seven of them, losing to Sullivan only in the eleventh precinct, the Third Ward, which was the heart of Finntown. In the remaining five northeast precincts in the Fifth Ward and in the northern portion of the Seventh Ward, the proportion of Irish immigrant voters was much lower, ranging from 11.3 to 6.3 per cent. Sullivan emerged the victor in four of them. In the six remaining precincts where Sullivan bested Driscoll, the percentage of working-class voters ranged from 56 to 75 per cent. All six precincts had a relatively small proportion of Irish immigrant voters, ranging from 4 to 7 per cent.

The Socialists drew their support from two working-class constituencies: unskilled immigrant workers and both foreign and native-born skilled and semiskilled workers. In the five Northeast precincts carried by Sullivan, the mean percentage of immigrant voters was fifty; slightly more than eight out of ten were manual workers, most of them miners. The proportion of Irish immigrant voters was low in comparison to the remaining Northeast Butte precincts. In the remaining precincts carried by Sullivan, all were located in The Flats, where only one-third of the voters were immigrants. Approximately seven out of ten were manual workers, but a much higher proportion worked in skilled and semiskilled occupations. There were few Irish immigrant voters.

The Socialists enjoyed substantial working-class support in the 1912 election with the relative exception of working-class Irish voters. In Northeast Butte, Socialist voters were likely to be miners and immigrants; in The Flats, they were probably native-born or immigrants employed in skilled or semiskilled manual occupations.

Socialists might have done better in the heavily Irish working-class precincts of the Northeast were it not for the traditional Irish allegiance to the Democratic Party and the anti-Socialist propaganda of the Catholic church. The Irish working-class vote had helped the Democratic Party barely carry the day in the face of a strong Socialist challenge.[29] If the Socialists were to win in the future, they would have to cut into the proletarian base that continued to vote Democratic. If they could not, the opposition would continue to hold the high ground.

While the Socialists and their opponents battled for political supremacy at the polls, another struggle for control was being waged within the huge and powerful Butte Miners' Union. Within this union a kind of two-party system had been in place for several years, as "conservative" and "progressive" miners literally slugged it out over who would rule the roost. A protracted war was being fought between these two factions, a war that would lead to the physical destruction of the Butte Miners' Union, the imposition of martial law, and the impeachment of Mayor Duncan.

The election of conservative candidates with their well-known policy of amicable relations with the mining companies, their disposition to favor peace and good times, is a matter of general congratulation.
— *Anaconda Standard*,
June 3, 1913

7 | *Something Rotten in Gibraltar*

On Miners' Union Day, June 13, 1913, eight thousand workers marched in celebration of the union's thirty-fifth anniversary. It was "the most important of Butte's holidays," the *Standard* enthusiastically reported, a day when members of the Butte Miners' Union and all other unions marched in an impressive show of labor solidarity.[1]

Founded on June 13, 1878, the Butte Workingmen's Union grew and prospered along with the town. In 1885, the union reorganized and became the Butte Miners' Union, with miners as its only constituency. Created initially to defend a $3.50-a-day wage scale for miners, the union quickly established a closed shop in the mines, chartered branch affiliates in other Montana mining camps, and was instrumental in founding the militant Western Federation of Miners in 1893. In an era marked by employers' hostility toward labor unionism, the strength and the respectability enjoyed by the BMU was unusual.

The BMU had been founded and nurtured in Montana's peculiar political environment. The copper capitalists were at war during the 1890s, and Clark, Daly, and Heinze evinced a friendly attitude toward organized labor and its demands as each avidly courted and cultivated working-class votes.[2] But there was a sinister aspect to this courtship. There were reports that warring capitalists had bribed union leaders in return for helping "deliver" the miners' vote on election day. The WFM, through its *Miners Magazine*, condemned the corruption in the Butte Miners' Union and expressed equal distaste for the political conservatism of its leaders.[3] For example, in 1902 the WFM endorsed the Socialist Party, and the BMU refused to attend the annual meetings of the Montana Federation of Labor.[4] When the WFM participated officially in the founding convention of the Industrial Workers of the World in 1905, the Butte local protested loudly.[5] Later that same year, WFM President Charles Moyer, Secretary-Treasurer William D. "Big Bill" Haywood, and former WFM member George Pettibone were arrested in Denver and taken to Idaho to stand trial for murder. The three were charged with having conspired to murder former Gover-

71

nor Frank Steunenberg for his actions against the Federation. The WFM and nearly the whole of organized labor rallied to their defense, but the BMU refused to participate and to help pay for the expensive defense of the three Federation leaders.

At the 1906 WFM convention, acting President J. C. Williams condemned the BMU for its disloyalty. But the members of the Butte delegation did not hear Williams's censure; they had already bolted the convention to protest the seating of two "socialist" Butte miners who had been denied delegate credentials by the union's conservative leadership. Back in Butte, miners who had long objected to the union's conservatism packed the union hall and elected a new slate of "progressive" delegates to replace those who had bolted.[6] The split signaled the two-party system that was beginning to emerge in the internal politics of the BMU.

On one side of the controversy stood the union's temporarily discredited "conservative" faction, whose leaders were mostly Irish and Democrats. Their critics called them the "company crowd," because they believed that the conservatives were too friendly to the mining companies. On the other side were the ascendant progressives. Many of them were members and supporters of the Socialist Party, some were IWW men, and some were independents who simply objected to corporate influence in union affairs. Most of the progressive leaders were also apparently Irish.

The progressives subsequently were able to win control of the union in local elections as a consequence of a controversy over the signing of a five-year contract with the Anaconda Copper Mining Company in 1907. In late 1906, the union demanded a fifty-cent increase in the miners' daily wages, from $3.50 to $4.00 a day. Amalgamated President John D. Ryan made a counter offer: If the union would agree to a five-year contract, the Company would recognize the "Butte scale" of $3.50 a day as the guaranteed minimum wage regardless of the market price of copper. If the price went up by eighteen cents or more a pound, then the miners' wages would rise to four dollars a day. In what appears to have been a confused referendum vote, the rank and file accepted the Company's offer without fully realizing that the four dollar wage was tied to the price of copper or that the contract put to them by the union's leaders also violated the WFM's practice of never signing a contract with an employer.

When the union signed the contract on April 4, 1907, the progressives were furious. They counterattacked at the annual WFM convention a month later. The progressives told the delegates that the BMU's contract directly violated the WFM's no-contract policy, which was based on the presumption that there could never be a common interest between employer and employee. The progressives successfully pushed for the adoption of an amendment to the Federation's constitution: "No local union or unions of the Western Federation of Miners shall enter into any signed contract or verbal agreement for any specified length of time with their employers." But the Butte contract was already signed, and it was allowed to stand.[7]

The 1907 convention was a turning point in the history of the Western Federation of Miners. On the surface, it had been one of the most radical gatherings of that organization. The delegates had adopted a new preamble to the constitution, reaffirming the Federation's belief in the "class struggle," "industrial unionism," and "independent political action."[8] Quietly, however, the Federation was drifting to the right, the most dramatic indication being its withdrawal from the Industrial Workers of the World.

By 1906, only a year after it was founded in Chicago, the IWW was floundering badly. Contrary to expectations, disgruntled AFL affiliates had not rushed to join the IWW, nor had the understaffed and underfinanced union enjoyed much success in organizing the unorganized. The IWW was also plagued by ineffective leadership, probably the most decisive cause of the union's weak beginnings. IWW President Charles O. Sherman had allegedly misspent the union's meager funds. Equally damning, Sherman was a conservative trade unionist. His major critic and rival was IWW Secretary-Treasurer William Trautmann, a self-described revolutionary who had no experience in managing a labor organization. A logical choice to lead the IWW would have been "Big Bill" Haywood, but he was in Idaho standing trial with Moyer and Pettibone. The men who were temporarily in charge of the WFM in Haywood's absence were a conservative lot who had never been particularly happy with the Federation's affiliation with the IWW and who were looking for an excuse to sever the WFM's connection with the radical unionists.

Weakness and frustration often engender factionalism, and there was a great deal of it at the second IWW convention as the Sherman and Trautmann forces slugged it out. Chairing the chaotic gathering was the WFM's acting vice-president, Charles O. Mahoney. A Sherman man and a political conservative, Mahoney found that his rulings from the chair were repeatedly challenged and rejected by floor votes engineered by the dominant Trautmann group. Then the Trautmann forces eliminated Sherman by ramming through a resolution abolishing the office of president. Unhappy with this turn of events, Mahoney led a majority of WFM delegates out of the convention; shortly thereafter, the WFM formally withdrew from the IWW.[9] From his Idaho jail cell, President Moyer agreed with the action, but Bill Haywood pointedly did not. By the time Moyer and Haywood were acquitted in 1907, they were bitter enemies. Haywood left the Federation to become the IWW's secretary-treasurer, and Moyer resumed his post as WFM president.

Moyer guided the WFM in a more conservative direction, toward eventual affiliation with the American Federation of Labor. His opponents charged that Moyer was motivated by opportunism, but the Federation's drift to the right stemmed from many causes. Perhaps being jailed for a long period of time had changed Moyer. Perhaps his personal antipathy toward Haywood played a part. What *was* clear was that the WFM was making no headway in organizing metal miners. The union had lost in a violent struggle with Colorado mine owners; it had failed to organize the important Joplin, Missouri, mining district; it was invisible in the Michigan and Minnesota mines; and it was being locked out in the Black Hills of South Dakota.

In Moyer's view, the WFM's weakness flowed primarily from its self-imposed isolation as a "revolutionary" union. In its bitter struggle to survive, the union had chosen to stand alone, and it could expect neither moral nor material support from the AFL, which it had so often condemned. If the WFM was to survive, Moyer believed, it had to make accommodations. In 1908, Moyer told the WFM convention that "industrial unionism [the IWW] is by no means popular and I feel safe in saying that it is not wanted by the working class." He advised: "Let us confine our efforts, for the time being, in bringing into our ranks these people over which we have jurisdiction"—that is, recruiting men who worked in the metal mining industry. Moyer informed the delegates that two hundred thousand men worked in the industry and that the WFM represented only forty-two thousand of them. The WFM will have done its "duty" in "bringing about the emancipation of labor," Moyer argued, if it successfully organized the metal mining industry. One year later, Moyer repeated his warning that any "effort to launch a general industrial movement at this time as proposed by some" was "undertaking the impossible."[10]

The Butte progressives disagreed. They had not directly experienced the WFM's hard-fought and bitter defeats, and they admired Bill Haywood and his uncompromising revolutionism. They could see no legitimate basis for Moyer's suggested change of direction, and they believed that the union president had only corrupt and self-serving motives. Together with their allies in the WFM, the Butte progressives had bitterly fought Moyer and the majority of the Federation's delegates who followed his leadership. Failing in 1907 to pass a resolution urging the WFM's reaffiliation with the Industrial Workers of the World, they lined up two years later behind a series of constitutional amendments designed to make the Federation an organizational carbon copy of the IWW.[11] The proposed amendments called for the abolition of the offices of president and vice-president, an end to all regular salaries for WFM officials, and the direct yearly election of WFM officers by a rank-and-file referendum vote (which would replace the annual election by the convention). Convention delegates rejected the proposed changes.[12]

The progressives also vigorously opposed a Moyer-initiated proposal to affiliate with the AFL. Moyer and the Federation leadership urged the WFM membership to affiliate with the AFL on the grounds that it would increase inter-union cooperation and strength and that it would implicitly lead to possible amalgamation with the much larger and stronger United Mine Workers of America. The WFM leadership asked:

> Is it in our best interests to longer stand alone in the industrial field? Second, are we consistent in continuing to stand aloof from the American labor movement and appealing to them for moral and financial assistance when we are forced to engage in conflicts with employers? . . . Realizing as we must, our helplessness in standing alone, . . . why should we hesitate to join hands with the United Mine Workers, which is composed of many times our numbers, simply because they are part of the American Federation of Labor?[13]

With the issue presented this way, WFM members approved the formal proposal to accept a charter from the AFL in a referendum vote in early 1911.[14]

The progressives denounced this "sellout" to craft unionism and continued their attacks against Moyer. They accused Moyer of lying to the rank and file, claiming that he had no real desire to merge the WFM and the UMWA and that he only wanted to begin leading a comfortable life as a respected labor leader. Nothing ever came of the proposed WFM-UMWA merger, lending some credibility to the progressives' indictment.[15]

The progressives did prevail on one issue: changing the method for selecting Federation officers. Progressives believed that the election of national officers by delegates selected by WFM union locals had been too easily "controlled" by the incumbent Moyer leadership. The direct election of officers by the rank and file, the progressives predicted, would be more democratic and accurately expressive of the members' sentiments. At the 1911 convention, which was held in the progressives' stronghold of Butte, President Moyer was forced to concede that it was time to "settle the question" once and for all. The convention approved a motion to provide for the direct election of the president and the executive board by the entire membership.[16]

Seeking to take advantage of the change, the progressives entered an opposition slate in the Federation election scheduled for June 1912. Calling itself the "Industrial Union Organization," the opposition slate was headed by IWW sympathizer Tom Campbell of Butte as its candidate for president of the Federation. Most of the other opposition candidates were also from Butte, and all of Butte's Industrial Union candidates were members of the Socialist Party.

Moyer reacted quickly by making exaggerated claims that Campbell and the others were all "sound" IWW men. This was the key to the vicious enmity between Moyer and the Butte progressives. The IWW had never been reconciled to losing the WFM from its ranks, and it is fair to say that those who sympathized with the revolutionary industrial unionism would have liked to see the metal miners marching behind the Wobbly banner. This desire encouraged Moyer's belief in an IWW conspiracy to take over the WFM or, failing that, to destroy it. There is no substantive evidence that such a plot ever existed, but Moyer believed it, and that belief produced a hostile attitude toward all who criticized his leadership, especially those whom Moyer believed were "sound" IWW men.[17]

George Curry was president of the Butte Miners' Union when the Butte progressives fielded their "industrial" slate in January 1912. Curry was a member of the Socialist Party, as were most of the union's other officers.[18] Some may have carried Wobbly membership cards, but there was no IWW local in Butte at the time. Nevertheless, all of these men considered themselves to be "industrial unionists." They were fiercely antagonistic toward the craft unionism of the AFL and were opposed to the political conservatism that the AFL epitomized. Industrial unionists identified themselves with "independent political action" and the Socialist Party, holding to the belief that militant industrial unionism and Socialist politics went hand in hand.

The progressives had controlled the Butte Miners' Union since 1907 and had attempted to "educate" the rank and file by tapping the union's education fund to buy bulk subscriptions to Socialist and IWW newspapers. They had also used their positions to proselytize on behalf of the Socialist ticket and the idea of industrial unionism.[19] They opposed Moyer because he was moving the WFM away from the kind of radical labor unionism that they believed was necessary to build working-class consciousness and political solidarity. But Moyer only saw the specter of the IWW plotting to steal the WFM, and the headquarters of the imagined plot was the Butte Miners' Union. This perception seems to explain Moyer's failure to react to the employers' attack on the BMU in March 1912.

The Anaconda Copper Mining Company and the other mining operators had been keeping a close eye on the political coloration of the Butte Miners' Union. Their five-year contract with the union would expire in April, and the union and the companies had agreed that negotiations over a new contract would not begin until after the local had selected a new slate of officers in the June union election. If the progressive faction remained in control, the unionists would undoubtedly make demands that the companies would be most reluctant to accept. The progressives knew that the

1907 wage agreement had worked entirely to the miners' disadvantage. When the agreement was signed, copper was selling at eighteen cents a pound and miners were receiving four dollars a day. But after a few months the price had dropped; it would not reach eighteen cents again until 1918. As a consequence, miners were still earning $3.50 a day in 1912, the same wage that Butte miners had received in 1878.[20] A progressive negotiating committee would have demanded a substantial increase in the daily wage and an end to the sliding scale. It is also likely that the committee would have demanded a dramatic improvement in health and safety conditions. It was in the companies' best interests, therefore, to do what they could to ensure the progressives' defeat in the upcoming union election.

Also pressing was the April 1912 Butte aldermanic election. If the Socialists could win four of those races they would gain majority control of the city council, and the Duncan administration might enact legislation that could be troublesome for the mining companies. Therefore, the companies also had a strong incentive to do what they could to prevent the Socialists from achieving their electoral goal.

The mining companies made their move on March 19 and 20. In a coordinated assault, operators summarily fired an estimated five hundred "socialist" miners.[21] The officers of the Butte Miners' Union reacted by calling for a mass protest meeting on the following day. At the meeting, the union appointed a committee to go to the operators and demand the reinstatement of those who had been fired. Three days later the committee reported that the managers had refused to take back any of the fired workers and, with two dissents, recommended that a strike be called immediately. Anticipating the recommendation, the BMU's conservative faction had packed the hall. Conservative members supported the counter-resolution offered by the two dissenting committeemen who opposed the immediate calling of a strike and urged instead that the walkout be postponed until the entire membership had voiced its sentiments in a referendum vote.[22]

If the companies had hoped to precipitate conservative opposition to a strike, they had picked their target well. Although all of those fired were probably not party members, most of those who lost their jobs were Finns. The companies had to have been aware that Cornish and Irish miners saw the Finns as competitors for their jobs and that they were unlikely to go on strike to force their reinstatement.[23] Miner Korven Kossi bitterly described for the Finnish Socialist paper, *Työmies*, the significance of the conservatives' resolution:

> The committee brought this recommendation to the union meeting, but several company stooges began to question the proposal: What do we, the majority, care about the fate of the Finns and the socialists—let them starve! They began to twist the matter toward a general vote, knowing full well that they would win.[24]

The resolution carried.

The next order of business was the election of the judges and clerks who would count the vote in the pending strike referendum. Finnish miner and progressive laborite K. O. Katuri described the crowded and emotional scene and the actions of the alleged "company stooges":

As the vote was being taken by ballot, a disturbance arose when the stooges of the companies began shouting and acting belligerent, even attempting in a group to physically attack the union president [George Curry], who took refuge in his chair behind the head table. One stooge reached the president's table and waved a hammer, but he was dragged away. Then about 200 Finns, whom the president had picked as bodyguards, began to move in from the other side of the room, pushing themselves between the president's chair and the bloodthirsty troublemakers.[25]

The strike vote was taken on March 29. The companies had given the men the day off to vote, and turnout was heavy. The strike was rejected by a decisive 1,121 to 4,460 votes.[26] The sharp divisions in the ranks of the miners, fostered by ethnic and political antagonisms, were apparent to everyone.[27] It was also evident that the union's progressive leaders had been repudiated. The way was now prepared for a resurgent conservative faction in the June elections.

The mass firing had also added to the tension between the progressives and WFM President Moyer. After the rank and file had rejected the call for a strike, BMU leaders had appealed to the WFM for assistance. They received none, with Moyer arguing that the Federation could do nothing because the local had voted officially *not* to strike. The Finns found it reprehensible that Moyer failed even to censure the miners for their unwillingness to defend their union brothers. The Finns argued that they had always been strong union men and that the union had deserted them. One Finnish miner said that the WFM could "rot" for all he cared and that the Finns wanted "real industrial unionism." After March 1912, Butte's Finns would be the IWW's strongest supporters in the mining city.[28] Because Charles Moyer had not come to the aid of the Butte progressives, he had implicitly made common cause with the BMU's conservative faction, the mining companies, and all those who opposed the Socialists in Butte. Both Moyer and the WFM would eventually pay a heavy price for his refusal to act.

As the June union elections approached, the conservatives took the offensive. The conservatives were there with the votes on the day that the union elected the judges and clerks who would supervise the election. On election day, the companies once again gave the men the day off to vote. It was a straight-out contest between the conservative slate, headed by Dennis Murphy for president, and the progressives, who picked Socialist Mike Houghton as their candidate. When the results were announced several days after the balloting, Murphy had bested Houghton by about five hundred votes; the rest of the conservative slate was elected by similar margins. In the race for national union offices, Campbell and the "industrial" faction were defeated.[29]

The progressives refused to accept the election results, charging that the conservative judges and clerks had "counted them out." Tom Campbell took the progressives' appeal for a new local election to the WFM convention in Victor, Colorado. Campbell met a cold reception from the majority of delegates, who were Moyer partisans. Rather than investigate Campbell's allegations, the delegates voted to expel him from the Federation for being the leader of the feared IWW plot to destroy the WFM.[30]

In Butte, the companies got the deal they wanted. The new conservative union officers presented the contract to the rank and file as follows: "To accept the offer made by the mining companies—yes or no." The answer was yes by 3,101 to 1,133 votes.

The new three-year pact retained the $3.50 minimum with a sliding scale based on the market price of copper. Under the new contract, the maximum theoretical wage was $4.25 a day if copper sold for eighteen cents a pound. When the contract was signed, copper was selling at seventeen cents, which gave miners a four dollar wage rate. When it dropped to sixteen cents, wages fell with it to $3.75. By the end of 1913 the price had fallen again, and the miners were once again back to the minimum of $3.50.[31] The contract contained no provisions concerning health and safety issues. The progressive miners talked about how the conservative union leaders were misleading the miners and were selling them out, but the rank and file was not listening yet.

In December 1912, the mining companies made what appeared to be a direct assault on the union's progressive faction by announcing a change in employment policy. From now on, the companies announced, a man seeking work in the mines would have to get a permit, a "rustling card," before he would be hired. To get the card, the man would have to fill out an application at a company employment office. His employment references would then be checked in a process that took two to three weeks. If the investigation proved satisfactory, the man would be given the card and he could look for work. He had to surrender the rustling card when he was hired. If he was subsequently fired or laid off, he had to apply for the permit all over again. If the worker's employers gave him unsatisfactory recommendations—for example, if he was a "troublemaker" or a "union agitator"—he would not get the card. Without it, he could not work for any mining company in Butte.[32] The unilateral declaration of the new policy appeared to undermine the very legitimacy of the union itself. Membership in the Butte Miners' Union would no longer be a guarantee of employment if

"Here's Food for Thought for the Cost of Living Experts
Headed by Mr. C. J. Kelly"
Montana Socialist, March 15, 1914

jobs were available. Employers could hire non-union miners who received a rustling card, and it was up to the union to get the new men to join.

The progressives reacted angrily to the announcement of the companies' new employment system. The system constituted a "blacklist" against union men, they charged, and the progressives took their complaints to a special union meeting held on December 6, 1912. The meeting was chaotic as progressives and conservatives cursed and shouted at each other. The conservatives backed a resolution calling for appointment of a committee to discuss the rustling card system with the managers. The progressives backed a proposal offered by George Tompkins, a Socialist and IWW supporter, demanding that the union go on strike to force the companies to drop the new policy.

In the wild and angry confusion, the conservative resolution was voted down. Before Tompkins's proposal was put to a vote, however, President Murphy entertained a motion to adjourn the meeting and then declared the motion carried. Amid hoots and hollers, Murphy left the platform and retreated from the hall with his supporters. Undeterred, the progressives continued the meeting and elected Joe Shannon, a well-known progressive and IWW man, to chair it. Tompkins's resolution was debated and adopted without a dissenting vote.[33]

On December 10, the conservatives packed the hall and voted down Tompkins's resolution. The progressives overwhelmed the conservatives at the next meeting a week later and passed a new resolution calling for a rank-and-file referendum vote on the question: "Will we abolish the card system now in vogue in the mines—yes or no?" In a close contest on December 21, the miners voted 1,856 to 1,627 to "abolish" the rustling card system. There the matter suddenly ended. The conservative leaders ignored the referendum and did nothing, and the progressives did not press the point. The IWW's western newspaper, the *Industrial Worker*, observed: "Late developments in Butte, Mont., have given plausibility to the general belief that many officials of the Western Federation of Miners are simply the tools of the Copper Trust."[34]

The progressives may have failed to act because of their preoccupation with the widening split between the Socialist Party and the IWW over the issue of sabotage and the subsequent recall of Bill Haywood from the party's National Executive Committee. As a consequence of the split, the badly divided progressives presented separate IWW and Socialist tickets in the June 1913 union elections. Divided, they were easily whipped by the conservative slate headed by Bert Riley.[35] But the division was only temporary. The progressives may have been beaten, but they were not broken. A Butte correspondent wrote to the *Industrial Worker*:

> The miners of Butte are dissatisfied and discontented, and are beginning to realize that the W.F. of M. is a thing of the past. No stronger proof of this can be shown than the number of men who quit paying their dues . . . and the way union job delegates are sometimes treated at the mines when they are examining cards. On one or two occasions I have heard of them getting beat up.

"A Miner" predicted that the tyranny of the rustling card system, excessive special assessments levied by the union, and the awful working conditions were "educating" the rank and file in the class struggle and persuading them of the need for a class-conscious industrial union.[36] "A Miner" and those he spoke for were moving toward a final break with the Butte Miners' Union.

We feel that we are right; we feel that the only hope for the miner in Silver Bow County is to have an economic organization sufficiently strong to control the situation, so far as work conditions are concerned. And this is what we intend to do if it is humanly possible for us to do so.
                                                    —Butte Mine Workers' Union,
                                                         September 5, 1914

8 | *The Destruction of the Butte Miners' Union*

Confident and complacent, the conservative faction of the Butte Miners' Union seemed oblivious to the discontent and anger boiling around them—a discontent that the progressive miners no doubt encouraged and exploited. In April 1914, the progressives made their final move to gain control of the union. At a regular union meeting, Daniel Shovlin, a leader of the progressive faction, made a motion that the union borrow the city's voting machines for the June union elections. Shovlin's motion was predicated on the assumption that if paper ballots were used the conservatives would count themselves in and the opposition out. BMU President Bert Riley first refused to accept the motion but then allowed a vote on it. Riley declared Shovlin's proposal defeated by a voice vote. He then accepted a motion from the floor to throw Shovlin's resolution in the wastebasket and declared that the motion had carried.[1]

Riley's arrogant handling of Shovlin's proposal was the "straw that broke the camel's back," as one conservative later admitted.[2] Had the progressives' proposal been accepted and had the conservatives won the election, the progressives would have been in no position to claim that they had been cheated. But because the union was going to use paper ballots (a system that both factions admitted was abused), the progressives charged that the union election would be a farce and withdrew from the contest. Consequently, the conservative slate ran unopposed with Frank O'Connor as its presidential candidate. O'Connor's nomination also demonstrated the conservatives' belligerent insensitivity. O'Connor, the man who had led the conservative faction out of the 1906 WFM convention, was a rabid enemy of the progressives.[3] Putting O'Connor on the ticket was a gross and intentional insult aimed at the progressives, but Riley's dictatorial handling of Shovlin's motion had already sealed the doom of the Butte Miners' Union. By the end of May, rumors were circulating that the progressives were planning to establish a new independent union of miners.[4]

With only about two thousand miners bothering to vote, O'Connor and the other conservatives were duly elected on June 2. On June 11, a union jurisdiction com-

81

mittee appeared at the North Butte Mining Company's Speculator Mine to inspect the union cards of the men going on the night shift, a routine that allowed the Butte Miners' Union to maintain its closed shop.[5] Several workers showed the committee their cards, but then a young miner—later identified as Michael "Muckie" McDonald—refused: "You'll not see my card. I'm not showing it." The rest of the miners followed McDonald's lead, refusing to show their cards and then roughly driving the committeemen away. The rebels then posted the following notice:

> Brother Members of the Day Shift, We your Brothers on the Night Shift have decided not to show our cards to the delegates of the Western Federation of Miners, Butte Local No. 1, and most respectfully request that you do the same.

The day shift agreed and refused to show their cards to the union committeemen, who turned the recalcitrant workers away from their jobs. The Speculator Mine was then closed for the day.[6]

On the evening of June 12, two thousand miners attended a protest meeting. With Daniel Shovlin as chairman, the men voiced their grievances against the Butte Miners' Union. Many were particularly upset about the continued levying of special assessments to support a WFM strike in Michigan that had clearly failed some months before. A rumor was circulating that the Michigan miners were not receiving the money from WFM headquarters, and the miners demanded to know where the money was going. Were WFM officials appropriating money from the strike fund for their own use?

The assembled miners argued over what action to take. One miner made a motion that the men storm Miners' Union Hall and seize the local's financial records. The motion was rejected. One unionist moved that everyone appear at the next union meeting and demand that the recent union election be annulled and a new one held. This proposal also was turned down. The workers finally agreed to establish a new miners' union and to boycott the Miners' Union Day parade and celebration the next morning.[7]

Only a few hundred "conservative" miners marched in the parade. Most of the miners either stayed home or watched the procession silently from the sidewalks. At the intersection of Dakota and Park streets, the quiet was broken when a mob of men suddenly attacked the head of the parade. The angry crowd, which was swelling rapidly, then marched on the nearby Miners' Union Hall and sacked it, throwing furniture out of the broken windows and scattering the union's papers and records. Informed that a riot was in progress, Alderman Frank Curran, who was acting mayor in Duncan's absence, rushed to the hall. Talking from the hall's second-story window, he tried to calm the crowd, but suddenly somebody pushed Curran out the window. The alderman fell to the pavement, seriously injured.

Realizing that they were outnumbered and that the crowd was out of control, police officers and sheriff's deputies made no attempt to stop the destruction. They did try to protect the union's safe by removing it from the hall; but the crowd muscled the safe away from them, hauled it to a nearby lot, and dynamited it open. The papers inside were scattered, and some enterprising crooks made off with an estimated sixteen hundred dollars in cash. Having done its work, the crowd then quietly dispersed.[8]

The next morning, Sheriff Tim Driscoll called Governor Samuel V. Stewart to plead for the mobilization of the national guard to restore order. Stewart mobilized the guard, but he did not want to put the troops on the train to Butte until he could assess the situation in person. When Stewart arrived in the city on the evening of June 14, he was surprised to find everything peaceful and he quietly demobilized the national guard.[9]

It is likely that the June 13 riot was a spontaneous affair fueled by a number of long-standing grievances. In addition to the complaint about the special assessments for the Michigan strike and Riley's arrogant handling of the progressives' motion on voting procedures, the *Montana Socialist* listed "grafting" and "abuse of official power" by union officials, the miners' hatred of the rustling card system, "corporate dictation" and "corporate espionage" directed at the Butte Miners' Union, "political discrimination" in employer hiring practices, and the "disruptive tendencies of a militant, anarchistic minority" stirring up discontent among the miners.[10] Rarely mentioned in the surge of charge and countercharge was the way in which both factions had taken advantage of a flaw in their union's operation. The Miners' Union Hall, built in the 1880s, was simply too small to accommodate effective participation by the rank and file. Only a few hundred men could comfortably sit in the hall, so it was easy for either side to "pack" a meeting.[11]

But perhaps the union's most fatal defect was its unsophisticated nature. Initially created to defend the miners' accustomed daily wages, the union had never become a protector of its members' health and safety. Although the union did pay out sick and death benefits, it never directly confronted employers on health and safety conditions and its two contracts were silent on these important issues. As one critic noted:

> The union has never been responsible for an increase in wages or for the reduction of hours; never has bettered a single condition; never has pretended to protect the men in their jobs, except in a futile attempt of the anti-company [Socialist] officials to protect the members discharged for political reasons in 1912, and never has really been representative of the rank and file. It has been anti-Socialist, anti-democratic, discriminatory, inefficient, oppressive, cumbersome, and, in election matters, dishonest.[12]

But these weaknesses were not discussed in the days following the June 13 riot.

The daily press blamed the IWW for the riot, a position that was readily shared by the shocked Charles Moyer: "There has been a movement on foot for years to secure control of the Federation for the IWW, or failing that, to destroy it."[13] The *Miners Magazine* alleged that "several hundred" Wobblies had been ordered to Butte before the June 13 rebellion and that they were the ones who had attacked the Butte Miners' Union Hall.[14] Many leaders of the progressive faction were IWW members, but many were not. Of the eight men indicted for various crimes committed on June 13, not one was an IWW man or a recognized leader of the progressive faction.[15] At best, the progressive union leaders had created the preconditions for the unpleasantness, but there was no reasonable evidence that they had conspired to precipitate the riot on June 13.

Charles Moyer arrived in the city four days after the riot to try to save the remains of Butte Local No. 1. He demanded and got resignations from O'Connor and the other discredited conservative officers. He promised that the WFM would supervise new elections in the near future. The gesture might have saved the Butte Miners' Union, except that Moyer would only allow those with paid-up WFM cards to vote in the proposed election. Moyer offered too little and too late.[16]

On the day that Moyer arrived, the insurgents held a referendum on whether or not Butte's miners would remain with the WFM. By a lopsided vote of 6,384 to 243, the miners repudiated the Federation. With this mandate, the rebels called a mass meeting on June 22. The four thousand miners who attended the meeting agreed to form an independent union of miners, the Butte Mine Workers' Union. Elected as provisional president was the young Irishman who had kindled the spark at the Speculator Mine, "Muckie" McDonald who, contrary to what Moyer might allege, was neither a Socialist nor a Wobbly. The miners elected IWW member Joe Bradley as vice-president, IWW man "Red Jack" Sullivan as recording secretary, and ex-Socialist Phil Christian as secretary-treasurer.[17]

To Moyer and the WFM leaders, the composition of the insurgent leadership was further evidence of an IWW conspiracy.[18] The truth was more complex. Witnesses as disparate as Mayor Duncan, Daniel Shovlin, and Jacob Oliver, a leader of the conservative faction, believed that the IWW comprised only a small minority in the new union.[19] The Wobblies made up an admittedly influential minority, but they were only part of a broad coalition of disaffected miners. Further, Butte's Wobblies never advocated BMWU affiliation with the IWW, either at the time of its founding or at any time during its brief existence.[20]

For his part, Charles Moyer simply refused to recognize the depth of the workers' antagonism for the Butte Miners' Union and the WFM, and he went ahead with his plans for a June 23 meeting of union loyalists. Mayor Duncan asked Moyer to postpone the meeting until tempers had cooled, but Moyer insisted. Receiving assurances from the leaders of the insurgent union that they had no plans to disrupt the meeting, Duncan let Moyer go ahead; but he put the police on full alert in case trouble developed.[21]

If Moyer expected hundreds of loyal WFM men to appear at the Miners' Union Hall on the night of June 23, he must have been disappointed when only a few dozen local men showed up. About two thousand curious onlookers assembled on the street outside, but the crowd was generally peaceful. Catcalls and hoots greeted the few men who entered the hall, while the insurgent leaders walked among the crowd urging them to keep the peace and go home.[22]

Inside the hall, the few men who came were uneasy and frightened. Shortly after eight o'clock, a loyal WFM miner entered the hall and began to climb the stairs to the second floor. Someone inside panicked and shot the "intruder," who fell back down the stairs, seriously wounded. More shots were fired from inside the hall in the general direction of the crowd, one bullet killing a clerk standing on a nearby street corner. Some men in the crowd returned the fire as people ran for cover. Mayor Duncan immediately ordered police officers to close all saloons and gunshops.

Men rushed to the nearby West Stewart Mine and seized some dynamite, apparently intending to blow up the building and everyone in it. By the time they got back, police officers had already secretly escorted the men inside the hall out the back way.[23] When the dynamiting began, Duncan remembered, he "didn't know quite how to handle the situation." Then taking hold of himself, he ordered Chief of Police Jerry Murphy to cordon off the area. Reasoning that the use of force could only result in the loss of innocent lives, Duncan told Murphy not to try to stop the destruction of the hall.[24] The hall was reduced to rubble, but there was no other significant property damage and no one else was killed.

As dynamite blasts echoed in the city and rattled the windows, Duncan reported to Governor Stewart that local authorities were making the best of a bad situation and predicted that peace would return once the angry miners had finished their grim work of destruction. Stewart was apparently reassured, and he decided not to mobilize the state's national guard. Clearly worried, however, he secretly wired Washington, D.C., to ask that federal troops be stationed at Fort Harrison and Fort Missoula.[25] By morning, Butte was quiet once more.

In the riot's aftermath, the WFM accused the Socialists of complicity in the alleged IWW conspiracy.[26] The Socialist Party replied: "Many of those conducting a movement for an independent miners' organization had been and are the most consistent and uncompromising enemies of the Socialist administration, the party paper, and the mayor."[27] In fact, not a single member of the party served on the new union's eighteen-member executive board.

The distance between the Butte Mine Workers' Union and the Socialist administration was widened in a tragic and ugly incident involving Butte's Finnish workers, who were strong supporters of the new union. Frank Aaltonen, a WFM executive board member and fellow countryman, had arrived in Butte on July 1 to assess the situation. When a delegation of Finns demanded that Mayor Duncan drive Aaltonen out of town, the mayor refused, saying that Aaltonen had a constitutional right to be in the city. Two days later, Finnish miner Erick Lantala visited the mayor and an argument ensued. Lantala, who was apparently drunk, attacked Duncan with a knife, and Duncan pulled out a pistol and shot Lantala in apparent self-defense. Critically wounded, Lantala died two days later. The slightly injured Duncan was emotionally shaken and took a leave of absence.[28]

Throughout the crisis the mining companies had taken a neutral position toward the warring factions. Now they faced the apparent victors. By the first week in August, the Butte Mine Workers' Union had signed up five thousand miners, but the new union was not yet the workers' official representative.[29] First, the union had to assert its jurisdiction in the district by imposing its own closed shop and by forcing the companies to acknowledge it as the miners' sole and legitimate bargaining agent.

It was not a good time for the new union to make its move. On August 1, the ACM Company reacted to a severe depression in the copper market by laying off two thousand workers. The outbreak of the war in Europe had temporarily shut down the market, as the *Engineering and Mining Journal* lamented: "There is no market in copper. There being no transactions it naturally follows that there can be no quotations based on transactions, and we are obliged to suspend our record of the market because there is none." The *Journal* then predicted:

> When the demand [for recognition] is made it will put up to the companies squarely the question of whether they will recognize the new union or the

Western Federation union. In view of the fact that the companies are not anxious to operate their mines at present, such a demand by the new union might come opportunely for the companies and inopportunely for the union.[30]

But the new union could not wait on the market. It had to assert itself or lose the tenuous hold it had on the miners. On August 26, a BMWU jurisdiction committee appeared at the ACM Company's Anaconda Mine to inspect the cards of the men going on shift. Thirty-four miners had no BMWU cards and were not allowed to go to work. The committee marched the men to a nearby vacant lot to undergo a ritual that the Butte Miners' Union had followed for years. The "scabs" were put on "trial" with a crowd of onlookers as the "jury." Committee Chairman James Chapman presided, assisted by President McDonald. Thirty-one of the men were released after they promised to join the union. The remaining three, WFM loyalists and suspected gunmen, were found "guilty" of being enemies of the new union. The three were escorted to the depot, put on the train, and told never to return. The next day the committee appeared at the ACM Company's St. Lawrence Mine and tried and "deported" another miner. None of the men who were "deported" were physically harmed, and Sheriff Driscoll brought all of them back to town on the same day. The BMWU committee promised that they would cover every mine in the district during the following week.[31]

Simultaneously with the beginning of its jurisdiction drive the new union posted a list of job conditions that it promised to enforce. The notice appeared at all of the mines:

MINE WORKERS, ATTENTION!

Pursuant to an action taken at the regular meeting of the Butte Mine Workers' Union, August 17, 1914, wherein your executive committee was empowered to wait upon the different heads of the mining companies and lay before them the matter of abolishing the system of blasting at dinner hour, and dampening the dust, the ventilation of blind workings and hot box by means of fans—

This is to notify you that your union has made arrangements with the companies whereby these conditions will be corrected at the earliest possible moment. And you are hereby notified that after this date there will be no more blasting at dinner hour or during the shift, and any infraction of this order must be promptly reported to the union. A water system will be installed as quickly as possible, and it will be your duty to report to the union any places you consider wholly unfit to work in, and the union will see to it that such condition is corrected. The workers are admonished in the interests of health, sanitation, and common decency, to use the toilet tanks wherever they are provided, and where there are none to report that fact directly to the union.

Do not throw foodstuffs around the levels and in the stopes and workings, as decaying food in the mine is a dangerous source of disease infection, and careless workers doing so should be promptly reported to the grievance committee or your union. Report to your grievance committee on the job any grievance which may arise, and in case you are unable to settle it, fail not to bring it before your union. Treat the boss in the mine upon that reciprocal basis and relation upon which most justly should rest the traffic between individuals of all mankind and no other. Treat him as every man who is a man should treat every other man. Stand up in full dignity of real manhood, and do not, under any circumstances, tolerate in the future as in the past, from any boss any bulldozing, browbeating, bamboozling or abuse of any kind, and if you receive such treatment, do not be slow in letting it be known to the grievance committee or the union. If you feel you have been unjustly discharged without warrant or sufficient cause, do not be slow in letting it be known. And let us work, pull and co-operate together to build a union for, by and in the interest of all workers.

(Signed)   GEO. R. TOMPKINS
JOS. SHANNON
MIKE SULLIVAN
WM. STODDARD
Executive Committee[32]

Here was a new kind of militant unionism, and the operators did not like it. Even though the union never threatened property or counseled violence, the operators had already hired more private guards. The ACM Company made it known that it was prepared to shut down its mines rather than recognize the new union.[33]

As soon as the BMWU committees began to appear at the mines, leading Butte businessmen told Governor Stewart that an "insurrection" was in progress, and they demanded that the national guard be sent to restore order. On August 29, the governor wired Mayor Duncan and Sheriff Driscoll: "Serious and persistent complaints of disorders . . . continue to be made to me. Can you protect lives and property?" Driscoll replied that it had become "impossible" for his deputies to "cope with the situation," and he begged the governor to send "regular troops." Mayor Duncan wired that neither lives nor property were being threatened and added in a letter that followed: "If things get to a point where I am unable to handle the situation I shall notify you."[34]

The governor's inquiries to Butte's mayor and sheriff were *pro forma*, for he was already moving in the direction requested by the petitioning businessmen. On August 28, Stewart had invited the commander of the national guard to "come to Helena immediately on important confidential matter connected with the Butte situation." On the same day, he had advised Montana's two U.S. senators, Henry L. Myers and Thomas J. Walsh, that "conditions" in Butte were "growing worse" and that he might have "to take some action within twenty-four hours."[35] But the governor still hesitated. No matter how desperate the situation was being portrayed, it was not as volatile as the June riots had been. It took one more incident before the governor took action.

At approximately one-thirty on the morning of Sunday, August 30, someone dynamited the employment office at the ACM Company's Parrot Mine. The damage was slight and nobody was injured; the night watchman had been pulled out of the area by an anonymous phone call moments before the blast. But the act was violent enough to prompt an official response. The governor was told immediately, and he mobilized the national guard.[36] In the process, he neglected to involve local authorities in the decision; and Mayor Duncan, the Socialist Party, and the Butte Mine Workers'

Union issued strenuous protests.[37] Despite local opposition, the national guard arrived in Butte on the evening of September 1 to declare martial law. The military ordered the closing of saloons, imposed press censorship, prohibited public assemblies, and created court martials to try civilians for violations of its orders. Warrants were issued for the arrest of several union leaders, charging them with kidnapping in connection with the "deportations" of non-union workers.[38]

The Socialists and the union accused the ACM Company of manufacturing the Parrot Mine incident so that it and the other operators could use the soldiers' bayonets to break the new union.[39] Subsequent events seemed to support the accusation. On September 2, the Company announced that BMWU committees were not allowed on its property. On September 8, ACM and the other mining companies announced an open shop:

> The attitude of the Mine Workers' organization toward the employer as expressed in its published notices and constitution adopted by it, put the organization beyond the possibility of being recognized or dealt with in any way, and so far as that organization is concerned, the undersigned companies will not now, or any time in the future, recognize its jurisdiction.[40]

Closing the circle, the companies also announced that they would not recognize the authority of the Butte Miners' Union either.

Following closely on the heels of martial law and the open shop, impeachment proceedings were instituted against Mayor Duncan and Sheriff Driscoll on a complaint made by several prominent business and professional men. Both officials were accused of dereliction in their official duties for failing to protect property and for tolerating lawless behavior. At their trials in late September, both were found guilty. Neither was repentant. Duncan said:

> I have been ousted, not because I neglected my duty, but because I had the courage to act by a higher and humaner principle than is approved by the capitalistic class. I have regarded human life as of greater moment and value than property. . . .[41]

As chairman of the city council, Clarence Smith assumed the post of mayor, and a deputy replaced Sheriff Driscoll.

In the interim, the state's business interests flooded the governor's office with praise for his firm action against "lawlessness, intimidation, and crime." Amalgamated President John D. Ryan was pleased, confiding to Senator Walsh that no one should be "finicky" about the methods used to suppress the "dynamiters" who had "terrorized" the city.[42] Governor Stewart dismissed any criticism of his action as coming from "Socialists and others who have a deep-seated prejudice against the use of militia under any circumstances."[43] Not so easy to dismiss was Senator Walsh's assessment that Stewart had gone too far in authorizing the use of military courts to try civilians. Walsh predicted that the governor's action would "engender a bitterness that you cannot eradicate."[44]

In Butte, the military intrusion was most keenly felt in the censoring of the *Butte Socialist* and in the sometimes draconian sentences the military courts imposed for the most trivial of offenses.[45] Most of the military's judicial business was handled in the

From *International Socialist Review,* July 1911, p. 5

IWW leader William D. "Big Bill" Haywood lectured the crowd at Columbia Gardens on June 13, 1911, sharing the platform with (from left) Butte Mayor Louis Duncan, BMU Vice-president George Curry, and BMU President Dan Sullivan.

N. A. Forsyth, photographer, MHS Photograph Archives

Thousands participated each year in the Miners' Union Day parade in Butte, the largest union celebration in the state.

Louis J. Duncan promoted the Socialist cause as mayor of Butte from 1911 to 1914.

William F. Dunne was the outspoken editor of the *Butte Bulletin*.

Joe Shannon, a member of the radical IWW, was a leader of the BMWU.

Cornelius F. "Con" Kelley was a prominent ACM Company official when workers were shot on the Anaconda Road in 1920.

Thomas Campbell led workers in the 1917 Butte miners' strike.

For weeks, opposing factions of the Butte Miners' Union had fought for control of their union. Then, on June 13, 1914, rioters stormed Miners' Union Hall after the Miners' Union Day parade had been disrupted.

On June 13, 1914, BMU dissidents stole the safe from the Miners' Union Hall, dragged it to a vacant lot near the Colorado Smelter, and dynamited the safe open.

The Miners' Union Hall was in ruins after over twenty dynamite blasts rocked the building throughout the night of June 23, 1914.

From *International Socialist Review*, September 1917

In a show of solidarity, thousands of mourners gathered in August 1917 at Mountain View Cemetery to bury murdered IWW organizer Frank Little.

Butte-Silver Bow Archives

Red-sashed pallbearers carried the coffin of martyred radical unionist Frank Little from Duggan's Mortuary in Butte.

Montana National Guard troops posed for a photographer in downtown Butte on September 6, 1914, not long after occupying the city.

In August 1914, Governor Samuel V. Stewart ordered the Montana National Guard to occupy Butte in what would be the first of several periods of martial law in the mining city.

Facing extreme working conditions and a lack of political power, thousands of Butte's miners acted in their own behalf as radical unionists and as supporters of the Socialist Party.

court of Major Jesse Roote, a prominent Butte attorney. Swelled up with new-found authority, Roote worked with patriotic zeal to punish those who had insulted the flag, the national guard, and the country. A barber was sentenced to sixty days in jail for refusing to cut the hair of guardsmen. A miner who cursed the military was threatened with imprisonment but was forgiven when he saluted the flag in the court's presence. These kinds of actions, H. L. Maury wrote to Walsh, were "pitiful parodies" conducted by "martinets."[46]

Maury did more than write letters. On behalf of the Socialist Party and the union he filed suit before the Montana Supreme Court, charging that the governor's declaration of martial law was unconstitutional. On October 8, the court ruled that it was unconstitutional for military courts to try civilians, voiding all of the sentences the military court in Butte had imposed.[47] While the decision was a victory for individual civil liberty, it had little substantive significance for the Butte Mine Workers' Union.

The union was locked out, many of its leaders were in jail, and high unemployment made even a non-union job preferable to no job for the working miners. After the beginning of the new year, the mining companies officially announced a blacklist of BMWU leaders and supporters. The ACM Company was quite frank in its defense of the blacklist:

> This company has refused employment to certain men. . . . The plain purpose of the company is to give preference at all times to peaceful, law-abiding, permanent residents of Butte. . . . No fair-minded person . . . can reasonably expect this company to make places in its mines for men who precipitated a condition of practical anarchy last summer.[48]

The BMWU appealed to the Silver Bow Trades and Labor Council, which represented all unions in the city, and asked that a committee be formed to investigate the blacklist in the mines. Divided, and perhaps intimidated by fear of Company retaliation, the Council turned down the request.[49] Wobbly poet "Dublin Dan" Liston gave a bitter reply:

> So these so-called Union men
> Tools of Kelley's A.C.M.,
> Have declared to help the miners
>   They're not able;
> 'Twould infringe upon their laws
> To investigate the cause,
> So the motion has been laid upon the table.[50]

Ironically, only the Socialist Party came to the aid of the Butte Mine Workers' Union by giving it full editorial support in the columns of the *Montana Socialist* and by actively participating in a union-sponsored and short-lived League of Blacklisted Workers.[51] But the damage had already been done. Under the combined hammer blows of the jailing of its leaders, the declarations of open shop, high unemployment, and the blacklist, the infant union withered and died.

The national guard was withdrawn from Butte in early November. Later that month, Muckie McDonald, Joe Bradley, and Joe Shannon were tried in district court in Boulder on the charge of kidnapping. The jury found McDonald and Bradley guilty;

McDonald was sentenced to three years in the state prison at Deer Lodge and Bradley to five. Shannon, who had taken no part in the "deportations," was acquitted, and he returned to Butte. McDonald was paroled in December 1916 and left the state. Bradley died in prison.[52]

The authorities seemed unable to apprehend and convict others who had committed more serious offenses. No one was tried for inciting the June 13 riot or for dynamiting the Miners' Union Hall on June 23, although one man was sentenced to five years in prison for stealing the dynamite that was used.[53] And no one was ever indicted for dynamiting the Parrot Mine employment office.

Indicted but conspicuously absent from the bar of justice were two prominent insurgent leaders: James Chapman, the head of the union's jurisdiction committee, and William O'Brien, a self-described IWW militant and the author of the union's constitution. They had been charged with kidnapping, but the military had released both of them with no explanation and allowed them to leave the state. Chapman and O'Brien later appeared in other states posing as radical union organizers. Although the evidence is circumstantial, both may have been private detectives who acted for the mining companies as spies and *agents provocateurs*.[54]

The major historical question remaining concerns the role the IWW played in these events. The WFM and the daily press were convinced that the insurgent union was an IWW front and that the Butte Miners' Union was brought down as the result of a deliberate IWW conspiracy.[55] But a close examination of the available evidence does not support either allegation.

It is true that among those who led the progressive faction of miners were local men who held IWW membership cards. This was especially the case after the Socialist Party split in 1913. It is also true that local IWW men like Joe Shannon helped found and lead the Butte Mine Workers' Union, but they were acting independently and received no advice or material assistance from the IWW. This is not to say that the IWW was unhappy with events in Butte. On the contrary, the Wobblies were elated by the crushing defeat that the WFM had suffered. For example, the secretary of the IWW local in Redding, California, wrote Joe Bradley on July 11: "I am glad the 'coup' was a success. . . . The radicals made a good job of it and I hope the example will be followed by several locals of the Western Federation of Miners." Dan Buckley, the Redding IWW man, also told Bradley: "I hope the new union will prove to be a sturdy one and that it will know its parents when the time is ripe." Another Wobbly in Redding sent a mixed message:

> Hurrah for Butte. Butte leads the way, others follow. . . . Moyer says it is only a blind and the new union is the I.W.'s but you know I wouldn't believe him. . . . Well, Joe, I'm awful sorry to know that you and that bunch of I.W.W.'s have doublecrossed us and started an independent union. I know how the Saint [IWW Secretary-Treasurer Vincent St. John] feels about it.[56]

Local Wobblies clearly had an important role in the new union, but letters printed in the local papers after Bradley's arrest reveal that there were Wobblies outside Butte who wished that the new union would become part of the IWW. Again, there is no clear evidence of an IWW plot.

In reality, the IWW virtually ignored the events in Butte until after martial law was declared. Aside from a brief account of the June 13 riot in the IWW newspaper *Solidarity*, the radical union was officially silent on the matter and did not even bother to report the June 23 dynamiting. At least one analyst has found *Solidarity*'s silence "strange," but there is no mystery. The IWW's attention was focused on raising financial and moral support for the defense of two organizers accused of serious crimes during an IWW strike in Wheatland, California. The union was also deeply troubled by its own failures, caused in part by its contradictory support of revolutionary agitation and its concern for workers' wages and their health and safety. By 1915, the IWW had become a strong advocate for agricultural and lumber workers and was behaving more like a traditional labor union; but in the summer and fall of 1914, the IWW was still weak, ineffective, and demoralized. In that condition, it would have happily broadcast any successful IWW effort to organize the miners. But it did not. As an organization, the IWW had played no part in the conflict. The Federation itself must assume the larger responsibility for destroying the Butte Miners' Union.

The WFM had ignored the concerns of Butte's Finnish miners in 1912 and had made common cause with the most reactionary elements in the Butte Miners' Union to defeat the progressive opposition. Moyer had sealed the doom of the WFM in Butte by refusing to acknowledge the depth of feeling that existed against the old union. He might have saved the situation by offering to help reform the Butte Miners' Union without preconditions, but he was unwilling to concede that much. He lost Butte as a result.

The Butte Miners' Union failed for many reasons, but chief among them were the actions and attitudes of the local union itself. Established to defend a scale of wages and to distribute injury and death benefits, the union never actively promoted the improvement of health and safety conditions in the mines. When the conservatives were in power, the union's inaction signaled indifference; when the progressives assumed control, they were seen as political agitators. Because most of the progressives were Socialists, they used their union positions to stump for the Socialist ticket rather than to transform the BMU into a vehicle of militant industrial unionism. They, too, failed to appreciate the role the union could play in directly ameliorating health and safety conditions on the job. For all their faults, however, the leaders of the progressive faction after 1913 understood and acted on the fundamental point that Bill Haywood made on Miners' Union Day in 1911. "To improve [working] conditions," Haywood urged, the miners must look to their union and not wait for legislative action in the state capital.[57]

In the wake of the destruction of the Butte Miners' Union in the summer and the impeachment of Louis Duncan in early fall, the Socialists faced a tough battle for their political survival. The critics who had always opposed Socialism pointed to the miners' revolt as yet another example of Socialist-inspired "anarchy." But had Butte's working class turned against the party as well? The November 1914 elections were the first test. Louis Duncan was the party's candidate for Congress, and the party hoped to see the ousted mayor "vindicated" in the election returns.

The greatest instrument of the mining companies is the
sympathetic vote of the working man.
— *Butte Socialist*,
October 31, 1914

9 | *Vindication and Defeat*

As the November 1914 general election approached, the Socialist Party of Montana
was confident that the voters would elect some of their candidates to county and
legislative offices. With 2,214 members organized in 89 local branches, the strong and
politically active party fielded slates of candidates in most of Montana's counties.[1]
Socialists had already been elected to a number of local offices, and they held majority
control in two major metropolitan centers, Butte and Missoula. In Missoula,
Socialists Andy Getchell, a locomotive engineer, and Dale Hodson, a stonemason,
were elected to the three-member commission in the April 1914 municipal elections.[2]
Like their comrades in Butte, Missoula Socialists also established a bimonthly campaign newspaper, the *Missoula Socialist*.[3]

With a seemingly strong base in urban centers, the Socialists saw the pending
general elections as the time to break into state politics, and they offered their most
detailed manifesto to the voting public. The Socialist Party state platform made the
usual demand for public ownership and expressed the party's continued support for
woman suffrage and a workmen's compensation law (both issues were on the ballot).
The party platform also condemned the war in Europe and expressed a fervent hope
that the United States would stay out of it. It chastised Governor Stewart for imposing military rule in Butte, which, the party charged, was motivated by a "brutal conspiracy to intimidate and enslave the people of Silver Bow County in the interests of
the Amalgamated Copper Company."

The platform also pledged Socialist support for state government development of
irrigation projects and water and electric power. It also demanded a system of state-
owned warehouses, stockyards, and grain elevators. The Socialists advocated low-
interest loans to working farmers and urged enactment of a law that would exempt
homes, tools, equipment, and improvements from farmers' property taxes. Finally,
the platform called for legislation that would limit the interest rates charged by private
lenders and argued that all land held for speculative purposes by corporate interests
should be heavily taxed.

Addressing the workers' concerns, the Socialists once again called for the election of the state mine inspector, effective legislation to improve ventilation and sanitation in the mines, and public works jobs for the unemployed. The platform also reacted to the recent events in Butte by urging the legislature to enact a law prohibiting the "importation" of private armed guards into the state.[4]

The generally positive attitude of the Socialists was counterbalanced by the extreme negativism of their traditional enemies. In Butte, the opposition decided once more to make Socialist government the central issue in the election campaign. Even though the war in Europe was responsible for the high rate of unemployment in the mines, the opposition blamed the Socialists and predicted that the mining companies would hesitate to reopen the mines if the voters were foolish enough to elect "demagogues" and "agitators" to public office.[5]

Joining the Butte daily press in its anti-Socialist propaganda was a new and scurrilous weekly called the *Butte American*. In the journalistic tradition of Heinze's *Reveille* (to which it claimed some vague lineage), the *Butte American* was, according to Louis Duncan, a "mushroom sheet" funded by the ACM Company. The little paper's motto read: "LET US MAKE BUTTE ONCE MORE AN AMERICAN CITY . . . NO CITY EVER THRIVED UNDER THE RED FLAG OF SOCIALISM." Typical of its style, editor Byron Cooney asked: "Who made Butte an easy place for the thief, the dip, the vagrant, the man who glorifies in the phrase, 'Hallalauja [*sic*], I'm a bum?'" Cooney answered himself: "Look at semi-educated freaks who captured the city hall and sowed the poison of civic treason. . . ."[6]

Because their opponents had decided to make the quality of the city's governance and the character of its candidates the major issues in the campaign, the Socialists decided to join the issue head on. Mayor Duncan was running for a seat in the U.S. Congress, and the Socialists argued that his decisions during the summer's riots had been "courageous" and "practical." The issue was not Socialists holding elected office, the party claimed, but whether or not the ACM Company was to be the "political as well as the economic ruler of Silver Bow County." The *Montana Socialist* predicted:

> Should this autocratic and unscrupulous industrial concern, which is closely allied with and representative of the greatest and most powerful capitalist interests in the nation, succeed in its crafty and sordid purpose; should it destroy, as it proposed to destroy, the solidarity of labor here, and to establish in this Gibraltar of unionism in America open shop conditions, it requires no great wisdom to foresee that soon whatever liberty and independence the working people, the small merchants and property owners—the common people—of Silver Bow County still retain will be lost in everything except an empty legal fiction. We shall be, as the residents of the coal fields of West Virginia and Colorado or the copper districts of Michigan, the groaning and sorely exploited slaves of a tyrannical and soulless employing company that is a political dictator and a law unto itself.[7]

In this way, the Socialists attempted to turn the question of "Who governs?" in another direction. The issue was government by the Socialists, who had already proven that they were the friends of the "common people," or government by a "soulless" corporation, which had demonstrated time and time again that it had no concern for the workers. This was a highly serviceable theme for the Socialists. F. A. Heinze had used it with great success in his fight with the Company, and there were strong echoes of his florid rhetoric in Socialist electoral propaganda. Anti-corporatism was a theme for all seasons and for a variety of political persuasions in Montana politics. But the Socialists distanced themselves from other anti-corporate critics by setting their message within the larger anti-capitalist framework of Marxist theory. Because they were Socialists they wanted even more: "We would abolish economic lordship over the lives of others. The industrial democracy to which this leads is the inspiration and aim of our political activities."[8]

When the votes were counted, it was clear that the Socialists continued to enjoy substantial working-class support. In his race for Congress, Louis Duncan received 3,810 votes (33 per cent) and ran second in Silver Bow County. Two Socialist candidates for the state House of Representatives were elected as well (Table 7). In the forty-eight-candidate field for the twelve legislative seats, Socialist Alex Mackel finished seventh with 3,648 votes and Leslie Bechtel finished twelfth with 3,628. Given the "poisonous ordure and cffluvia" that had been heaped on the party by the "subsidized political sewers," the *Montana Socialist* announced that it was pleased with the party's electoral performance.[9]

TABLE 7: *Each Party's Share of the Popular Vote in the November 1914 Election in Silver Bow County*

	Democrat	Socialist	Republican	Progressive
Congress	38.8%	33.2%	25.5%	2.5%
County Attorney	40.4	32.3	25.2	2.1
Sheriff	30.3	27.6	38.9	3.2
State senator	40.0	32.1	25.4	2.5
State representative	34.8	32.6	29.6	3.0

Source: Official Election Returns for Silver Bow County, November 3, 1914, Office of the Secretary of State, Helena.

Regrettably, the workmen's compensation initiative, which the Socialists and the labor unions had worked hard to pass, was defeated, thanks to a massive propaganda campaign waged against it by a business front called the Montana Advancement Association.[10] But in Silver Bow County, the initiative received easy approval with 64.7 per cent of the vote. Even so, not all Butte voters were as supportive. While workmen's compensation was massively supported in Northeast Butte and The Flats, it was rejected by a narrow margin in the Middle-Class Enclave.

In contrast, woman suffrage, which the Socialist Party had strenuously supported since its founding, won state-wide approval with 52.2 per cent of the vote. In Silver Bow County, however, the suffrage referendum lost, with 4,471 voting in favor and 4,505 voting against. Interestingly, woman suffrage was supported in Butte's working-class communities and was defeated in middle-class neighborhoods west of Main, suggesting that support for women's right to vote by the Socialists and most of organized labor had paid off.

Duncan won easily in The Flats, but he failed to win in Northeast Butte. Socialist state senate candidate Edmund Landendorff's total of 3,574 was typical of that received by most of the party's slate. Like Duncan, he won in The Flats, finished second in Northeast Butte, and placed a dismal third in the Middle-Class Enclave.

The sheriff's race was an exception to the overall pattern in which the Democrat and the Socialist placed first and second. The unfortunate Tim Driscoll, who had been impeached and removed from office, was the official Democratic candidate (it had been too late to remove his name from the ballot). Rather than attempt a write-in campaign for another Democrat, the Democratic establishment and the daily press swung their support to Republican Charles Henderson, who was elected sheriff in November.[11] But the Irish Democratic voters in Northeast Butte refused to go along with the advice of the Democratic dailies and made Driscoll the victor there with 38.2 per cent of the vote. The vote for Driscoll was an expression of that community's intense identification with the Democratic Party, and its ethnic identification; perhaps it was also a demonstration of support for the sheriff who had restrained his deputies during the June riots (Table 8).

TABLE 8: *Selected Votes in Butte's Social Communities in the 1914 Election*

	Middle-Class Enclave	The Flats	Northeast Butte
Congress			
Evans (D)	45.5%	31.9%	43.7%
McCormick (R)	31.6	26.8	19.0
Duncan (S)	22.9	41.3	37.3
State Senator			
Gallwey (D)	47.6	30.5	44.1
Grigg (R)	29.6	28.3	18.8
Landendorff (S)	22.8	41.2	37.1
Sheriff			
Driscoll (D)	25.4	21.2	38.2
Henderson (R)	51.3	41.8	29.0
Smith (S)	23.3	37.0	32.8
Ballot Issues*			
Workmen's Compensation	49.9	66.1	70.6
Woman Suffrage	46.5	52.4	52.3

Source: Official Election Returns for Silver Bow County, November 3, 1914, Office of the Secretary of State, Helena.

*Percentage of vote favoring issue

The Socialists held their ground in Butte and Silver Bow County in the November 1914 elections, but they made no important gains except for the election of two candidates to the state legislature. The party had even slipped a bit, receiving an average of about two hundred fewer votes than it had gotten two years before.[12] Now it faced a changed political landscape. Women would be voting in the next election, and the battle for control of Butte's city government was just months away.

In the interim, the economic depression that had begun in Butte shortly after the onset of the war in Europe continued unabated. A miner described the situation in the *International Socialist Review*:

Union activity is at a standstill all along the line. The industrial conditions are positively the worst that Butte has ever experienced. Not one third of the usual quota of men are employed. Business failures are the order of the day. Suffering and want among the poor is great.[13]

Private charities provided shelter and food for the unemployed; city government, fifty thousand dollars in debt due to reduced revenues brought on by the desperate economic climate, was in no position to offer relief of its own. Mayor Smith's most substantive response to the municipal fiscal crisis was to lay off some of the city's work force.[14]

The decision to lay off city workers immediately rekindled factionalism in the local Socialist Party. Those party members who were laid off charged that they had been singled out for punishment because they opposed the Duncan-Smith "machine." "Red" leader William Sullivan, who had just been readmitted to membership in the party, led the charge of the discontented, with the apparent support of Street Commissioner Dan Sullivan, Judge Booher, and former City Attorney Maury.[15]

Hoping to prevent Clarence Smith's nomination for mayor in the party's city convention, the dissidents backed George R. McDonald, a rank-and-file party member, as their candidate. In February 1915, the party held its convention to endorse candidates for the March primary. The vote for mayor was close, with Smith receiving 142 votes to McDonald's 105. But members of the Finnish branch had not been allowed to participate in the vote, and the dissidents questioned the validity of the convention results. Had the Finns been allowed to vote, the dissidents charged, McDonald would have been nominated. Sullivan and the others appealed to the party's State Executive Committee, asking it to annul the convention endorsement and order a new convention in which the Finns would be permitted to vote.[16]

The Finns had been barred from the convention because the county central committee had stripped them of their branch charter in January. The committee's action was in response to a National Executive Committee order that directed all state parties not to recognize Finnish locals that had been expelled from the Finnish Socialist Federation for pro-IWW sentiments.[17] The Butte dissidents argued that the NEC had no authority to dictate to state parties which branch charters should or should not be granted. That authority was exercised exclusively by the state parties that created and dissolved party locals.[18] The state committee agreed, ruling that the NEC directive was contrary to the party's national constitution. Therefore, the Silver Bow County central committee had no authority to strip the Finns of their branch charter. The state committee urged the county committee to recognize the Finnish branch; if the committee balked, the state committee would do it. But the state committee refused to annul the results of the convention, ruling that party members would have to decide between Smith and McDonald in the March primary.[19] The decision was a hollow victory for the Finns. The immigrant Finns could participate in a party convention, but most were barred from voting in the March primary because they were not citizens.

Clarence Smith's opponents decided to back McDonald for mayor in the primary, and they selected City Treasurer Shovlin for the treasurer's spot, even though Shovlin had refused to renew his membership in the party after the 1913 faction fight.

The Smith forces, the majority in the English-speaking branch, backed Alderman Curran as their candidate for city treasurer and suspended McDonald from party membership. In protest, H. L. Maury resigned, but his resignation was rejected.[20]

In the March primary, Smith easily whipped McDonald by 1,078 to 510 votes, and Curran defeated Shovlin by a similar margin. Clearly, while some "old-time Socialists" were disenchanted, the majority of the party's members and supporters were not. The "red" faction, which had always argued that it was the heart and soul of the party, was in fact a minority within a minority.[21]

The disunity and disarray in the local party was accompanied by a certain lethargy of spirit and timidity in the city administration. The Smith administration proposed and passed an ordinance indicating the city's intention to purchase the privately owned waterworks, but the matter was still being deliberated when the April 1915 election took place. The municipal fuel-yard bill never came to a vote after City Attorney Mackel advised the administration that it was not permitted under state law.[22] These two bills exhausted the legislative initiatives that the Smith administration was willing to take, and the fourth year of Socialist government in Butte was a disappointing one. It is not surprising, then, that in the 1915 election campaign the Socialists stressed that four years of Socialist government had been at least "good" government, the best that Butte had ever experienced. The party platform declared:

> The Socialists are the first in Butte ever to have mastered the science of municipal government IN THE INTERESTS OF THE PEOPLE. They are prepared in the future to make more substantial progress in the direction of good government, clean government, and efficient government than the people of Butte have ever believed possible.[23]

"Good," "clean," and "efficient" government—a "reform" ticket fielded by either of the old parties could promise and presumably deliver as much. Ready to accept the challenge and the opportunity, the Democrats nominated Charles Lane, a "leading citizen and businessman," as their candidate for mayor. Lane radiated honesty and integrity, and the Democrats pledged that they too were in favor of public ownership of municipal utilities.[24]

The daily press showed less initiative and imagination. The *Standard* and the *Miner* trotted out the usual anti-Socialist diatribes, particularly emphasizing the economic consequences of a Socialist victory. The *Standard* advised:

> If Socialist rule is continued, capital will continue to show reluctance to invest in Butte . . . for capital is wary of towns where property is destroyed, where lives are endangered and authorities show themselves unable or unwilling to suppress lawlessness.

The *Miner* predicted: "If the Socialists are voted down, I.W.W.ism will never have a chance to raise its head again in this community."[25]

Responding to journalistic attacks and the Democrats' sudden discovery of the reform theme, the Socialist Party rediscovered itself as the party of the workers. The Socialists argued that big business was looking for a "friendly" city government that would readily "club Butte's workers into submission."[26] The Socialists asked voters to review the events of the last four years in this city. The Socialist Party has been in control of city government. They have always stood by YOU. They have cleaned and improved the streets where YOU live. They have promoted public works that employed YOU. . . . They have raised your wages. They have protected your pickets and banners against unfair employers. They have refused to shoot YOU down like dogs in the street, when the hired thugs of the masters provoked disorders and riots. For YOU a Socialist mayor was unjustly ousted from office. . . . When you were blacklisted, Socialists protested against this injustice to YOU.[27]

The Socialists also directly appealed to newly enfranchised women voters, stressing the party's long-time commitment to equal rights and pointing to the improved quality of life in Butte since the Socialists had assumed office. Hoping to crack the Democratic hold on Irish voters, the Socialists accused Charles Lane of being a member of the nativist, anti-immigrant, and anti-Catholic American Protective Association.[28] But the severe economic depression remained a fact of life, and the daily newspapers darkly hinted that depression and unemployment would certainly continue unless the Socialists were turned out of office.[29]

The mines were closed on election day, and turnout was heavy, especially among women. When the votes were counted, the Socialists had been soundly defeated. Lane polled 6,681 votes to Smith's 3,698, and Republican Arthur Ellingswood trailed with 2,714. Curran and Booher lost by similar margins. Not one Socialist aldermanic candidate was elected; each had received an average of only 28 per cent of the votes cast.[30]

Upset and bitter about the results, the Socialists complained:

The majority of the voters of Butte, and particularly the newly-enfranchised women voters, have spit upon the hand that helped them, and in a frenzy of unreason and blind folly slapped the face of their faithful servant and protector, the Socialist Party, and discharged that servant to re-engage the one who brought them municipal debt, dishonor, disease, and death. . . .

. . . The whole thing in a nut shell is that the company holds the key to the breadbox of Butte. Few families there are in this camp who have not heard the prowling of the wolf of hunger during the last winter. . . . The sources of information, the press, the pulpit, the platform, the schools all have been used to foster the conviction that it was the Socialists and Socialism that are responsible for the empty stores, the silent mines, the closed banks, the unrest and discontent to be found. . . . The women voted against what they had been led to believe (and wanted to believe) was an invidious power menacing their food supply.[31]

The victorious Charles Lane thanked the women voters for their support, as well he might. Turnout statistics suggest that most women had voted for the old party candidates. Voter turnout in 1915 was 13,097, compared to the all-male turnout of 7,133 two years before. In the 1913 election, the combined old party vote total was 3,266; in 1915, the old party vote stood at 9,399, a net gain of 6,133. At the same time, the Socialist vote total had declined somewhat. In 1915, Clarence Smith received 3,698 votes compared to the 3,867 votes that Duncan had gathered in 1913, a net loss of 169. It appears that the Socialists had held on to their core supporters, but they had failed to pick up any support from women voters. The Socialists could only hope that the women would learn from their "mistake" and vote for the party in the future.[32]

The defeat in Butte effectively marked the end of the Socialist Party as a significant political force in the city and in the state. By 1916, state-wide membership had declined to 749 people. In the November 1916 election, the party's national ticket of Allen Benson and George Kirkpatrick polled only 9,564 votes in Montana (5.4 per cent of the total), and the party elected no legislative or local candidates.[33]

In Butte, the Socialist Party was the victim of violence. In June 1915, the printing plant of the Butte Socialist Publishing Company was destroyed by dynamite. The plant was rebuilt and the Socialist Hall on Harrison Avenue in The Flats was opened, but by then party membership had declined by two-thirds.[34] With declining membership and revenue, the *Butte Socialist* ceased publication in December 1915:

> Our friends and supporters through wholesale blacklisting have been driven away by the hundreds. Advertisers have been driven from our columns by direct and indirect threats of boycott by powerful privileged interests. Criminals in the pay of our adversaries have destroyed our property by dynamite. The subsidized capitalist press . . . have stopped at no misrepresentation, vilification, innuendo, and downright falsehood with which to affect our destruction. We have not been destroyed or silenced, but the burden of the conflict has increased.[35]

Turnout was low in the 1916 aldermanic elections, and the Socialists received an average of only 29 per cent of the votes cast. In April 1917, the Socialists fielded Duncan as their candidate for mayor in what would be his last race in Butte. Duncan received 1,612 votes, just 16 per cent of the total.[36] The Socialist era in Montana politics was over.

In Butte and in hundreds of other American communities, the Socialist Party had tried to implement its grand strategy for the peaceful coming of the "Cooperative Commonwealth," but it had failed. Electoral successes at the local level, so numerous in 1910-1912, were seen as the first step toward national political power. But as it turned out, the party could advance no further in Butte or anyplace else. The Socialist Party had risen briefly as a political and economic force and had then quietly faded into oblivion. We must ask why.

First, Butte was a working-class city with a strong union tradition, an environment that should have been extraordinarily receptive to the party's message. Yet, the Socialists remained a minority movement in Butte because they were unable to capture permanently the support of the proletarian majority. The workers remained divided by ethnic ties and many were loyal to the old parties. The Socialists were unable to substitute the politics of class for these loyalties in the minds of many working-class voters, especially the Irish.

Second, the party was hamstrung by the severe limits that restrictive state laws placed on the authority of local governments.[37] Working with the legal authority it had, the Duncan administration did "make good" in office, but only as a reform government. It could not "deliver" on party promises that were more explicitly Socialist in content. Nonetheless, it was clear from election returns that the workers who gave their votes to the party were satisfied with the modest results achieved, as long as they could afford to express their support. The economic depression of 1914-1915 made voting for Socialism in Butte too risky and gave substance to the daily press charges that Socialist government brought with it punishing economic consequences. By 1915, enough voters—especially the newly enfranchised women—were willing to believe those charges.

Third, the party was handicapped by the electoral rules of the game. In addition to malapportioned wards, the Socialists, like all third parties, faced the bias inherent in single-member districts and multi-member at-large elections. In both, getting the most votes was the only thing that counted. The party with the largest bloc of voters won all the prizes, even though the votes received by the second-place finisher might also be large. Because of the way in which votes were counted, the number of Socialist candidates elected always lagged behind the party's share of the popular vote. This was especially the case in the at-large elections to the Montana legislative assembly. An electoral system based on proportional representation would have eliminated such bias by awarding to each party its proportionate share of elected candidates based on its share of the popular vote received. To have adopted such a system would have required that the Socialists at least capture control of the state legislature or join in a coalitional alliance with one of the major parties to adopt proportional representation, but neither appeared to be even a remote possibility.

Fourth, the Socialists were weakened by the threat and sometimes the application of economic coercion and political manipulation. In 1912, the mining companies discharged suspected Socialists just before the aldermanic election. In 1913, the opposition tried fusion. In 1914, miners had to work a full shift on election day. There is little doubt that the companies had one objective in mind: the defeat of the Socialist Party.

The Socialists wanted to believe that their failures were caused primarily by external, hostile forces; but the party had discomforting internal problems as well. In Butte, the party had been plagued by endemic factionalism. The fight between the IWW and non-IWW elements in the local organization and later between the "reds" outside the party and the "yellows" who remained inside was nasty and debilitating. The daily press, which had its own partisan political axes to grind, had exacerbated the conflict by thoroughly publicizing it. Disenchanted Socialists and ex-Socialists flayed the party unmercifully with accusations that "bossism" and corruption were running rampant in the local and in Butte's Socialist government.

All of this was ammunition for the anti-Socialist daily press. Was there any truth to the accusations? In an article published in the May 1915 *International Socialist Review*, H. L. Maury, a late convert to the dissidents, claimed that the party had become infested with and corrupted by patronage-driven ambitions. Using its power over city jobs, Maury claimed, the "Duncan-Smith machine" had driven out all independent-minded party members and replaced them with loyal government payrollers.[38] Maury exaggerated. The fact of the matter is that some who refused to rejoin the party and who remained supporters of the IWW were kept on the city payroll. For example, Joe Shannon, a Wobbly and leader of the Butte Mine Workers'

Union, was given a city job after the mining companies blacklisted him. Nonetheless, factionalism bred a certain degree of intolerance within the party. Those who criticized the party were called "traitors," and it was suggested that some of the dissidents were in fact private detectives in the hire of the mining companies. Intolerance of dissent was most evident in the shabby treatment given the Finnish branch, which was denied the right to fully participate in the party's affairs. Factionalism and the appearance of intolerance toward dissent could not have helped the party's electoral efforts.[39]

Given the problems that the Butte Socialists faced, their record of achievement in city government was impressive. There is no doubt that Socialist government improved the quality of life in the city, especially in working-class neighborhoods. Streets were paved, sidewalks were constructed, sanitation was improved, and health regulations governing businesses and rental properties were systematically and rigorously enforced. The Socialists established a new standard of municipal government in the mining city.[40] Equally important, the Socialist government's pro-working-class stance led to restraint on the night of June 23, 1914, when the Miners' Union Hall was dynamited—a restraint that probably saved lives and property. The city's reaction also provided an environment in which the insurgent Butte Mine Workers' Union was free to organize the mines. Despite what embittered radicals might say about "reformist" Socialist government in Butte, the ACM Company and its allies knew that the Socialist Party was an adversary to be reckoned with, and they were determined to crush it.[41]

But the defeat of the Socialist Party did not signal the end of working-class insurgency in Butte. The Socialist Party's fight was but a phase in the protracted struggle between capital and labor. The insurgency assumed new forms and ways of articulating itself and in the process so broadened and deepened that the Socialist era was quickly overshadowed.

In all the mines in this camp there is a slogan, and upon a miner's absolute obedience to the letter of this slogan depends his job. Shift bosses, foremen, superintendents, all, repeat it as the devout repeat the litany and the miner hears it from the day he starts work until he is burned to death or dies a victim of miner's consumption—GET THE ROCK IN THE BOX!

—handbill, June 11, 1917

10 ‖ *STRIKE!*

By the summer of 1915, the slump in the copper industry was over. The war in Europe had increased the demand for the red metal, and copper prices soared from 13.7 cents a pound at the beginning of the year to 17.6 cents by October. With rising prices, employment in the mines returned to the pre-depression levels of 1912-1913. Wages rose as well. By the end of the year, miners were receiving four dollars a day, and a Butte Wobbly wrote that "the camp is enjoying prosperity with a capital P, if the organs of the mine kings can be believed."[1] The price of copper continued to climb, reaching 28.5 cents a pound by 1916. In the following year, the price rose still higher to 29.2 cents and miners' wages reached $4.75 a day, producing an aggregate weekly payroll of $3.3 million.[2]

The war-induced boom had created good wages and full employment, but there were also less salutary side effects. The cost of living kept pace with and probably exceeded the workers' wage increases, and the perception that merchants were taking unfair advantage was causing unrest in working-class areas.[3] Even more disturbing, the accident rate in the mines was increasing. On October 16, 1915, a mine car containing 500 pounds of dynamite exploded at the Granite Mountain shaft of the North Butte Company's Speculator Mine, killing seventeen men instantly.[4] Handbills appeared in the streets:

North Butte Mining Company
Be Careful
Don't Get Hurt
There are Ten Men
Waiting For Your Job.[5]

Although the Butte Mine Workers' Union had long since disappeared and the IWW had no local in the city, the handbill signaled the presence of a hard core of union militants ready and willing to act. All they needed was a spark.

But the first manifestation of discontent to surface had nothing to do with either the high cost of living or the hazards of employment in the Butte mines. Following the U.S. entry into World War I in April 1917, Congress imposed conscription to build up the armed forces. On June 4, 1917, all adult males between the ages of eighteen and forty-six were required to register for the draft. Many American men, especially those native-born, were no doubt eager to rally to the colors, but a significant minority was opposed to the draft for religious and political reasons. Many Irish and Finnish immigrants did not want to take up arms to defend the interests of their countries' imperial oppressors, Great Britain and Russia. Many of these men also mistakenly believed that the act of registering for the draft meant automatic conscription into the armed forces.

On draft registration day, some native-born Americans joined a number of the Finns and Irish in street demonstrations to protest the draft. The crowd, which had probably gathered in response to crudely written handbills that had been spread throughout the city, was loud and militant. The handbills announced that "War is Hell" and advised "Don't Register" to "kill or be killed" for the benefit of the "money powers" and "the nation which has riveted the chains of slavery around Ireland." No organization claimed authorship of the handbills, but it was fair to assume that they had been distributed by men and women affiliated with or close to the Finnish Workers' Club and the Irish Pearce-Connelly Club. Assisted by a small contingent of national guardsmen, police officers broke up the anti-draft parade by firing guns into the air and clubbing demonstrators. Twenty-one people were arrested.[6] The daily press blamed the anti-draft demonstration on "outside agitators" who were "working in the interests of Germany." In the days following, a large number of "slackers" — men who had reportedly refused to register — were also arrested.[7]

The furor generated by the protests, however, was soon overshadowed by one of the greatest tragedies in American mining history. Late in the evening of June 8, fire broke out in the Granite Mountain shaft of the Speculator Mine. The fire, touched off by a shift boss when his carbide lamp ignited some oil-soaked electrical cable, spread quickly, enveloping the mine with gas and smoke. Of the 415 men on the night shift, 164 were trapped in the spreading inferno and lost their lives. Most died from gas and smoke inhalation. Rescue teams found many of the victims piled up in front of cement bulkheads that blocked escape to other tunnels. State law required that there be doors on the bulkheads to permit escape, but the law had been ignored.[8]

On June 11, the miners spontaneously began to walk off the job. The first to go out were the men employed at W. A. Clark's Elm Orlu Mine. Perhaps as many as three thousand more workers (half of the work force) followed over the next several days. On June 12, the men met in a mass meeting to form a new union of miners, the Metal Mine Workers' Union.[9] The union made the following demands:

1. Recognition of the Metal Mine Workers Union by all the Mining Companies of the Butte District in its official capacity.
2. The unconditional abolition of the Rustling Card system, and to reinstate all blacklisted miners.

3. A minimum wage of $6.00 per day for all men employed underground regardless of the price of Copper, as well as all surface men to receive an increase in wages in proportion to raise in miners' wages.

4. The mines to be examined at least once each month by a committee, half to be selected by this Union and half by the Company, the object being to avoid, as far as possible, fires and many other accidents.

5. That all men starting in mines shall be shown exits to all other mines so that they shall be able to escape in cases of fires or all other accidents.

6. All members getting seven or fifteen days lay off to be given a hearing before a Committee, three to be appointed by this Union, and an equal number to be selected by the Company. If the offense claimed is not proven, the miner or group of miners shall be immediately put to work, and paid in full for all the time lost.

7. That all bulkheads must be guarded FOR THE SAFETY OF THE MINERS by having manholes built into the concrete bulkheads.

> Signed:
> William Stoddard
> John Doran
> Dan Shovlin
> Joe Little
> Tom Campbell. [10]

From the beginning, the operating companies refused to recognize the new union. The companies issued a joint statement:

> This element [the new unionists] forms but a small proportion of our population, but is attempting to pursue its usual vicious methods of intimidation and violence. Their attempts to riot on registration day plainly indicated their motives. Neither this element nor any organization made or controlled by it will receive any consideration or recognition by the mine operators of Butte. [11]

As in 1914, the companies and the daily press tried to link the new union to the IWW. But the Metal Mine Workers' Union, like its predecessor, assured workers that it was independent and worked to prove it by prohibiting the distribution of IWW propaganda at union meetings. [12]

The mining operators ignored the demands made by the new union, claiming: "No grievance of the workers of the Butte mines have been brought to the attention of the operators and we believe none exists." W. A. Clark's rejection was more direct. He threatened to flood his mines rather than recognize or negotiate with "the anarchistic element in control of the so-called miners' union." [13]

The intransigent companies faced an equally determined union. With the support of Local 65 of the International Brotherhood of Electrical Workers (IBEW), the Metal Mine Workers' Union led a strike that completely shut down the mines by mid-June. The electricians were already on strike against the Montana Power Company, and at the urging of electrician William F. Dunne—a radical unionist—the IBEW local adopted the miners' demands as their own. The electricians threatened to call its members out of the mines unless the miners' demands were met.[14]

The operators responded by repeating their refusal to negotiate with the strikers. The union called out the electricians employed in the mines, who were soon joined by the machinists, blacksmiths, boilermakers, and other mine employees represented by unions of the Butte Metal Trades Council. To counter the "lies" of the daily press, the MMWU and the IBEW began to publish a weekly *Joint Strike Bulletin*, with Bill Dunne as editor.[15]

Unlike the strike in 1914, the miners did not picket or use union jurisdiction committees. Union leaders wanted to avoid any incident that might give the companies an excuse to engage in retaliatory violence or give the state cause to declare martial law and call in U.S. troops. The union advised: "Our members understand that it is our business to see that no detectives or stool pigeons be given the opportunity to create a disturbance and the result has been that the Companies have been . . . absolutely unable to start trouble."[16]

Also unlike the insurgents of 1914, the new union was willing to entertain affiliation with the AFL. The Silver Bow Trades and Labor Council pressed for the connection, intimating that the striking miners would receive unqualified support from all AFL unions if they did so. But the miners were being asked to join the generally despised International Union of Mine, Mill and Smelter Workers, the old WFM with a new name. Dunne told the striking miners that he knew that joining Moyer's union would be a "hard pill" to swallow, but he urged them to affiliate for the sake of labor solidarity.[17]

Operating on the assumption that the Metal Mine Workers' Union would be taken in as a group and given a charter in the IUMM & SW, the strike leaders called for a referendum vote on the question. The rank-and-file miners seemed inclined to favor the affiliation; but the day before the vote, the local representative of the IUMM & SW told strike leaders that if the result was affirmative his union would order the miners back to work immediately. Further, the IUMM & SW would not take the strikers in as a body and grant them a charter. Those who wanted representation would have to apply individually for membership. These last-minute "conditions" instantly stifled any inclination on the part of the strikers to join the AFL. In the referendum, the miners decisively rejected affiliation by a vote of 4,528 to 437.[18]

Because the mining companies refused to negotiate with the MMWU and realizing that the unionists could expect little sympathy from state and local authorities, the strikers appealed directly to the U.S. government for relief. They asked federal authorities to investigate conditions in the Butte mines and to mediate a settlement between the union and the companies. Responding to W. A. Clark's threat to flood his mines, the strikers also asked the federal government to consider seizing the mines and operating them in the national interest.[19] On July 4, striking miners met in a mass meeting and issued this declaration:

> We, the miners of Butte, Montana, in mass meeting assembled, do hereby
> unqualifiedly proclaim our devotion and adherence to this, the land of our
> birth and adoption, and to our duly elected representatives, and do call upon

our Government forthwith to ASSUME CONTROL AND MANAGE-
MENT OF EVERY MINE IN THIS DISTRICT. . . .[20]

In its efforts to secure federal intervention, the Metal Mine Workers' Union
found a ready and willing ally in Montana's first-term Republican congresswoman,
Jeannette Rankin. A progressive of deep humanitarian instincts and firm convictions,
Rankin had already earned the enmity of conservative and super-patriotic Montanans
by acting on her pacifist beliefs and voting against America's declaration of war.[21] On
August 7, Rankin introduced a bill in Congress mandating the federal takeover of
Butte's mines, and she pressed for a federal investigation of mine conditions and
mediation of the strike. She told her colleagues in Congress: "The conditions in the
mines have grown more and more unsafe. I have had heartbreaking letters from the
wives of miners saying that when their husbands went to work they never knew
whether or not they would ever return, and that they lived in constant anxiety."[22]

The House of Representatives never seriously considered Rankin's mine seizure
bill, but the striking miners were pleased with her efforts and said so. In July, spokesmen for the Metal Mine Workers' Union told Rankin that if President Wilson would
appoint her as federal mediator they would call off the strike as soon as she was "com-
missioned to make permanent settlement." Rankin was willing.[23] The ACM Company
was not. Company Manager Cornelius Kelley wrote Rankin: "The unwarranted attack
made by you without investigation upon the Anaconda Company and its officials
precludes your being acceptable as mediator or my conferring with you relative to the
existing conditions."[24]

The strikers' request for Rankin was also a reaction to their extreme dissatisfac-
tion with W. H. Rodgers, a federal mediator who had arrived in Butte in early July.
Rodgers had apparently persuaded the companies to make separate settlements with
the electricians and other striking craft unionists. In this way, the companies hoped
that the miners' strike would be undermined and eventually broken and that copper
production could be resumed without granting legitimacy to a union that carried the
taint of the IWW.[25]

The striking craftsmen voted to return to work in mid-July. Prodded by Rodgers,
the companies made some concessions, most notably by announcing a slight
modification in the rustling card system: Any man applying for a card would be given
one immediately unless there was some "reason for denying it." The companies also
granted a slight increase in the workers' daily wages. Working conditions and recognition of the new union were not addressed. Rodgers told the MMWU that the offer
was the best he could do under the circumstances, and he advised the union to call off
the strike. MMWU members coolly received Rodgers's advice and then rejected it.[26]

The return of the craft unions and the mild concessions unilaterally doled out by
the companies were having a dampening effect on the strike. The men had to eat, and
they had to feed their families. Some miners went back to work. Thousands more,
the *Strike Bulletin* claimed, left the district to seek work elsewhere.[27] Confident, the
companies overplayed their hand.

Strike sentiment was kept ablaze by the arrogance of ACM-hired gunmen who
swaggered through the streets of Northeast Butte and threatened men they thought
were strikers. On July 28, the *Strike Bulletin* reported that gunmen had beaten two

men on the Anaconda Road. The weekly would later identify William Oates, Herman Gillis, Pete Beaudin, "a rat named Middleton," and a leader named "Ryan" as particularly arrogant and vicious.[28]

The strikers began to fear for their safety. They knew that violence had accompanied strikes elsewhere. At Bisbee, Arizona, for example, a small army of vigilantes had rounded up striking copper miners and left them in the desert. The *Strike Bulletin* predicted a "revolution" if a Bisbee-style roundup were attempted in Butte. On July 13, the miners' union wired Jeannette Rankin:

> Union advised deportation and violence by gunmen imminent here. Governor Stewart advises no protection beyond county peace officers. Gunmen deputized. Union request you demand Federal protection in event of violence.[29]

Rankin sought an immediate audience with President Wilson, but Wilson could not—or would not—see her. Presidential Secretary J. P. Tummulty told Rankin that the situation in Butte was receiving the president's "constant and anxious attention." Rankin told the union on July 17 that while she had failed to meet with the president she had apprised Labor Secretary Will Wilson of the situation, who was "much interested and promised to help." There the matter rested until the end of the month. On July 30, Mary O'Neill, a confidante of the congresswoman, wired Rankin that there were rumors that the mine operators intended to round up and drive the strike leaders out of town that night. "Gunmen, game wardens, soldiers all ready for the work," O'Neill reported.[30] The situation had grown ugly. The change in mood coincided with the arrival of Frank Little, a member of the IWW's General Executive Board and a leader of the IWW metal miners' union.

Little came to Butte on about July 20 to try to win the striking miners over to the IWW. An uncompromising revolutionary, Little had openly stated his opposition to the war in Europe and his hatred of the capitalist system. In the July 21 issue of *Solidarity*, he articulated his and the IWW's labor philosophy:

> An injury to one is an injury to all! So all together, you diggers and muckers, boost for the organization that is going to get you the things that will really make life worth living. Force the bosses off your backs, put them to work down in the hole with the producers; hand them their muck sticks and make them *earn* a living for a change.[31]

Little spoke at several meetings in Butte, but what he actually said is not known. The daily press sensationalized his remarks in an attempt to picture the Wobbly leader as a dangerous subversive who ought to be arrested, or worse.[32] We can assume that Little "disdained to conceal his views" and that the daily press was only a little less reticent in holding back theirs. The *Anaconda Standard* editorialized:

> The Industrial Workers of the World has arrayed itself in open rebellion to our country and our government. It is against America, it is against the institutions of this land. It is against law and order and in favor of anarchy. . . . The leaders, by their acts and utterances, have placed themselves outside consideration as American citizens. . . . As enemies of this country they

should be given the consideration and treatment to which enemies are entitled and no more.[33]

The *Standard*'s denunciation of "enemies" was prompted by Little's remarks to a crowd at Finlander Hall the evening before. The IWW leader had reportedly called soldiers who were used in strike situations "uniformed thugs," reiterated his opposition to the draft and the war, and hoped for the day when organized miners would force "the officials on the sixth floor [of the Hennessy Building, ACM Company headquarters] down below with a muckstick."[34]

Local political and corporate leaders put pressure on U.S. District Attorney Burton K. Wheeler to arrest Little for his "treasonable utterances." "Besieged by demands" that he do something, Wheeler reviewed the Espionage Act of 1917, which made it a crime to "convey false reports or false statements" about the armed forces, to "attempt to cause insubordination, disloyalty, mutiny, or refusal of duty" in the armed forces, or to attempt to "willfully obstruct recruiting or enlistment service." With the reluctant agreement of L. O. Evans, chief counsel for the ACM Company, Wheeler concluded that the evidence did not warrant an indictment of Little.[35] The fiery Wobbly leader may have violated no law, but his speeches did cost him his life. Early on the morning after Wheeler and Evans had consulted the statutory law, Little was murdered.

At approximately three o'clock on the morning of August 1 six men in a large black automobile pulled up in front of Little's boarding house on North Wyoming Street. Five of the men entered the building and found the landlady, Mrs. Nora Byrne, who asked what they wanted. They replied: "We are officers and we want Frank Little." The frightened landlady told the men the number of Little's room. They dragged Little outside in his underclothing. Still recovering from a broken leg suffered in an automobile accident in Arizona, the victim could offer little resistance. The "officers" forced Little into the car and sped away. After driving a short distance, the men stopped the car and tied Little behind it. The murderers dragged him over the pavement before savagely beating the severely injured man. Then Frank Little was hanged from a nearby railroad trestle. Early that morning, a passing workman discovered Little's body with a vigilante placard hanging around his neck: "Others take notice, first and last warning, 3-7-77." Below were the letters "L-D-C-S-S-W-T," with the "L" circled. The others "warned" were Bill Dunne, Tom Campbell, Daniel Shovlin, Joe Shannon, John Williams, and John Tomich—all leaders of the strike.[36]

No one was ever indicted for Little's murder. The coroner's jury determined that Little had been murdered by "persons unknown." The *Strike Bulletin* claimed that the murderers' names were known and promised to reveal them. It never did, instead reporting that "two of the men were in business, two are gunmen, and one is connected with LAW ENFORCEMENT."[37] Over the following years, hints were dropped and names were named in the daily *Butte Bulletin* (previously the *Strike Bulletin*) concerning who was responsible for Little's murder. Three years after the killing, Burton K. Wheeler accused ACM Company attorney D'Gay Stivers of knowing who the murderers were. In July 1923, Bill Dunne claimed that Little had been murdered by "agents of the Anaconda Mining Company" and named men who he believed had knowledge of or had participated in the killing: lawyer Roy Alley, John D. Ryan's private secretary and alleged commander of the Company's private army of guards;

Stivers; L. O. Evans; John Berkin, sometime deputy sheriff and notorious gunman; J. F. Taylor, described as a "stool pigeon" and "gunman" from Seattle; Oscar Rohn, head of the Pittsmont Mining Company; and James Rowe, a prominent Butte businessman. Dunne also theorized that Little had been killed in the hopes that the incident would "get the striking miners to riot so that they could be shot down and driven back to work. . . ."[38]

The strike leaders had considered that motive and had counseled the strikers to remain peaceful in the face of the outrage. The workers heeded that advice without dissent. In an impressive display of labor solidarity, sixty-eight hundred men, women, and children marched in Little's funeral procession as red-sashed pallbearers carried his body to Mountain View Cemetery.[39] On August 17, Wheeler reported to the U.S. attorney general that "thousands of miners" still remained on strike and noted that the strike was continuing without "violence or disorder" of any kind. For their part, Dunne, Campbell, and Shannon took precautions to protect their own lives by staying in a different place each night. After observing men in a car watching his house, Shannon sent his small children to Iowa to stay with relatives. Dunne secured a license to carry a pistol and made it no secret that he was armed.[40]

Frank Little had failed in his mission to win the Metal Mine Workers' Union over to the IWW cause. But in death the tough revolutionary became a martyr, and his murder gave new energy to the flagging miners' strike. On August 23, the Anaconda smeltermen, long chafing under the tutelage of the ineffective International Union of Mine, Mill and Smelter Workers, went out on strike and joined the Metal Mine Workers' Union. The Butte streetcarmen struck on the same day. The mines, which had begun to operate, were shut down once more.[41]

On September 5, in a raid that paralleled a planned and coordinated nation-wide roundup of IWW leaders, federal agents invaded the Metal Mine Workers' Union headquarters in a search for "seditious" material. They found nothing. The *Strike Bulletin* lampooned:

> The raid yesterday was a Hoosier performance. . . . The vigilante raiders crawl[ed] into every hole and corner in the hall, winding up eventually on the roof, where, judging from their attitudes, they were looking for Zeppelins, or for German money which might fall from the heavens.[42]

Jeannette Rankin continued to press for a federal investigation and mediation in the strike, but without success. The studied indifference by the responsible federal authorities was partly caused by their perception that the Butte strike would soon be quietly over. And they were right. By the end of September, the Anaconda smelter was operating normally, thanks to the employment of strikebreakers and demoralized smeltermen who were drifting back to work. The mining companies' obdurate attitude combined with government indifference and occasional hostility toward strikers' demands had been too much for the workers to withstand. On December 20, 1917, the Metal Mine Workers' Union officially declared that the strike was over.[43] Speaking on behalf of the union, George Tompkins thanked Jeannette Rankin for "the effort you have put forth on behalf of our cause in Washington." Tompkins continued: ". . . we are frank to state that there seems to be little or no confidence on the part of the workers in general that they can expect any relief or aid from the government forces."

He ended by predicting that "the workers have come to the conclusion that any betterment of their conditions will be secured only through their own economic power, through industrial strikes and other means which they are beginning to employ to attain their desired results."[44]

Tompkins's observation was prescient. The union's long and peaceful strike and its careful lobbying for federal government intervention had failed, but in the wake of that failure those who had led and supported the strike re-examined strategy. Some would turn resolutely toward the IWW's anti-political philosophy; others would advocate militant unionism and a new brand of independent political action. The insurgent community was becoming divided in much the same way as the Socialist Party had been five years earlier, even though the division was not immediately apparent to the participants.[45]

One product of the strike was the transformation of the miners' *Strike Bulletin* - into a regular labor newspaper. Established as a weekly at the end of 1917, the *Butte Weekly Bulletin* became the alternative newspaper in the mining city, providing news and analysis for the workers that the daily press failed to supply. Bill Dunne was principal editorial writer, and Robert B. Smith was the editor. With growing financial assistance from several local unions in the state, the weekly became a daily in August 1918.

The *Butte Bulletin* was unabashedly revolutionary in its editorial philosophy. Declaring itself to be the voice of the "producing classes," the *Bulletin* announced: "We believe in the abolition of classes in society; in the right of all equally to participate in the wealth which they help to create." Its motto was: "WE PREACH THE CLASS STRUGGLE IN THE INTERESTS OF THE WORKERS AS A CLASS." The paper warmly applauded the Bolshevik Revolution in Russia and gave regular coverage to what it believed were the positive accomplishments of the struggling Soviet Republic. On the home front, it reported on the struggle between capital and labor throughout the nation and took every opportunity to damn the ACM Company and its economic and political allies. The paper condemned the high cost of living in Butte and regularly exposed instances of corruption in municipal and county government. Written with style and dash, the *Butte Bulletin* was a constant thorn in the side of its enemies. Governor Sam Stewart once exclaimed in exasperation: "I defy anyone to produce a more radical or revolutionary sheet in the United States; certainly none can be found among the daily papers. Why it is allowed to circulate through the mails is more than I can understand."[46]

Eclectic in its advocacy of tactics, the *Bulletin* occasionally made cloudy references to the necessity for a "dictatorship of the producers" and the revolutionary general strike. But its primary focus was to urge independent working-class political action, not only through contesting elections but also through grassroots organizations that could put pressure on local government authorities. In time, both of these efforts would score some dramatic successes. But in the opening months of 1918, a newly organized IWW was just beginning to recruit members and build its strength. With national headquarters in Butte under the leadership of A. S. "Sam" Embree, an experienced and tough Wobbly militant, the IWW's Metal Mine Workers' Industrial Union No. 800 promised that any strikes it led would be short ones. Embree exhorted: "We want 10,000 members in Butte to abolish the rustling card without a strike. Be one of them!"[47] Those who had been disappointed and at least temporarily demoralized by the long and unsuccessful MMWU strike gravitated to the IWW. Among these were MMWU leaders Joe Shannon and Joe Kennedy. With such men as these the IWW Miners' Union No. 800 was able to seize the initiative in its efforts to organize the Butte miners, and the employers were worried.

Employers' fears of worker unrest stemmed in large part from marginal changes in the social character of the labor force. Many experienced miners, both native- and foreign-born, were in the armed forces. As a consequence, the number of native-born, Cornish, and Canadian miners was less than it had been before the war, while the relative numbers of Finnish and Slavic employees had increased noticeably. Interestingly, there were fewer Irish miners in the work force during the war, but many of them were apparently recent immigrants and, along with the immigrant Slavs and the Finns, the Irish were responsive to Wobbly organizing efforts.[48] J. H. Rowe, the chairman of the county draft board, complained that these immigrants were particularly prone to resist conscription:

> Thousands of immigrants here, and doubtlessly elsewhere, have assimilated no more American sentiment or aspiration for democracy than the peasant who remained at home. A day's pay in Butte is more than they could earn by hard labor in Europe in a month and they have come here for . . . food and shelter.

These "foreigners," wrote Roy Alley, were "an unassimilated mass [that] needs but leadership at any time to become a dangerous menace."[49]

The fact was that during the war a "sentiment and aspiration for democracy" was particularly absent among both business and government officials at all levels. Nationally, Socialists, Wobblies, and pacifists were jailed. The mails were closed to seditious newspapers, and proceedings were begun to deport subversive aliens. It was a time of intense intolerance against all forms of dissent; and Butte, with its long history of labor unrest, was typical of the intolerance that fueled repression. In Butte, the IWW and the *Butte Bulletin* represented sedition and treason to most local business and political leaders, who were quite prepared to jettison constitutional guarantees in order to stop such troublemakers.

In February 1918, Governor Stewart called the Montana legislature into special session, and it dutifully enacted laws to suppress dissent. First, the legislature passed a criminal syndicalism law that made it a crime to belong to the IWW or similar organizations. Second, the Montana Sedition Act made it illegal to criticize the government or to "incite or inflame resistance" to it. Finally, the legislators provided a legal basis for the Montana Council of Defense, which the governor had created in 1917 in response to a request from President Wilson that such councils be established to assist the U.S. government in "the carrying on of the war." Montana legislators empowered the Council to issue orders that carried the force of law. Its first order, handed down on March 15, 1918, ruled that "no parade, procession or other public demonstration" could be held in the state without the governor's written permission. Other repressive orders soon followed. The Council forbade the use of the German language and German books in the schools, made it a crime to hitch a ride on a train (a measure aimed primarily at migratory farm workers, who were a strong base of support for the IWW), and tried unsuccessfully to stop the publication of the *Butte Bulletin*.[50]

Nationally, Congress amended the Espionage Act to prohibit "political" strikes and strikes that interfered with the war effort. Congress also approved laws against "enemy aliens" authorizing the arrest and deportation of any alien who was a member of the IWW or similar organizations. Finally, "sedition"—uttering "disloyal" words— was made a crime. The "sentiment" for democracy had so weakened in official circles that it was thought quite proper to declare thought, belief, and association a crime punishable by imprisonment or deportation.[51]

To root out sedition and treason, the U.S. government initiated a massive program of political surveillance directed at dissidents and aliens. Assisted by private detectives employed by corporations and volunteers from the American Protective League, a civilian organization of patriots, the Justice Department's Bureau of Investigation (later the FBI) and Military Intelligence engaged in systematic spying directed at the economic (labor union) and political activities of Butte miners. The Bureau of Investigation relied heavily on information from private detectives. For example, when agent F. W. Byrn wanted information on Bill Dunne in July 1918, he sent one of his men to see Roy Alley, who was only too glad to supply the file the Company had been keeping on the radical leader.[52]

Finally, on August 17, 1917, federal troops were garrisoned in the Butte mining district to ensure order. They would remain there until January 1921. Much like civilian government officials, the military saw its mission as one of preventing outbreaks of sedition, and it was quite willing to ignore constitutional guarantees to accomplish that goal.[53]

Some government officials refused to join the stampede to temporarily suspend democratic rights in order to ensure the presumed greater good of winning the war. Both U.S. District Judge George Bourquin and U.S. District Attorney Burton K. Wheeler attempted to apply the laws fairly even though it was the unpopular thing to do. Wheeler was not about to indict those who merely criticized government policies, nor would he indict men who had failed to register for the draft out of ignorance. Judge Bourquin refused to convict defendants who had engaged in "loose talk," and he preferred to sentence draft resisters to public service rather than to prison. Not unexpectedly, other public officials were upset with Bourquin and Wheeler and repeatedly pressed for their removal. Because federal jurists were appointed for life and could only be removed for "treason," "bribery," and "high crimes and misdemeanors," Bourquin could only be removed through the impeachment process. But Wheeler's tenure was subject to periodic renewal. Wheeler was originally appointed district attorney in the fall of 1913 on the recommendation of his close friend and political ally Senator Walsh, but his term of office had expired in November 1917. Walsh, who was up for re-election in 1918, was in a difficult situation. If he recommended Wheeler's reappointment it would surely undermine the support he enjoyed in the Democratic Party. If he abandoned Wheeler and recommended someone else, he would not only be deserting a friend, but he would also be giving aid and comfort to those who were eager to suppress public criticism of official policy. Wheeler did the generous thing and spared Walsh by resigning in October 1918.[54]

Only two incidents broke the quiet in Butte between the end of the long strike of 1917 and September of the following year. On St. Patrick's Day 1918, the Pearce-Connelly Club attempted to hold a parade that had been forbidden by municipal authorities. Troops broke up the demonstration and arrested approximately one hundred people. Later that month, police raided the IWW hall and arrested forty men on unspecified charges. All were later released.[55]

By the summer of 1918, the divisions in the ranks of the insurgent miners had solidified. The Metal Mine Workers' Union (independent), with an estimated five hundred active members, formed a close relationship with the *Butte Bulletin*. Both were devoting their attentions to fielding a radical labor ticket in the coming election. For them, the experiences of 1917 had demonstrated the necessity of winning political control of the local sources of government power.

The 1917 strike had different lessons for the other miners' organization. The local affiliate of the IWW metal miners' organization had about a thousand members in the summer of 1918. Its leaders were confident of their organization's power to compel the companies to recognize the miners' demands for better working conditions, higher wages, and an end to the rustling card employment system.[56] While one part of the insurgent community was preparing for the fall elections, the IWW was planning a fall strike. It would be the first of three major miners' strikes that the IWW would lead.

There is no escaping the conclusion that "class antagonism" and "class prejudice" exists [*sic*] to an alarming degree
in some of the industrial centers of the State. This feeling
is particularly noticeable in Butte where the men, as a
rule, look upon their employers as opponents and antag-
onists who control the production of metals in the Butte
mining district despotically and autocratically.

– Commissioner William J.
Swindlehurst, Montana
Department of Labor and
Industry, July 16, 1919

11 ‖ *To the Anaconda Road*

Originating in the city's First Ward and then wending its way uphill in a northeasterly
direction through Dublin Gulch, the Anaconda Road led to many of the district's
major mines, including the Neversweat, the Anaconda, the High Ore, the Diamond,
and the Speculator. Miners went to and from work on this road, and it was here on a
spring day in 1920 that corporate gunmen opened fire on miners picketing the
Neversweat Mine, killing one man and wounding sixteen others. The strikers were
gunned down as they fled down the road in search of safety. The authorities were
either unable or unwilling to bring the gunmen to justice, prompting Wobbly essayist,
poet, and songwriter Ralph Chaplin to exclaim bitterly:

The overlords of Butte will not permit their right to exploit to be challenged.
Drunk with unbridled power and the countless millions profiteered during
the war, with lying phrases of "law and order" on their lips, the blood of
workingmen dripping from their hands and the gold of the government
bursting their coffers they face the nation unreprimanded and unashamed –
reaction militant, capitalism at its worst. The copper trust can murder its
slaves in broad daylight on any occasion and under any pretext. There is no
law to call a halt. In the confines of this greed-ruled city the gun-man has
replaced the Constitution. Butte is a law unto itself.[1]

The path that led to the shootings on the Anaconda Road began on August 17,
1918, when the national leaders of the IWW were convicted in Chicago for violating
the Espionage Act. The guilty verdict was expected, and the battered and bruised
IWW was determined to react with a dramatic gesture of defiance. The Wobblies
decided to call a general strike to protest the imprisonment of their fellow workers and
all other "class war prisoners," an action in direct violation of the Espionage Act. But
the IWW was heavily infiltrated by undercover operatives of the Bureau of Investigation, Military Intelligence, and private detective agencies; and federal authorities knew
about the strike plans from the start.[2]

In Butte, Military Intelligence agents in close cooperation with private detectives were not only fully aware of the Wobbly strike plans in the city, but they seemed interested in ensuring that the strike actually took place. On August 23, an army intelligence officer from Spokane, Washington, arrived in Butte and informed the local BI office that the committee planning the nation-wide IWW strike was headquartered in the mining city. Surprised, Agent F. W. Byrn countered that his agents knew of no such committee and that in his opinion it did not exist. In his report to BI headquarters in Spokane, Byrn observed that Military Intelligence seemed overeager and "extremely anxious to get results."[3] On September 11, BI Director A. Bruce Bielaski wired Byrn that Military Intelligence was predicting an IWW strike for the next day, but Byrn thought that the army was overreacting. Intelligence officers had predicted that the Wobblies would strike on September 10, but nothing had happened.[4]

September 12 was draft registration day, when all unregistered men between the ages of eighteen and forty-six had to register. Contrary to the dire prediction of Military Intelligence, the registration proceeded peacefully and without incident.[5] But the army was soon vindicated. On that evening, the Butte local of the Metal Mine Workers' Industrial Union No. 800 met and called a strike for the next morning. The union demanded an eight-hour day, a six dollar per day wage, abolition of the rustling card system, and the liberation of "all economic and class war prisoners." Agent Byrn believed that the miners had little sympathy for a strike and predicted that it would soon fizzle.[6]

If the army and the local authorities had ignored the strike call, Byrn might have been right. Instead, Military Intelligence agents, local policemen, and private detectives raided the offices of the *Butte Bulletin*, the independent Metal Mine Workers' Union, and the IWW. Without search warrants, these enthusiastic enforcers of law arrested dozens of men and held them without charge "for the [Montana] Council of Defense." Additional sweeps uncovered "slackers," who were arrested without the authority of warrants.[7]

District Attorney Burton K. Wheeler and Agent Byrn were outraged. Byrn wired Bielaski that the raids had given life to the IWW strike and that men were walking off the job in protest. He reported:

> The whole attitude of the Military Intelligence in this locality is such that I feel that the best interests of this Bureau will not permit us to co-operate for the reason that the Military Intelligence acts in many cases *without the slightest regard for the law*, and this office cannot, by co-operating with the Military Intelligence, countenance any such actions.

Wheeler's appraisal, wired in code to the U.S. attorney general, was succinct: "Labor conditions Butte. Many arrests being made by soldiers. . . . Prisoners brutally treated and held without warrant or hearing."[8]

Two thousand to three thousand miners were out, enough to effectively cripple copper production. On the evening of September 18, an ACM Company gunman shot and killed miner John Carroll in the street after an argument between the two. The gunman, Herman Gillis, was arrested and charged with murder. The local chief of Military Intelligence, Lieutenant Will H. Germer, told his enlisted chauffeur that the Carroll killing "will probably not amount to much — if it does, we'll kill some more."[9]

Germer's violent antipathy was not unusual. Governor Stewart was eager to see the military continue its actions and argued strenuously that the "slacker" raids should continue. General Enoch H. Crowder, the U.S. Provost Marshal, disagreed: "As you are aware, it is the view of the Department . . . that under any and all circumstances it is opposed to military participation with the civil authorities in the work of arresting slackers in a general roundup." Crowder told the governor that it would be ill-advised to conduct the raids in Butte's tense environment.[10]

Meanwhile, Wheeler, assisted by Thomas Barker, a representative of the War Labor Board, was seeking a peaceful solution to end the strike. Wheeler and Barker told the IWW that the war was still on and copper was needed. They promised that if the strike was called off they would urge the federal government to investigate the conditions complained about in the strikers' demands.[11] Local IWW leaders were reluctant to agree to the plan. They wanted to check with IWW headquarters in Chicago on the progress of what they wrongly believed was a nation-wide general strike.

On September 22, three thousand men attended a strike rally at the Butte baseball park. Dunne, Tom Campbell, and Assistant U.S. Attorney James H. Baldwin pleaded for an end to the strike, but two Wobbly leaders, B. Y. Thorpe and H. R. Shirley, hotly urged that the strike should continue until the miners' demands were met.[12] Wheeler then played his hole card. He called Shirley and Thorpe into his office and accused them of being private detectives. One of the men (probably Shirley) admitted that it was true. In an open letter to Dan Kelly, legal counsel for the ACM Company, Wheeler leveled his charge: "The I.W.W. organization did herald or call the strike in Butte. That much is true. They were encouraged to do so by the paid agents of your company. These agents are high in the counsel of the I.W.W. local union."[13]

Wheeler's letter was a bombshell. It ended the 1918 miners' strike, with the IWW officially calling it off on September 28. The *Butte Bulletin* theorized that the ACM Company had conspired to encourage the strike, confident that it would surely fail. The Company hoped that the failure would so demoralize the miners and so discredit both miners' unions that there would be no labor unrest in the future, especially when wages fell, as they surely would when the war ended.[14] The strike also revealed the close cooperation between the army and the corporation, with the army serving as both a source of muscle and intelligence. With the end of the war, the military would continue to supply its strong arm in strike situations, while the surveillance function would be largely assumed by the Bureau of Investigation.[15]

The price of copper began its predictable slide after November 1918. By the end of the year, several mines were closed and thousands of miners were out of work.[16] The ranks of the unemployed were further swelled by soldiers who returned to find that their old jobs no longer were available to them. On December 27, 1918, the *Butte Bulletin* predicted that the Company would soon announce a wage cut and suggested: "Only control of the industries by the workers themselves can prevent the misery and suffering that comes from unemployment; if they are good enough to fight the battles of the nation, they are good enough to run its industries."[17]

Governor Stewart was expecting trouble. He wrote Major General J. F. Morrison, commander of the army's Western Department, pleading for the garrisoning of federal troops in Butte. The governor told the general: "You are no doubt familiar with the situation in Butte. It is a big labor camp and many foreigners are employed.

Thousands of people who speak very little English and are more or less affected by Bolshevik doctrines are there." Morrison promised that some federal troops would remain in the mining city.[18]

The situation in Butte was approaching the flash point. Large numbers of unemployed men roamed the streets, many of them veterans still wearing their uniforms. The city government was broke. Banks would not honor the city's pay warrants, and firemen and police officers were threatening to quit in protest.[19]

Bureau of Investigation agents kept a close watch on the increasingly tense situation. Byrn instructed Special Agent D. H. Dickason to circulate in the pool halls and cafes to gauge working-class sentiment. Dickason's reports for January 1919 indicated that discontent was growing by the day but that there was no significant support for a strike. More ominous was the formation of a "workers' council," which Dickason characterized as "a local eruption of a malady, or condition, more deeply seated and more insidious than any I.W.W.ism."[20]

The origins of the Butte Workers' Council, which was created in December 1918, remain unclear. IWW men and some craft unionists were active in the Council, and the *Butte Bulletin* gave it full editorial support. It was clear that the Council was an ongoing open meeting to which all workers were invited and that the Council had been modeled after the workers' councils (soviets) formed in Russia after the overthrow of the Tsarist regime. In a sense, the founders appear to have seen the Council as something of an alternative shadow government of the workers. Through it, the workers would be energized, organized, and united. But for what? On January 22, 1919, the Butte Workers' Council hinted at its goals. It announced that it was in constant communication with "workers', soldiers' and sailors' councils" that were forming throughout the country and that it was preparing "to act in concert with them at a moment's notice." In the wilder fantasies of some of the participants, the Council may have been preparing for some kind of proletarian insurrection similar to the Bolsheviks' seizure of power in Russia. Officially, however, the Workers' Council said it was organizing to fight for a six-hour day, freedom for "class war prisoners," and the withdrawal of American troops who were occupying a part of eastern Siberia.[21]

The nascent workers' council movement, whose actual scope was much more limited and ephemeral than the Butte radicals could have imagined, might have quietly expired except for the example provided by a general strike in Seattle, the first of its kind in the United States. The Seattle General Strike, which had grown out of a wage dispute in the shipyards, began on February 6. On the same day, the Anaconda Copper Mining Company announced an immediate reduction in wages by one dollar a day. Nothing could have more effectively incited the miners to strike.[22]

On February 7, the miners began to walk off the job, and the Workers' Council boldly announced that it would "take hold" and "handle the general strike situation." In fact, it appears that the IWW was the main driving force behind the strike, even though it never officially claimed responsibility. Mass picketing of the mines began almost at once; companies of strikers, often led by returned veterans and marching in military formations, covered the hill and shut it down. Within a few days, eight thousand men, virtually the entire employed work force, were out.[23]

In the crisis, the banks underwrote the city's finances to at least temporarily avert the threatened walkout of the firefighters and police force. Governor Stewart wired frantically for more federal troops to prevent what he believed was "an arranged plan of agitators to precipitate violence and general disorder." Three companies from the 44th U.S. Infantry arrived on February 9 under the command of Major A. M. Jones. Jones sent his troops into action on the following day to break up the picket lines with fixed bayonets. Eight strikers were wounded. That evening, the soldiers raided IWW headquarters at Finlander Hall. In the ensuing melee, John Kinari was bayoneted in the stomach.[24]

The soldiers' brutal handling of the strikers further inflamed the situation. The craft unions now inclined toward the Butte Workers' Council, so that five days into the strike the Council comprised sixty-five delegates representing both miners' unions plus twenty-six craft unions, including electricians, blacksmiths, streetcarmen, iron workers, laborers, plumbers, pipefitters, boilermakers, and bakers. Completing its superficial resemblance to the soviets, the Council admitted returned military veterans and changed its name to the Soldiers', Sailors' and Workers' Council.[25]

After the bloody confrontations of February 10, the army stepped back by taking the troops off the streets and assigning them to guard mine property. For their part, the leaders of the strike temporarily suspended the mass picketing.

It was a time of testing. The Silver Bow Trades and Labor Council called on the AFL unions to consider calling a general strike. Two days later, the Butte Metal Trades Council did the same. More companies of troops were moved into the area. Stewart called on Major Jones to treat the "seditious, disloyal, and revolutionary" in "the most forceful and determined manner" and said that he was ready and willing to declare martial law. But both Mayor W. H. Maloney and the military commanders in Butte counseled patience. They wanted to see if the general strike the radicals were hoping for would actually come off.[26]

The key was whether or not the hoisting engineers would vote to join the strike. If they walked out, it would be extremely difficult for the companies to reopen the mines. On February 15, the engineers voted by two to one to stay on the job. Suddenly, the rush was on. First this and then that craft union local voted to call off the strike. The streetcarmen, who had not run their cars since the beginning of the strike, voted to return. In vain, Shannon and Embree pleaded with the electricians to stay the course. Then the IWW, true to its promise to conduct only short and successful strikes, officially announced the end of its participation on February 17. The independent Metal Mine Workers' Union followed suit later that day. The third miners' strike was at an end; shortly thereafter, the Workers' Council was dissolved.[27]

Nevertheless, the 1919 miners' strike did have an effect. Although the daily press and the army might have believed that the strike was a sinister expression of the "Bolshevik desire to paralyse industry," the ACM Company and other big business leaders were not so simpleminded. They knew that the cost of living in Butte was high, and a committee of the local elite was formed to put pressure on the merchants to reduce prices. As a consequence, prices did come down slightly.[28] At the same time, the *Butte Bulletin* put intense editorial pressure on city government to do something; in July, the city responded by opening a public produce market. Also in July, the operating companies, which were again experiencing more profits, announced the restoration of wages to their pre-February 6 levels. Perhaps most important, the strike had not demoralized the miners nor weakened the growing influence of the IWW.[29]

Later that year, the federal troops were quietly withdrawn from the district, but the labor situation was far from quiet.[30] On July 4, members of both miners' unions went out on a one-day strike to protest the imprisonment of Tom Mooney, a California labor union activist who, along with Warren Billings, had allegedly dynamited a Preparedness Day parade in San Francisco in 1916. The next day, a dynamite blast severely damaged the entrance of the ACM Company's pay office. The perpetrators were never apprehended, and the *Bulletin* theorized that the Company had attacked itself in order to place blame on the radical unionists.[31] The dynamiting did coincide with a convention in Butte organized by the One Big Union, a Canadian labor federation. The OBU was similar in many respects to the IWW in its tendency to denigrate independent labor political action and to advocate the revolutionary general strike. The Butte meeting was part of its effort to invade the Pacific Northwest and draw the unorganized, as well as the AFL unions, within its orbit. But the OBU drive did not amount to much, and nothing came of the Butte meeting except a decision by the Metal Mine Workers' Union to affiliate with it. The miners' union changed its name to the Metal Mine Workers' of America Local No. 1 of the One Big Union, a long title for an almost moribund organization. Wobbly leader A. S. Embree had told the OBU delegates that the IWW was the principal miners' organization in the Butte district, and he was right.[32]

The 1919 strike season concluded with a two-month, state-wide walkout by the metal trades unions in August. Rejecting an offer of assistance from the IWW, the Metal Trades Council fought on alone and in October was compelled to accept the operators' contract offer.[33]

During the following months, the IWW quietly prepared for another go at it. There can be no doubt that government authorities and the ACM Company knew of the union's plans. Agents of both had infiltrated the Butte local and reported its every move, and post office authorities routinely intercepted IWW mail and forwarded the contents to the BI. In March 1920, the BI received the text of a letter from post office officials written by Nick Verbanec, secretary-treasurer *pro tem* of the MMWU No. 800. In the letter, Verbanec noted the "good spirit among the workers here in Butte toward Industrial Union #800. . . . the Butte branch is gaining more power every day." On April 16, another Butte Wobbly wrote in an intercepted letter: "Butte is looking good for the IWW. I think we will make the boss sit up and take notice. This year the miners are waking up fast."[34] On the evening of April 16, the IWW held a meeting and voted to call out the miners the next morning. The usual demands were posted, and the IWW asked the AFL unions to join it in a "general strike against the organized masters of greed until such times as all our demands are granted." As in the 1919 strike, the IWW organized mass picketing on the roads leading to the mines. By day's end, almost the entire labor force was out on strike.[35]

On Monday, April 19, Governor Stewart wired General Hunter Liggett, commander of the army's Western Department, asking for troops. Liggett responded immediately and reported that soldiers from Fort Lewis, Washington, were on the way. But the governor was impatient. On April 21, he pleaded again with the army: "Conditions in Butte growing worse. I respectfully urge as much haste as possible in getting troops on the ground." Soldiers boarded a train for Butte that afternoon.[36]

Governor Stewart's impatience was justified. The IWW was ready for a fight, and the governor knew that the ACM Company was eager for a final showdown. Roy Alley had intimated as much to the governor a year before. Stewart had asked Alley his opinion about what would happen if U.S. troops were withdrawn. Alley replied that the "revolutionary movement in Butte has grown to such proportions that the Government must soon take cognizance of it." He predicted a "showdown" if the troops left, and he welcomed it:

> It might be just as well, however, that things came to a show-down here, as to allow them to drag on indefinitely. The removal of troops will be the signal for open demonstrations against the Government within a very short time, and as stated above might as well come soon as late.[37]

On Tuesday morning, April 20, as mass picketing continued, the *Butte Bulletin* ran the following editorial:

ALLEY OPENLY URGES MURDER

"The wobblies [*sic*] have got us tied up again. It wouldn't be so bad if they only quit themselves but they are interfering with our own loyal men.

"We need some more killings and hangings here, and if there were any red-blooded Americans in this camp it would be done."—Roy Alley, secretary to John D. Ryan of the A.C.M., in the Thornton Hotel barber shop about 9:30 yesterday morning.

So ROY ALLEY wants to hang someone AGAIN!

He wants MORE killings and hangings!

WE need some more killings!

WHOM does ROY ALLEY mean by WE?

WHAT does he want by MORE?[38]

Things were getting rough. On the first day of the strike, Company gunmen threatened the pickets on the Anaconda Road. When the editorial hit the streets the gunmen began to assault pickets, some of whom were severely beaten. The biennial report of the Montana Department of Labor and Industry laconically described the action:

> . . . the following day, April 21, a force of deputies were [*sic*] employed by the Anaconda Copper Mining Company to guard the property and prevent pickets from interfering with men on their way to work. All of the guards were deputies appointed by Sheriff [John] O'Rourke and all of them were paid by the mining company. Many clashes occurred between mine guards and picketers at various properties during the day. According to all reports the mine guards were unusually active, as many picketers were badly beaten, some of them quite seriously. In several places the fight was bitter, but in every instance the mine guards got the better of the encounter.[39]

At approximately four-thirty in the afternoon, Sheriff O'Rourke along with several deputies and city policemen walked into a tense situation at the Neversweat Mine. Pickets on the Anaconda Road were jeering and hooting at several dozen mine guards who occupied the railroad embankment above them and in front of the mine.

The sheriff tried to persuade the pickets to leave peacefully, but they refused. Embree allegedly told the sheriff that the men had a perfect right to be on a public road, and several strikers produced road tax receipts to show that they had helped pay for its maintenance. The sheriff gave up and reportedly exploded in exasperation: "All right. Stay here!" But the strikers wanted more. Some demanded that O'Rourke arrest those gunmen whom the strikers claimed had beaten and clubbed their comrades. O'Rourke supposedly replied: "All right. I'll investigate this. We're here to give protection to everybody." Immediately after O'Rourke spoke, the gunmen, without a word of warning, began firing into the group from the embankment above. According to the *Butte Bulletin*, Roy Alley allegedly gave the signal: "Go get 'em boys! Give the sons of bitches hell!" The pickets ran back down the road to escape the bullets. Sixteen were wounded, all of them shot in the back. Tom Manning died from his wounds a few days later. Sheriff's deputies and police officers at the scene did nothing to stop the assault.[40]

At the coroner's inquest into the cause of Manning's death, several witnesses testified that the attack was unprovoked and that the mine guards did all the shooting. Especially devastating testimony was offered by law officers who witnessed the scene. City Chief of Detectives Jim Larkin remembered that the gunmen on the embankment fired all of the shots. No shots, Larkin said, were fired by either the pickets or someone from a nearby boarding house. Police officer Sam Haltunen testified that the gunmen had run down the hill, firing as they went. One of them had mistaken Haltunen, who had been wearing a khaki uniform, for a picket and clubbed him, shouting: "You get down the hill, you s— of a b——." Another gunman, who Haltunen identified as John Berkin, had intervened, telling the gunman that he had just clubbed a policeman. The gunman had apologized and then run down the hill in pursuit of the fleeing pickets. Because it was impossible to determine precisely which gunman had fired the shots that killed Thomas Manning, the coroner's jury determined only that the victim had died from wounds caused by a .32 calibre bullet "fired from a pistol in the hands of some person to this jury unknown." The *Butte Bulletin*'s headline dripped with sarcasm: "THOM MANNING DEAD ACCORDING TO VERDICT RENDERED BY CORONER'S JURY." Even though several witnesses identified a man fitting the description of Roy Alley as present at the scene and in apparent command of the gunmen, County Attorney Nick Rodering did not indict him or any mine guard under his command.[41]

The local office of the Bureau of Investigation was entirely sympathetic with the ACM Company's desire to rid itself of the IWW and seemed to view the shooting as a reasonable response to the conflict. In his April 22 report, for example, Special Agent J. L. Webb noted his perception that eight of the men who were wounded on the Anaconda Road "were not citizens of the United States and all were members of the I.W.W."[42] Special Agent W. D. Bolling expressed his attitude succinctly in testimony given at a trial involving an unsuccessful attempt by the federal government to deport IWW leader Nick Radivoeff. This exchange was recorded between the BI agent and Radivoeff's attorney:

Bolling: I haven't any fault to find with the gunmen who shot people on Anaconda Road.
Question: That meets with your approval?

Bolling: It does.

Question: Entirely your approval?

Bolling: Yes sir.[43]

On the evening of April 22, one day after the Anaconda Road shootings, U.S. troops arrived in Butte. There was no further violence. The IWW called its pickets off the roads leading to the mines and tried unsuccessfully to enlist the other unions' support, but no other union would join the strike. Some miners began to drift back to work; others left the camp to find employment elsewhere.[44] On May 13, the IWW officially called off the strike and advised miners to continue to strike "on the job." The Metal Mine Workers' Industrial Union No. 800 exhorted:

> Avenge the death of your martyred dead—Tom Manning and Frank Little—by slowing down on the job and refusing longer to produce wealth that gluts to overflowing the coffers of the A. C. M. Co.
> Slow down on the job and save your tired bodies from the "con" ward and the undertaker!
> Slow down on the job and force the masters to give you more of the wealth you alone produce!
> Slow down on the job and force the six-hour day, and freedom for all the prisoners of the class war!
> Slow down on the job and make Montana "safe for democracy"— safe for the workers!
> Slow down on the job and destroy the "contract system," the "bonus system," and the "efficiency system!"
> Slow down![45]

These were brave words, but the IWW's power in Butte had been broken. On May 10, the ACM Company posted notices announcing that it would not knowingly hire an IWW man, a policy that had been at least implicit in the rustling card system in December 1912.[46]

The blacklist was an effective one; both the Company and the BI knew who the Wobblies were because government agents and private detectives had heavily infiltrated the union. These undercover operatives were also busy sowing the seeds of discord and distrust among the ranks of Wobbly men. BI records reveal that two Finnish miners working for the Bureau had infiltrated the IWW during the 1920 strike. These infiltrators continuously lobbied for an end to the strike, which created dissension between the Finns and the Irish, the latter apparently being more solidly in support of the strike. In reporting on the IWW meeting in which the strike was called off, BI agent Thomas F. Price happily noted: "The atmosphere of the whole meeting, from beginning to close, seemed to be one of depression, despair and misunderstanding. . . . Individuals and groups departed from the hall, each one apparently suspicious of the other."[47] In July, one of the BI's "confidential informants" reported that the IWW was "too much broken to come out again [on strike]."[48]

In October, the Wobblies discovered that their recording secretary was an operative of the Thiel Detective Agency.[49] The discovery clearly upset one BI informant, who wrote: "This thing has made a deep impression and operative will have to be careful for some time to come. Everybody suspects everybody now." Regaining confidence, the informant then boasted to the BI: "If they [the Wobblies] only knew who are the stools and how many of them there are, they would sure be a dismayed bunch. To think that so many of their supposed best men are paid agents makes me laugh every time I think of it."[50]

The informal policy of exchanging information on "radicals" with the ACM Company was well developed by 1920. In the Radivoeff deportation hearing before Judge George Bourquin, Agent Bolling readily admitted that he had routinely "gossiped" with Roy Alley, D'Gay Stivers, Con Kelley, L. O. Evans, and Dan Kelly about the men they were mutually spying on. Bolling said he had supplied these Company officials with what he characterized as "unofficial" information from the BI files. When asked if he saw himself as the representative of an "impartial government," Bolling said that he thought so.[51]

But the record clearly demonstrated the opposite. From the 1917 strike on, the federal government was far from "impartial." It had studiously ignored the miners' grievances, its soldiers had acted with ruthless determination to suppress "disorder," and its agents had infiltrated and spied on the IWW, which the government's inaction and indifference had helped to create. There was no IWW presence in Butte when the Speculator tragedy occurred. It took the murder of Frank Little and the failure of the Metal Mine Workers' Union to bring the IWW to Butte.

The Wobblies had pluck and determination and a single-minded devotion to the miners' cause, yet only a minority of miners were IWW men. This minority was drawn principally from the ranks of newer immigrants and transient single men who formed such a large proportion of the men employed underground.[52] To such groups, the Wobblies' call for "direct action" and their rejection of electoral politics made sense; they could not vote, and they could see little evidence that voting had made any difference in working conditions.

But most workers *could* vote, and despite the slim legislative results achieved by independent political action, many workers were still willing in 1917-1920 to seek change through the electoral process. The Socialist Party may have been dead, but the idea of proletarian political action was not. It had been given new inspiration from a most unlikely source—the farmers of North Dakota.

Feeling exploited and shortchanged by banks, grain companies, and railroads, North Dakota farmers had discovered a political remedy in the direct primary. In 1915, a handful of men met and formed the Nonpartisan League. Led by organizer Arthur C. Townley, a former farmer and Socialist Party member from Beach, North Dakota, the NPL advocated a form of agrarian socialism that had immense popular appeal among North Dakota's embittered and exploited farmers. The NPL called for state ownership of grain elevators, mills, and packing houses; demanded the establishment of a state bank that would advance credit at low interest rates; and advocated a system of state hail insurance, exemption of farm improvements from taxation, and state administration of grain grading. To bring this modest prairie socialist plan into being, the Nonpartisan League fielded a slate of candidates in the 1916 Republican primary. The League's slate, headed by Lynn Frazier for governor, swept the North Dakota primary. It had captured the state's dominant party, and its candidates were elected that November. For the next three years, the Nonpartisan League would battle with some success in implementing its program, while the League's electoral triumph would capture the imagination of radicals in other states.[53]

In Butte, the insurgents who remained committed to political action viewed the developments in North Dakota with growing interest and enthusiasm. Former Socialists and other radicals who supported the independent Metal Mine Workers' Union and the *Butte Bulletin* made contact with the League in the spring of 1918. The League had already penetrated the farming counties of northeastern Montana and was about to establish its state headquarters in Great Falls. By the summer of 1918, the Nonpartisan idea had found an organizational vehicle in Butte, the Nonpartisan Club of Silver Bow County. Operating out of the headquarters of the Metal Mine Workers' Union on South Idaho Street, the Nonpartisan Club drew up a platform demanding, among other things, "one hundred percent taxation on all war profits," a shortened workday to provide employment for all who wanted to work, the election of state mine inspectors, and an improved workmen's compensation law. During the summer, the Club announced a partial slate of candidates pledged to its platform. All would enter the Montana Democratic primary in 1918.[54]

The entrenched and privileged interests in this camp are
badly scared.

—Butte Bulletin, August 27, 1918

12 | *The Nonpartisan Challenge*

The ranks of the local economic and political elite were horrified at the formation of
the Nonpartisan Club and its decision to enter candidates in the Democratic primary.
To them, the Socialist Party had been resurrected in a different form. The *Anaconda
Standard* warned:

> There are Bolshevik candidates in the primaries . . . who have expressed their
> antagonism to America and everything American at every opportunity.
> . . . If America is not a good enough country to believe in, it is not a good
> enough country to hold office in. . . . Let them run for office in Germany or
> in Russia.

It was, therefore, "the patriotic duty" of every citizen to vote against the "socialist and
I.W.W. candidates."[1] It was true that former Socialist Party members were on the
Nonpartisan Club slate, but the press aimed its biggest guns at that "I.W.W. sympa-
thizer," "red Socialist," and "arch troublemaker" Bill Dunne.[2]

William Francis Dunne was thirty years old in 1918. Born in Kansas City on
October 15, 1887, he was the oldest in a family of eight children. In 1894, the Dunne
family moved to a Minnesota farm, and Bill Dunne later attended college in that state
for a time. After dropping out of college, Dunne was an electrician's apprentice until
1907, when he emigrated to Montana. He worked for several employers in the state,
including the Northern Pacific Railroad and the Montana Power Company. In
1912, he moved to Vancouver, British Columbia, where he was elected the district
organizer for the International Brotherhood of Electrical Workers. Dunne returned to
Montana in 1915 and worked again for the Montana Power Company and the
Milwaukee Railroad. In January 1916, he landed in Butte and found a job with the
ACM Company. After the 1917 miners' strike, in which he played a large part, Dunne
became the major editorial writer for the *Butte Bulletin* and an active player in the
Nonpartisan Club's political drive.

Not since F. A. Heinze had one man so captured Butte's attention and in so doing marked an era. Physically, Dunne stood apart from those around him. A heavily muscled man with short, close-cropped hair cut in the Prussian style, he was an imposing—some thought menacing—person. Many saw him as the personification of a revolutionary agitator. To his admirers, Dunne was a tough, proletarian version of Louis Duncan. To the ACM Company, he was one of "the cleverest agitators in Butte." In 1918, he demonstrated his "extraordinary impudence" by filing as a Democratic candidate for the Montana House of Representatives. Even more than the quasi-socialist Nonpartisan Club, Dunne became a major issue in the August primary.[3]

Forty-seven Democrats competed for twelve legislative positions on the ballot, and Dunne finished sixth with 3,260 votes. The only other Nonpartisan candidate to win nomination was Jerry J. Harrington, who finished fourth with 3,425 votes. The other seven Nonpartisan candidates for the legislature finished thirteenth, fourteenth, fifteenth, sixteenth, eighteenth, twenty-first, and twenty-second with an average vote of 2,537. The totals were so close that a shift in the sentiments of only a hundred or so voters would have resulted in the nomination of four more Nonpartisan Club candidates.

Of particular interest was Jeannette Rankin's race as a Republican candidate for the U.S. Senate. Her principal opponent for the nomination was Dr. Oscar Lanstrum, a Helena physician. Because she had championed the miners' cause in the 1917 strike, Rankin enjoyed the full support of the *Butte Bulletin* and the endorsement of the Montana Nonpartisan League. In Silver Bow County, she easily beat Lanstrum by 1,818 to 1,307 votes, but she narrowly lost the state-wide contest, with 17,091 votes to Lanstrum's 18,805.[4] Rankin subsequently filed as a candidate in the general election under the Nationalist Party label, creating a three-way race between herself, Lanstrum, and incumbent Democratic Senator Tom Walsh.

Across the state, the Nonpartisan League had done rather well in its first outing. Fourteen League-endorsed state senate candidates had been nominated, ten Democrats and four Republicans. Twenty-eight League candidates—seventeen Democrats and eleven Republicans—won nomination for the state House of Representatives. Also nominated were Charles H. Cooper, League candidate for associate justice of the Montana Supreme Court, on the Republican ticket, and Democrat J. H. Hall for railroad commissioner.[5]

While the Nonpartisans were making their drive in the primary races, their enemies were trying to silence the *Butte Bulletin*. The *Bulletin* had long planned its transformation from a weekly to a daily newspaper, which had prompted Eugene Carroll, the president of the Silver Bow County Council of Defense, to write the Montana Council of Defense urging "that steps should be taken as soon as possible to prevent such publication." Carroll suggested that an August 5 decision of the U.S. War Industries Board had established a legal basis for the MCD to issue the order. To conserve the supply of newsprint, the Board had announced that the establishment of any new daily newspapers should be prohibited. On August 12, in direct response to Carroll's suggestion, the Montana Council of Defense issued the ban on new dailies, an order directly aimed at the *Butte Bulletin*.[6]

In an angry editorial, the August 16, 1918, *Bulletin* called the Montana Council a "slimy political gang, whose actions are a stench in the nostrils of decent people. . . .

Fortunately," the editorial concluded, "they have no legal status or authority. They can fulminate to their heart's content against anything and everything that menaces their master's interest, but—no one need pay any attention to them." On August 20, the first daily issue of the *Butte Bulletin* was published.

In early September, the Council hauled Dunne, managing editor Smith, and business manager Leo Daly before it to explain themselves. Speaking for the paper, Dunne told the Council that under guarantees provided in the Bill of Rights the *Butte Bulletin* should be able to freely criticize the Montana Council of Defense. He dared the Council to prosecute him. The Council obliged. All three men were indicted for violating the Montana Sedition Act, and both Dunne and Smith were found guilty in Helena district court a few months later. They appealed their convictions to the Montana Supreme Court, which reversed the convictions in May 1920.[7]

In Butte, the general election season of 1918 was drawing to a close, and the *Butte Miner* and allied papers editorialized in the usual fashion. When the county central committee "excommunicated" Bill Dunne from the Democratic Party, Dunne responded by expressing "his deepest gratitude" for the honor bestowed on him.[8]

In the 1918 campaign, the character of the League candidates, particularly Bill Dunne and Jeannette Rankin, became the issue. Dunne ran under the slogan "For Real Democracy, Not the Corporate Kind" and said little of substance. Rankin did not actively campaign in the mining city, but the *Butte Bulletin* worked in her behalf by running full-page ads identifying her as a candidate of the "toilers" and by providing editorial support:

> With steadfast courage that puts most of her male colleagues to shame, Miss Rankin has constantly spoken for the lowly and the oppressed; with no possibility of reward other than knowing that she has followed the right course, she has used her time and energy in trying to obtain some small measure of justice for the workers, and from them and them alone . . . must her support come.[9]

On November 5, the people of Butte and Silver Bow County went to the polls. When the votes were counted, it was clear that Rankin had run a very strong race against incumbent Tom Walsh. Although he had won re-election in the state-wide totals, the senator just squeaked by in Silver Bow County with 5,877 votes compared to Rankin's 5,798, while Lanstrum trailed with 4,587 votes. Rankin had badly beaten Walsh in The Flats, come in a poor third in the Middle-Class Enclave, and almost passed him in Northeast Butte, losing by only twenty-two votes. The old class lines had once more been drawn.[10]

Bill Dunne, the workers' other champion, won his election to the Montana House of Representatives. He had received 6,935 votes, finishing fifth in total votes received for the county's twelve legislative seats. Joining him and fifteen other newly elected Nonpartisan legislators were two Democratic candidates, Charles Boulware and Jerry Harrington, who had also been endorsed by the Nonpartisan Club. Charles H. Cooper, who also had Nonpartisan support, won his seat on the Supreme Court.[11]

On January 6, 1919, the Sixteenth Montana Legislative Assembly convened for its sixty-day biennial session. The *Butte Bulletin* expected nothing positive to come of it:

The legislators, the majority of them servants of the Anaconda Copper Company . . . are now getting busy and caucusing every night that the Sixteenth Assembly may leave no stone unturned to make Montana even safer than in the past for the A.C.M.[12]

Representative Dunne apparently shared the *Bulletin's* sentiment, for he frequently absented himself from the daily legislative sessions. When he did attend, however, he made his presence felt. On one occasion, he took the floor to denounce the ACM Company as a "gigantic bloodsucking corporation which has its fingers on the throats of practically every man, woman and child in the state of Montana. . . ." On another, Dunne asked his colleagues: "What sane man would crook a finger to save and perpetuate a system of society that can only save millions from starvation by slaughtering millions in battle?"[13]

Dunne saw the legislature as an arena in which he could speak for the workers and for world revolution. But he also engaged in more traditional lawmaking efforts. He introduced House Bill 195, which would have provided for a new workmen's compensation system. H.B. 195 called for substantially increasing the level of payments to injured workers and to surviving dependents, extending compensation to

"Under Which Flag Will You Serve?"
Butte Miner, April 2, 1919

dependents not currently living in the United States (many of the younger immigrant miners had left wives and children in their native countries), and extending coverage to include injury and death by occupational diseases, such as miners' consumption. The legislature's Joint Committee on Compensation killed H.B. 195 and substituted a weaker bill that provided for only a slight increase in the compensation rate. The new bill passed the House, 69 to 7, with Dunne and six other Nonpartisan legislators voting against it.[14]

As the Assembly plodded toward adjournment, Dunne was preoccupied by his sedition trial. On February 24, 1919, both he and Smith were found guilty, and Dunne's enemies made a move to have him expelled from the legislature; but the House voted to allow Dunne to remain until the Montana Supreme Court resolved the case on appeal.[15] By that time, however, Dunne had grown weary of serving in a legislature where nothing that he considered substantive could be accomplished. By the end of February, he had decided to seek another elective office; he would run for mayor of Butte.

On March 2, Bill Dunne formally entered the mayoral race on the Democratic ticket. A few days later, the Nonpartisan Club met and endorsed Dunne's candidacy and also gave the nod to James J. McCarthy for city treasurer and old-time Socialist Mike Allen for police judge. The Nonpartisans also selected a full slate of aldermanic candidates.[16]

Dunne promised that he would deliver "a clean, honest, efficient and just administration." Acknowledging his reputation for being "somewhat radical," Dunne took great pride that his candidacy was "opposed by every interest that has been identified with the corrupt administration [of city affairs]."[17] His candidacy also inspired some rather bad poetry, as evident in "Dunn and Democracy":

> What Duncan did
> Why Dunn can do;
> He's honest and he's able, too—
> Butte need's a man,
> Virile and true.
> We've got the man;
> It's up to you. . . .[18]

But Dunne was not the reincarnation of Louis Duncan, and the Nonpartisan Club was not the Socialist Party parading about with a new name. It was true, as the established press was happy to point out, that former Socialists were in the ranks of this latest insurgency, but there the parallels ended. The Socialist Party had been a stable membership organization that had nominated candidates from within its ranks. The party had stressed its platform and not the individual qualities of its candidates. In contrast, Dunne was very much his own man, and the Nonpartisan Club was nothing more than a loosely organized electoral vehicle in which platform and principles played but a secondary role. In the 1919 campaign, the Nonpartisan Club did not even bother to draft a platform; consequently, each candidate was free to fashion his own. For his part, Dunne announced his commitment to setting up a public produce market to combat the high cost of living, to constructing public toilet facilities, and to improving city sanitation.[19] But the real issue in the campaign was Bill Dunne himself. And he wanted it that way. Dunne delighted in playing the part of the revolutionary ogre.

Dunne's opponent in the primary was Captain William Cutts, a regular Democrat who had earned his military rank doing guard duty in the spruce forests of the Northwest during the war. The *Anaconda Standard* and the *Butte Miner* gave their enthusiastic editorial support to "Billy" Cutts, while firing vituperative volleys at the insurgent ticket.[20]

Turnout was heavy on March 24, with 10,183 (76 per cent) of the registered electorate casting ballots. On the morning of March 25, the *Butte Bulletin* triumphantly announced that unofficial tallies had given Dunne the nomination over Cutts by 113 votes. The *Bulletin* also reported an assault on Dunne pollwatchers by police and gunmen at two precincts and at the city hall. The paper advised its readers to be at city hall to prevent a "steal" when the official election canvass was made.[21]

It was a tempestuous scene in the city hall as members of the canvassing board read the totals from the precinct tally sheets. The announced totals showed Cutts the winner by 102 votes. The difference between the precinct judges' announced returns and the official canvass was significant:

	Judges' Returns	*Official Canvass*
Cutts	4,509	4,621
Dunne	4,622	4,519

The *Anaconda Standard* was exultant: "AMERICANISM TRIUMPHS IN BUTTE OVER DUNNE, DISASTER, DISGRACE, SEDITION AND SOVIET," the headline read. "BALLOT RAVAGED BY CROOKS," countered the *Butte Bulletin*.[22] The appearance of fraud was manifest. In four precincts there were differences in the totals on the tally sheets turned in by the precinct judges and the announced results in the official returns, the differences in every case adding to Cutts's column. Only one of the sixteen ballot boxes stored in city hall was locked and sealed, and when the ballot box from one precinct was opened it was empty. Judges in two precincts claimed that the tally sheet totals they had turned in had been altered; one of them pointed out where several sheets had been changed, presumably after they were delivered to city hall. Consequently, Dunne's narrow "victory" was turned into a win for Cutts.[23]

Even with the irregularities and discrepancies in the count, the official canvass revealed the intense class polarization that Dunne's candidacy had sparked. Dunne had beaten Cutts in four of the eight wards, and his support came essentially from those neighborhoods that had earlier supported the Socialist Party. Dunne carried Northeast Butte and The Flats, but he was trounced in the middle-class neighborhoods west of Main Street. The final results were:

	Northeast Butte	*The Flats*	*Middle-Class Enclave*
Dunne	1,699 (57%)	1,242 (57%)	1,578
Cutts	1,289	945	2,386 (60%)

The *Butte Miner* opined that Dunne's near-victory had "disgraced" the city, and the paper accused the 4,519 who had voted for him with "disloyalty."[24] Nor was the *Miner*'s embarrassment finished. While Dunne and McCarthy appeared to have been defeated, Nonpartisan candidate Mike Allen won the Democratic nomination for police judge, and six out of the eight Nonpartisan aldermanic candidates had also won nomination: John Sullivan, Barry O'Leary, Bernard McVeigh, Con Lynch, Walter Kyle, and E. G. Johnson.[25]

Not surprisingly, Dunne and McCarthy announced that they would challenge the Democratic primary results in court and threatened to file as independent candidates should the court rule against them. On April 1, the challenge was heard in the chambers of District Court Judge Edwin Lamb. The testimony revealed the substantial irregularities and violations of the law in the conduct of the election, which suggested that either gross incompetence or strenuous fraud had been committed. Attorneys Louis Donovan and B. K. Wheeler, representing the plaintiffs, pressed Lamb to make a decision in the case before the deadline for filing by independent candidates was passed. But Lamb delayed. On April 3, the last filing day, the two attorneys asked that their suit be dismissed. Lamb denied the motion. Desperately,

"Democracy in Butte"
Butte Bulletin, April 3, 1919

Dunne and McCarthy rushed to the city clerk's office with their filing petitions. The city clerk refused to accept them, saying that neither could file as an independent as long as their status as Democratic candidates was in doubt. The following morning, Judge Lamb announced his decision. In essence, he ruled that there was strong evidence that electoral fraud had been committed in the Democratic primary but that the district court had no legal authority to supply a remedy. Donovan and Wheeler would have to appeal to the Montana Supreme Court for relief.

Upon hearing Lamb's decision, Dunne and McCarthy returned to the city clerk's office and demanded that they be allowed to file as independents. The city clerk refused, reminding them that the deadline for filing had passed. Donovan and Wheeler then petitioned the Montana Supreme Court and asked it to issue a *writ of mandamus* ordering the city clerk to put the two candidates on the ballot. The state Supreme Court denied the petition. In an unsigned opinion, the court claimed that "it could not intelligently examine and determine the important questions" that were presented in the appeal with the general election only two days away. With that, Dunne's and McCarthy's attempt to get on the ballot ended.[26]

Dunne urged all "honest voters" to boycott the municipal election. Even though it meant certain defeat by their Republican opponents, the Nonpartisan candidates urged the same action. Wheeler was angry: "You cannot expect justice in the district court or in the supreme court. You might as well throw your law books away and use them for fuel as they are no longer of any use in Montana."[27]

Only 7,159 people finally voted, 3,024 fewer than in the primary election. The result was a Republican landslide. Republican William Stodden trounced Cutts by a margin of almost two to one. The other Republicans did just as well. The unfortunate Cutts received just 2,656 votes, 50 per cent of what he had presumably received in the primary. The *Butte Bulletin* bitterly suggested that he had received "the vote that he is really entitled to, and the vote that he actually received in the primary, for there are at least 2,656 gunmen, stool-pigeons, labor-fakirs, lickspittles and pimps in Butte. . . ." Two days later, the *Bulletin* predicted:

> The lines are sharply drawn, the issues are clearly defined, the movement knows its strength and from now on will devote all its energies to what will be the final battle on the political field, the general election a year from next November.[28]

Tanned farmers from the dry-land country met the
workers from the coal mines and smelters. They talked
about their work and found out that they both worked
hard for less than a living. They talked about wages and
prices and the press that slanders them impartially. They
talked about the war and the profiteers and found they
agreed on most questions. They agreed that government
had passed from the hands of such as they and thought
that it was time to re-establish majority rule.

—*Butte Bulletin*, March 5, 1920

13 | *The Final Battle*

To wage what the *Butte Bulletin* called the "final battle," the growing political insurgency of farmers and workers first had to defeat a determined effort to reduce, if not to eliminate, the Nonpartisan League's potential power in the state's direct primary. The vehicle to defeat the insurgents was Senate Bill 124, enacted by the Montana legislature in its January-March 1919 session. S.B. 124 proposed the abolition of the direct primary as the mechanism for nominating candidates for state and congressional office, replacing it with nomination by state party conventions. Local and state legislative candidates would still be nominated by direct primary, but with a difference. Montanans would no longer have "open" primaries, where voters did not have to publicly declare party affiliation. Under S.B. 124, there would be "closed" primaries, where the public declaration of party affiliation was required. Voters were to vote on S.B. 124 in a special referendum election scheduled for September 2, 1919, the timing probably selected to coincide with harvest time, when public attention toward politics is traditionally low.[1]

The obvious motive behind the legislature's action was to make it more difficult for the farmer-labor coalition to capture the two dominant parties through the primary nomination process. Immediately sensing the danger in the new system, the Nonpartisan League organized a petition drive to suspend the September referendum, which would have delayed a public vote on S.B. 124 until the November 1920 general election.[2] By June, the Nonpartisan League and its allies had gathered enough signatures (equivalent to 15 per cent of the vote cast in the previous gubernatorial election) to compel the secretary of state to cancel the special election.[3]

Undeterred, the League's enemies seized an opportunity to strike a blow against the insurgents when Governor Stewart called the legislature into special session for the last week of July 1919. Stewart ostensibly called the session to provide relief for Montana's farmers who were battling the economic and social effects of a three-year drought. But the legislators provided little relief. Instead, they resurrected part of S.B.

124 as S.B. 32 and defined it as an "emergency statute" that could not be suspended by referendum petition. S.B. 32 "closed" the open primary once more and—in obvious reaction to Dunne's candidacy for mayor—also prohibited a candidate who had been defeated in a primary from filing as an independent. The bill sailed through the upper chamber without a recorded vote and was approved by the House, 67 to 17, with ten of the negative votes coming from the Nonpartisan minority. Stewart signed the bill into law on August 11, 1919. Disgusted, Miles Romney, the crusading liberal editor of the Hamilton *Western News*, asked: "The flunkies of the Anaconda, drunk with power, have challenged the people. What are we going to do about it?"[4]

The Nonpartisan League responded with a second petition drive. To ensure that this effort would not be wasted, the farmer-labor coalition asked the Montana Supreme Court to declare the petitions valid, claiming that no "emergency" had existed when S.B. 32 was enacted. On January 30, 1920, the Supreme Court ruled by a three-to-two vote that the legislature had exceeded its authority. The justices reasoned that just because the legislature declared the statute an emergency did not make it one. The court's decision preserved the open primary for the 1920 campaign. It also saved the state's presidential preference primary. First used in 1916, the presidential primary was held in April to allow voters to indicate their preferences for a presidential candidate and to elect national convention delegates and party electors. No doubt fearing that the Nonpartisan League might try to influence the 1920 national conventions, the extraordinary session of the legislature had enacted another "emergency" statute, this one abolishing the presidential primary. A petition drive resulted in the suspension of that statute as well.[5]

These brazen and cynical attempts to change the electoral rules of the game had unintended and unhappy consequences for the opponents of the Nonpartisan League. The strenuous fight to save the primary had mobilized Montana's organized farmers and workers and had given them a new and vigorous commitment—one fueled by anger and hope. One symptom of this new awakening was the reformation of the Montana Federation of Labor. Under the direction of President Mortimer M. Donoghue, the MFL had become conservative, apolitical, and ineffective. By the fall of 1919, a new "progressive" faction had emerged to challenge Donoghue. Its candidate was Steve Ely, a United Mine Workers coal miner from Sand Coulee. When Ely won the endorsement of the central labor bodies in Great Falls, Helena, and Butte, Donoghue sensed that his defeat was certain and announced his retirement. Ely became the new president of the Montana Federation of Labor by acclamation.[6] A few weeks later, he announced where he thought the Federation should be headed:

> My conception of the functions of the federation is that its power and influence should be exercised on the political field for the promotion of the interests of the workers. The policy hitherto practiced by my predecessors in office by lobbying at the state capital, begging the legislature, as a dog beseeching his master for crumbs, for legislation beneficial to the workers of the state, has brought nothing but humiliation to them.

The farmers and workers were "the majority," Ely continued, and he predicted that once they were organized they would "soon be in control of the state administration and the legislature. . . ."[7] For organized labor, the vehicle for independent political action was the Montana Labor League.

Originally called the Citizen Labor Club, the Montana Labor League was founded by the Great Falls trade unions in May 1919. Its brief manifesto declared the League's desire to "educate the people along political and economic lines" and pledged that it would work "to secure for the producer the largest share of the wealth he creates." The Labor League's immediate demands were an improved workmen's compensation law along the lines suggested in Dunne's bill, the prohibition of corporate blacklisting of union members, the improvement of working conditions, and the provision of paid maternity leave for working mothers.[8] These demands echoed the reforms enunciated earlier by the Populist, Labor, and Socialist parties. Finally, the Labor League, like the Socialist Party, said it favored "public ownership and democratic control of industry." In February 1920, the Montana Federation of Labor's annual convention in Great Falls endorsed the Montana Labor League and adopted the *Butte Bulletin* as its official voice.[9]

The MFL's convention coincided with the Fifth Annual Co-operators Congress, organized by the Montana chapter of the American Society of Equity. The two organizations—one representing farmers, the other made up of workers—held several joint sessions. They heard Burton K. Wheeler denounce government repression of political dissent and Attorney General Sam Ford detail how the ACM Company had not paid its fair share of taxes. These joint meetings signaled a new degree of unity between the "producing classes." One concrete result of the new cooperation was the decision to work to place Dunne's compensation bill on the November ballot as an initiative.[10]

"The Trouble with Montana"
Butte Bulletin, October 3, 1920

Following the Great Falls gathering, the Silver Bow Trades and Labor Council organized a local chapter of the Montana Labor League. Membership in the organization would be open to all those "engaged in useful occupations." The steering committee was made up of *Bulletin* editor R. B. Smith, John Driscoll, Charles Gildea, and Con Lowney, the last three former members of Local Butte of the Socialist Party.[11]

In June, the Butte chapter of the Labor League endorsed Wheeler for governor. Its members instructed Dunne to take the endorsement to Great Falls, where a joint convention of the Nonpartisan League and the Montana Labor League was about to begin. At that meeting, delegates nominated Wheeler as the Nonpartisan candidate for governor. Nominated for lieutenant governor was Roland C. Arnold, a Nonpartisan League state representative from Valley County. After Wheeler announced that he would accept the nomination if he could run as a Democrat, the convention resolved to run all its state and congressional candidates in the Democratic primary.[12] The complete ticket was as follows:

Governor	Burton K. Wheeler	Silver Bow County
Lieutenant Governor	Roland C. Arnold	Valley
Secretary of State	R. A. Haste	Yellowstone
Attorney General	Louis Irvin	Glacier
Treasurer	Ella Lord	Cascade
Auditor	Ole Sanvik	Hill
R.R. Commissioner	J. P. Meadors	Richland
Superintendent of Public Instruction	Margaret Hannah	Sweet Grass
Associate Justices of the Supreme Court	Howard Pease	Beaverhead
	W. W. Palmer	Custer
	John A. Matthews	Broadwater
Western District Congress	Burton Watson	Missoula
Eastern District Congress	M. M. McCusker	Roosevelt

Not surprisingly, the ACM Company was the central issue in the campaign, with Wheeler promising: "If elected, I will not put the Anaconda Copper Mining Company out of business, but I will put it out of politics." The coalition's campaign slogan was: "WE ARE OPPOSED TO PRIVATE OWNERSHIP OF PUBLIC OFFICIALS."[13]

The *Butte Bulletin* warned that it was time for people to choose sides in the struggle between "the producers" and "the great financial combinations." In this fight, the paper continued, those who remained outside the farmer-labor insurgency were implicitly supporters of the status quo:

> In the present situation the term "independent" is synonymous with "corporation tool." The issue is so clear, the lines so closely drawn that there is no middle ground. An individual is either on one side or the other and no amount of wishy-washy sentiment can disguise the fact. Those who are not with the organized farmers and workers are against them. . . .[14]

Wheeler told his wife that it would be a "mean, dirty campaign." He was right. One week after the Great Falls convention, Wheeler went to Dillon to deliver a speech. When he arrived, he discovered that the city council had passed an ordinance denying him the use of city hall. When Wheeler attempted to speak on a street corner the chief of police threatened to arrest him. The rally was moved to a nearby farm where a "mob of rowdies," reportedly organized by the American Legion, broke up the meeting and threatened to lynch Wheeler. In the confusion, Wheeler escaped and was driven to the railroad station at nearby Bond. Some of the mob followed him to the station, which was a converted boxcar. When some of the mob tried to enter the locked station, Wheeler's guard—a local ranch hand—announced that he would shoot to kill. The mob's enthusiasm suddenly cooled and it dispersed. Wheeler stayed overnight in the station and was driven back to Butte the next day. Because of this incident, the anti-Wheeler press nicknamed the candidate "Boxcar Burt." He was labeled "Bolshevik Burt" in the same spirit.[15]

Never before had a radical insurgency posed such a threat to the established economic and political order in Montana. In response, the "regular" Democrats patched together a united opposition slate headed by W. W. McDowell, a former lieutenant governor. The establishment Democrats characterized the election as a "straight fight between the reds and the Americans."[16]

A few weeks after the attempted assault on Wheeler, the ACM Company moved against the workmen's compensation initiative. By the end of June, the Nonpartisan forces had gathered enough signatures to place the proposal on the November ballot. D'Gay Stivers, the Company's legal representative and troubleshooter, soon appeared at the office of Secretary of State Charles Stewart with petitions signed by thirty-five hundred "farmers and businessmen" asking that their names be withdrawn as supporters of the initiative. Stewart removed the names, and the initiative failed to qualify for the ballot. Federation President Ely appealed to the Montana Supreme Court to order Stewart to count the signatures that had been withdrawn. But on July 26, the court rejected Ely's appeal without comment and adjourned until September.[17]

Just as in 1914, the ACM Company's agents had waged a campaign of misinformation in selected rural counties to defeat a broad-based workmen's compensation statute. The lie was the same. Farmers were told that the proposed law would cover farm laborers and ranch hands, but only at great cost to the farmers. The initiative did no such thing, but many were persuaded by the Company's arguments. Thwarted in the legal process, the farmer-labor coalition devoted its attention to winning uncontested political control of the state of Montana.

During the last week in July 1920, the Butte local of the Montana Labor League fielded its county and legislative ticket. Larry Duggan, who had been a Labor Party state representative in 1903 and was now an acknowledged leader of the insurgent forces, was running for sheriff at the head of the county ticket. For county attorney, the Labor League endorsed George M. Bourquin, Jr., the son of the controversial federal judge. Bill Dunne once more was given the nod as candidate for the Montana House of Representatives. Former Socialists on the ticket were A. N. Alderman, Arthur E. Cox, John H. Driscoll, and Sam Spiegal, all running for the legislature, and Mike Allen for clerk and recorder.

The League's candidates for county government pledged to end corruption, prevent killings like the one on the Anaconda Road, stop electoral fraud, and drive the ACM Company out of local politics. The legislative slate was committed to a better workmen's compensation law, taxes based on ability to pay, bonuses for veterans to compensate for wages lost while in service, and the consolidation of the city and county governments.[18]

The obvious connections between this new insurgent movement and the Socialist Party should not obscure the fact that the Labor League was a much more heterogeneous formation, both socially and ideologically. The League's ticket was headed by Burton K. Wheeler, the progressive-minded former U.S. district attorney and close friend of incumbent Senator Thomas J. Walsh. Locally, the presence of Dunne, *Butte Bulletin* editor R. B. Smith, and former Socialists on the ticket was neatly balanced by the candidacies of Duggan, Bourquin, incumbent District Judge Jeremiah J. Lynch, Democratic alderman Louis Freudenstein, and Elizabeth Kennedy, the wife of a mine superintendent. Nor did the Labor League's platform simply parrot the old Socialist manifestos. Like the Nonpartisan League, which it consciously emulated, the Montana Labor League had borrowed some of its immediate demands from the Socialist Party and had added some of its own. Like the Socialist Party, the Labor League was a vehicle for the working class; unlike the party, the League had no articulated vision of the future beyond the realization of those reforms. Finally, the Labor League was a much broader coalition than the Socialist Party had ever been because it had the full and open endorsement of the Montana Federation of Labor and was openly in alliance with the organized farmers.

Because of the League's potentially broad electoral base, the enemies of the emerging radical coalition reacted with a fury of hate perhaps unparalleled in Montana history. The Democratic dailies described the make-up of the insurgent ticket as "indolent," "unscrupulous," "vicious scoundrels," "sedition-mongers," "professional agitators," "criminals," "breeders of anarchy and riot," "advocates of physical force," "hostile aliens," "ex-convicts and thugs," "Soviet laborites," and the "outcasts and pariahs of society" who "brought little more than a change of toothpicks with them."[19]

Local agents of the Bureau of Investigation agreed, and they kept a close watch on the Montana Labor League by infiltrating its meetings and rallies and by tapping the telephones of its prominent leaders. The insurgents knew there were spies among them, and they did some spying of their own. Bureau agents feared that their telephone lines and mail (as well as that of the ACM Company) were being subjected to radical surveillance carried out by telephone and postal workers who were sympathizers of the Labor League and the IWW.[20]

The primary campaign closed on the evening of August 23 with about five thousand people attending a Wheeler rally at the Butte Hotel. Gunmen hired by the mining companies were in the crowd. A BI informant dutifully recorded their remarks: "This would be a good time to get Dunne." "Let's shoot the son of a ———." The gunmen muttered but did nothing, for they had been spotted by Labor League members who were armed and were ready to act. The next morning, the *Anaconda Standard* hoped there were "enough decent men and women" in the community to defeat the "Soviet" party.[21]

Voter turnout was heavy. To ensure an honest election, U.S. deputy marshals observed the proceedings. When the votes were counted, the Labor League had almost swept the primary in Silver Bow County. Eight League candidates were nominated to run for the state legislature, including Dunne, who led the field with 4,096 votes. Larry Duggan beat incumbent Sheriff O'Rourke. Incumbent District Judge Edwin Lamb and incumbent County Attorney Nick Rodering were also defeated. George Bourquin, Jr., received the county attorney nomination. The other League members nominated were Judge Lynch and Louis Donovan for the district court. The League candidates for county commission, auditor, public administrator, superintendent of schools, and surveyor were also nominated. In the state and congressional races, the farmer-labor ticket captured every spot on the Democratic ticket. Wheeler buried McDowell by 35,228 to 17,798 (5,474 to 3,418 in Silver Bow County). The other Nonpartisan candidates also won easily.[22]

The insurgent push trickled down to county and legislative races across the state. In twenty-eight counties, League candidates won every nomination. In six other counties, including Silver Bow, the insurgents won the majority of the nominations. The election produced twenty-two farmer-labor candidates for the state senate and seventy-one for the state house of representatives. The National Nonpartisan League characterized the result as "one of the most sweeping victories in the history of the farmers' movement"; the *Butte Bulletin* called it a "repudiation of the sinister policies of the copper interests and their prostitute press."[23] The shock of the radical surge must have been palpable, for the establishment dailies fell into temporary and uncomfortable silence.

The discomfort was acute. It was bad enough for the ACM Company and its allies that Wheeler was the Democratic candidate for governor. Worse was the absence of a safe harbor in the Republican ranks. The Republicans had nominated Joseph M. Dixon as their gubernatorial candidate, and Dixon was no friend of the Company. A former congressman and U.S. senator, Dixon was a progressive who had managed Theodore Roosevelt's abortive Bull Moose ticket in 1912 and stood as the Progressive Party candidate for U.S. Senate in that same year. In 1912, Dixon's campaign slogan had been: "Put the Amalgamated out of Montana Politics." Dixon supported the open primary and had made much of the Company's ability to escape paying its fair share of taxes.[24]

Mine taxation might have been the issue in the 1920 campaign, but Dixon also saw a splendid opportunity to capture the support of the voters who were frightened and uneasy about the Democratic-Nonpartisan ticket. Consequently, he waged an unabashed anti-radical campaign, posing as a defender of the state from the evils of "half-baked state socialism." Anti-Wheeler Democrats openly supported Dixon and the Republican ticket through the Montana Democratic Club, which had been organized by Senator Henry Myers. Dixon fully appreciated the irony in the implicit support he was receiving:

> The business crowd everywhere are both scared and at work to save the state from the socialistic menace and I am doing my level best to keep them in that frame of mind. It is funny to see the strenuous support in many quarters that 3 months ago would have loved to have put flowers on my grave.[25]

The farmer-labor coalition counterattacked by charging that Dixon's new-found crusade was phony and self-serving. They offered plausible evidence showing that Dixon had courted the Nonpartisan League when he had first decided to run for governor. Dixon vigorously denied the charge. The *Butte Bulletin* devoted considerable attention to Dixon, characterizing his platform as an appeal to "ignorant prejudice" and labeling Dixon as nothing but a "pampered pet of all the big and little profiteers."[26]

In the polarized political atmosphere, Dixon's moderate credentials were ignored. It was "Dixon or the Deluge." Following the lead of their gubernatorial candidate, the Butte Republicans ran large ads. One warned: "DON'T LET THE RED HAND STRANGLE BUTTE. VOTE THE REPUBLICAN TICKET."[27] Dunne was the central scapegoat of these diatribes, and Wheeler was portrayed as the servile puppet of the "ruffian" Dunne. Wheeler, the *Standard* allowed, might not be as bad as Dunne, but if he was elected he would be forced to carry out the Nonpartisan program of "destruction." Wheeler retorted:

> I have a secret I don't want you to tell the Republicans. I saw Dunn the other day and Dunn gave me a deed to the half of me he owns, and if I see [A. C.] Townley [national leader of the NPL] I will get a deed from him for the half he owns and then I will own myself. If the Republican Party will get a release for Dixon for the first mortgage the Anaconda Company holds on him and a release on the second mortgage that the Montana Development Association holds on him, then it doesn't make any difference whether Dixon or I am elected.[28]

But there was precious little humor in the election. There was no middle ground between the Nonpartisan ticket and the swelling aggregation of opponents arrayed against it, which included the Republican Party, anti-Wheeler Democrats, most of the newspapers in the state, and the big business community. To the opposition, the Nonpartisan ticket represented a revolution that was about to devour them, and some began to contemplate violence if the Nonpartisans won.

On September 16, a "confidential informant" of the Bureau of Investigation reported that "the opposition" was preparing to use "any means possible to carry the polls [in November], fair means or foul, mostly foul." The covert preparations for a possible counterrevolution were apparently being organized by the "Citizens Committee of 800." A BI report on October 1 described the committee's intent:

> The organizers of the Citizens Committee of 800 are proceeding very carefully in selecting their men. . . . This committee will be prepared to meet any emergency that might arise should the radical candidates be elected. . . .
>
> Agent would not be in the least surprised to learn some morning that Dunn had been roughly handled and the *Butte Bulletin* plant destroyed.[29]

Even though the Bureau of Investigation characterized the committee as having a "vigilante conception," it felt no obligation to prevent such lawlessness.

Meanwhile, Wheeler hammered away at the Company and its domination of state politics, although little of what he said was reported in the hostile press. In the railroad town of Laurel, he boasted: "We stole the Democratic Party from the

Anaconda Copper Mining Company and we will give it back to the people." He promised: "If I am elected governor I am going to stop the shooting of miners in the back like dogs on Anaconda Road." On October 28, Wheeler declared: "The greatest aim of the Nonpartisan League is to place humanity above the dollar."[30] But the tide was running against the insurgents. In the August primary, Wheeler polled 32 per cent of the votes cast, and by October there was little evidence that he had acquired any additional support.

The insurgents' inability to broaden their social base was compounded by the growing unpopularity of the Democratic administration in Washington, D.C. In the grip of a postwar recession, the nation's voters were ready to punish the incumbents. In Montana, the recession manifested itself in low prices for agricultural commodities; for example, wheat had dropped from $2.40 a bushel in August to $1.25 in October. In Butte, fewer than half of the mines were operating, as the price of copper slumped to fourteen cents a pound compared to nineteen cents at the beginning of the year. In the fall of 1920, to be a radical and a Democrat was to be doubly damned. The result was a Republican landslide.[31]

Republican presidential candidate Warren G. Harding received 61 per cent of the vote in Montana and won in every county but one. Dixon received 60 per cent of the votes cast and carried forty-six out of fifty-three counties. The other Republican candidates for Congress and state office did just as well. The Democratic-Nonpartisan ticket went down in defeat. The best the farmer-labor coalition could claim, according to the *Nonpartisan Leader,* was four state senators and eleven or twelve state representatives whom it had endorsed.[32] None was from Silver Bow County.

In Butte, the *Anaconda Standard* exulted: "BUTTE KICKS OUT REDS AND ELECTS AMERICANS TO OFFICE." All eight of the Labor League candidates for the state legislature had been defeated. The League slate had polled an average of 7,874 votes, compared to 8,924 for the four "regular" Democratic candidates and 9,275 for the Republicans. The League candidate who received the most votes was A. N. Alderman, who placed sixteenth in the twenty-four-candidate field. Dunne finished nineteenth, receiving just 8,175 votes. The final tallies showed two "regular" Democrats and ten Republicans elected. Wheeler did beat Dixon in the county by a narrow 50.4 per cent to 49.6 per cent. It was a personal triumph. The other Nonpartisan candidates for state offices lost in the county by wide margins.

Some other League candidates did win their county races. Both Duggan and Bourquin were elected, as were the League candidates for county commissioner, auditor, superintendent of schools, and public administrator.[33] None of the winners had closely identified themselves with the Montana Labor League, and their victories were basically personal ones.

In the wake of its electoral disaster, the farmer-labor coalition may have taken some consolation in the voters' decisive rejection of the legislature's attempt to eliminate the state's open primary. A large majority had voted to retain the primary as an open election and to keep the presidential preference as well.[34] Silver Bow County rejected the three legislative referenda, and the social and economic splits were evident in the distribution of votes. Butte's working-class communities supported the primary system without reservation, but voters in the middle-class area west of Main Street cast ballots in favor of both closing the open primary and abolishing the direct primary for state and congressional office. The residents west of Main voted to keep the presidential primary. (The results on the legislature's referenda and the gubernatorial and sheriff's races are summarized in Table 9.)

TABLE 9: *Butte's Social Communities and Selected General Election Results, 1920*

	Middle-Class Enclave	The Flats	Northeast Butte
Governor			
Wheeler (D)	40.1%	52.6%	61.5%
Dixon (R)	59.9	47.4	38.5
Sheriff			
Duggan (D)	41.9	50.7	62.8
Carlson (R)	58.1	49.3	37.2
Legislative Referenda*			
Abolish the direct primary	50.2	41.5	38.6
Close the open primary	53.3	44.9	36.4
Abolish the presidential primary	48.2	42.8	39.4

Source: Data derived from the official canvass of the general election. The author wishes to thank Fred Quivik of the Butte Historical Society for supplying a copy of the canvass.

*Percentage voting in favor

Overall, the state-wide farmer-labor coalition had been badly beaten. The *Butte Bulletin* bravely predicted that "the fight" would continue, but by then the fight was all but over.[35] Although they did not know it, the year 1920 marked the final and decisive contest between organized capital and its opponents in Montana. The nation was settling in for a decade of "normalcy," a decade in which radicalism found precious little breathing space. A historic opportunity for the establishment of a permanent socialist presence in the main corridors of political life had come and was now gone.

Politically, the wage-earners of this nation are without an organ of expression except that meaningless outlet for resentment through the parties of their bosses and the bankers.

—Bill Dunne, *Butte Bulletin*, March 16, 1923

Afterword

Bill Dunne wrote these words in the *Butte Bulletin* long after leaving Butte. Over the years, he returned only occasionally and briefly to the mining city where he had gained his reputation as a radical working-class leader. Dunne became a devoted member of the Communist Party U.S.A., which was just emerging into full public view since its founding in September 1919. He had an uncritical admiration for the developing Soviet system of government in Russia and proved to be a good party man. His first major role for the party was as co-editor of the *Daily Worker* in 1924.[1]

Burton K. Wheeler's subsequent career was decidedly different. In 1922, he announced his candidacy for the U.S. Senate seat held by Henry Myers. Myers smoothed the way by announcing his retirement at the end of the term. This time, the ACM Company remained benevolently neutral. Perhaps the copper bosses were bowing to the inevitable, or maybe they were not particularly upset with having Wheeler far away in Washington, D.C. Wheeler won the election easily, accumulating 55 per cent of the vote and carrying thirty-one of the state's fifty-four counties.[2]

The ACM Company was preoccupied with other things, principally the activity of Governor Dixon, who was pushing strongly for a new tax on metal mining. But the legislature rejected Dixon's proposals, primarily because of the Company's well-oiled and efficient lobbying efforts. The governor then used his influence to get the metal mines tax on the ballot as an initiative. In November 1924, the people approved Initiative 28, but in the same election they replaced the Republican Dixon with Democrat John Erickson, whose campaign had been heavily backed by the ACM Company and other large business interests.[3] Dixon was out, the Company would pay a little bit more to operate in the state, and the working-class insurgency was only a faint whisper.

The *Butte Bulletin* was dead. Forced to return to weekly publication in late 1921 because of a sharp depression in the copper industry and the emigration of miners elsewhere, the paper struggled along but could not survive. In January 1924, the *Butte Bulletin* published its last issue.

145

As the *Bulletin* was dying, the handful of radicals who still believed in the possibility of independent political action was gathering under the banner of the Farmer-Labor Party of Montana. Representing the shattered remnants of the Labor League and the Nonpartisan League, the Farmer-Labor Party never got off the ground. It fielded no ticket in Silver Bow County, and Frank J. Edwards, the party's candidate for governor in 1924, received just 10,666 votes (6.1 per cent), of which only 380 came from Silver Bow County.[4] The Butte workers' long flirtation with third-party experiments was finally over.[5]

We should not forget that the working-class insurgency that gripped the city of Butte for almost three decades was part of the general labor and farmer unrest prevalent in other parts of the country. During those years, people did not accept large-scale corporate enterprise as part of the natural order of things. It was a time when many working-class people believed that their political rights and social status were being destroyed by the new, emerging order.

The workers resisted, and as they resisted some were inspired by a vision that was in opposition to the received truths embodied in the hoary shibboleths of "private property" and "free enterprise." At its simplest and most emotive level, the future the insurgents dared to imagine was the creation of a democratic community of producers in which human intelligence and labor would be consciously harnessed for the benefit of all. These believers called it socialism.

In their strivings, the insurgents encountered vigorous opponents who were sometimes cunning and sophisticated, but more often simply heavy-handed and brutal. They found that many of their fellow workers were indifferent or apathetic and that ethnic divisions and traditional political identifications were hard to break. Most of all, they encountered the sheer dominance of the capitalist culture in the minds of many workers. Consequently, taking one's stand for the alternative was more often than not a most frustrating experience. This frustration is evident in the anonymously penned "A Message," which appeared in the March 24, 1919, *Butte Bulletin*:

> Struggle, struggle working man
> How we wonder that you can;
> Stick around the world so cruel,
> And be such a brilliant fool.
>
> Harbor misery, shoulder strife,
> Starve your children and, self and wife;
> So the profits may pile up,
> For each parasitic pup.
>
> Love your master, kiss the shoe,
> That is always kicking you;
> Drudge along a slaver's path,
> And accept the driver's wrath.
>
> Fight war's battles for the plutes,
> Fill the world with prostitutes;
> Foot the bills which graft has made,
> While through all life's years you wade.

Wave the flag that's handed you,
Murder if they tell you to;
Glory in the blood you've spilled,
While some mother's joy you've stilled.

How about a spark of grit?
Can't you quite deliver it?
Reasons why will you please show,
If you choose to answer no.

Freedom never will be won,
With such slaving habits, son;
On such things let's place a ban,
Struggle, struggle, working man.[6]

The insurgents also fought among themselves and made mistakes. Should they pursue "political action" and try to vote themselves toward revolution? The Wobblies cried that only "direct action" would do. But they all believed in the palpable evils of capitalism, and such arguments seemed to be needlessly divisive and self-defeating. They were all searching for formulas that would work. In the end, none of them did.

In the final analysis, American electoral socialism's failure was found in demographic trends and the electoral rules of the game. In Marxian theory the advance of socialism presupposed the emergence of the working class as the electoral majority in advanced industrial societies. In their study of the history of democratic socialism, Adam Przworski and John Sprague wrote:

> At the end of the nineteenth century, as socialist parties entered into the competition for votes, they saw in universal suffrage an institution that would allow the working class to proceed from "political to social emancipation," as Marx put it fifty years earlier. Elections would open the "parliamentary road" to socialism; they would bring about a "peaceful revolution" from a society based on the exploitation of workers to one that would provide conditions for universal liberation. Barricades would no longer be needed when workers could cast ballots: votes would be "paper stones."[7]

But shortly after the turn of the century the larger socialist parties in Europe discovered that population trends were running contrary to theory and that the working class would never become the electoral majority that could vote socialism into power.[8] In the United States the trend was the same. At the time of the founding of the Socialist Party of America there were approximately eleven million wage workers in the United States, comprising 38 per cent of all employed persons. By 1910, the proportion of wage workers among the employed had climbed to 41 per cent, but at no subsequent time did the percentage of blue-collar workers among the gainfully employed exceed 45 per cent.[9] Further, even though American workers did form the largest single social class bloc, a large minority of them could not vote because they were immigrants, because they were women, and, in the case of black Americans, because of discriminatory election laws. Even among those workers who could cast ballots there were often sharp ethnic, racial, and religious divisions that undercut proletarian solidarity. Consequently, even though workers did constitute a numerical electoral majority in hundreds of American communities their votes often went to the candidates of the old parties. Even if local Socialists could win and retain their electoral base they still faced the insurmountable barrier presented by demographics – wage-workers would never constitute an electoral majority in the nation.

Nonetheless, the United States is the "great exception" in one critically important respect. Despite demographic trends, socialist parties in other industrial societies did establish themselves as major and permanent electoral movements while the Socialist Party in America sputtered and died. There are many reasons for the American exception, but three are particularly salient to the examination of socialism in one city and the concurrent and subsequent trends in American electoral history.[10]

First, European socialists struggled for recognition and power in societies in which social class distinctions were more obvious and rigid than those in the United States. In addition to the often gross inequalities of wealth, power, and status between classes, most European workers could not initially vote for socialism because the franchise was denied them. Consequently, their struggle for socialism was simultaneously a struggle for democracy, for the political emancipation of the working class. In this fight, European socialist parties created for themselves substantial and sustained proletarian support. As Selig Perlman perceptively wrote in 1928:

> In other countries, where the labor movement started while the working class was still denied the franchise, there was in the last analysis no need of a theory of "surplus value" to convince them that they were a class apart and should therefore be "class conscious."[11]

In the United States, what Perlman calls the "free gift" of the ballot dampened class consciousness and class solidarity and made it more difficult for Socialists to persuade workers that their interests could only be represented by an independent workers' party.

Second, as socialist movements elsewhere gained in influence they were able to successfully apply pressure for changes in election laws that would almost guarantee them a permanent and important place in the political landscape. Winner-take-all vote-counting systems (the single-member district and the multimember at-large systems still used in the United States) were discarded for a system of proportional representation in which each party receives parliamentary seats in proportion to its actual share of the popular vote.[12] In Sweden, for example, the adoption of proportional representation followed closely on the heels of working-class suffrage in 1907. In the first election after the change, the Social Democratic Party doubled its share of seats in parliament and was eventually able to routinely command 40 to 45 per cent of the popular vote.[13]

In the United States, however, the Socialists and other third-party movements were saddled with the winner-take-all system, which leaves even large minorities without representation after an election. In 1912, for example, the 172 Socialist candidates for the U.S. House of Representatives polled 902,865 votes, 6.4 per cent of the total popular vote. Because none of them came in first with a plurality of the vote, none was elected. Had a system of proportional representation been in place, the Socialists would have sent twenty-eight of their candidates to Congress. This would have given the Socialists a base for further political advance because voters who supported the

Socialist ticket would no longer be casting "wasted votes."[14] It is not surprising that Socialists continually advocated the proportional representation system.[15]

Finally, socialist parties in Europe often grew out of the trade union movement as the political expression of the workers' demand for political equality. European trade unions, often led by Socialists, helped maintain class unity on the economic front while simultaneously providing campaign financing and other forms of material support for the socialist parties. In a review of political parties in the democracies, Leon Epstein observed:

> American Socialists failed because they were unable to recruit large scale support in the working class. This was not because of the absence of trade unions, but because of the absence of enough socialist-organized and socialist-oriented ones. . . . The typical European "labor movement" had two expressions, one industrial and the other political, but both based on the assumption that the working class had interests that only its own organizations could serve.[16]

There was no such assumption in American political culture. Not only was there a denial of common working-class interests in the ethnic, racial, and religious divisions among workers, but organized labor as embodied in the American Federation of Labor was actively hostile to independent political action. The AFL counseled workers to vote within the two-party system by supporting "progressive" Democrats and Republicans.[17] Consequently, no trade union-Socialist Party alliance was ever accomplished in the United States. Without such an alliance the Socialist Party was almost certainly doomed as an electoral force.

Two obvious and glaring consequences have flowed from the failure of the Socialist Party to achieve a permanent foothold in American politics. First, as John D. Stephens has carefully documented, there is a strong correlation between the strength of organized labor and political socialism and the establishment of the social welfare state and the lessening of the inequalities of income and wealth.[18] Policies such as old-age pensions, unemployment, maternity leave, broad-based public health care and national health insurance, and progressive taxation of income and wealth are strongly associated with the strength of the trade union movement and the Socialist Party in industrial capitalist societies. The weakness of the American trade union movement and the absence of a socialist party help explain the weakness of America's social welfare commitments and how the distribution of income and wealth has remained substantially inegalitarian and virtually unchanged through a succession of Democratic and Republican administrations.[19]

The absence of a socialist or labor party has also produced a level of citizen non-involvement and nonparticipation unparalleled in the democratic world. While other democracies regularly experience an election turnout in excess of 80 per cent of eligible voters, in the United States only a slim majority bother to cast ballots in presidential elections, with the nonvoters drawn primarily from the ranks of the working class and those with lower-middle and low incomes.[20] The United States election laws not only tend to discourage participation (for example, elections are held during a workday, while most democracies hold elections on Sundays or on a national holiday), but also there is no party to organize and mobilize the working class. In Sweden, all classes vote at about the same rate, and the overall turnout is always in excess of 90 per cent.[21]

Where no class-specific political organization exists, as in the United States, participation by those in manual occupations and with modest to low incomes is invariably lower.[22] In his analysis of voter turnout in the United States, Paul Kleppner wrote:

> In modern European contexts, the presence of working-class parties and associational infrastructures provides a collective boost to participation rates and produces aggregate turnout profiles devoid of strong class and age biases. No similar parties and mechanisms for social class reinforcement emerged in the early twentieth century United States. Without the operation of mechanisms that offset economic and educational disadvantages, the participation of citizens who individually lack the resources and skills that stimulate turnout began to decline, and aggregate turnout measures came to exhibit strong and systematic class skews.[23]

Given its conspicuous failure, what has been the contribution of the socialist movement to American life? The Socialists offered practical political solutions that helped push society toward the amelioration of some of the worst features of industrial capitalism and the urban environment; the demands for a decent wage, healthy and safe working conditions, and union representation would be granted some legitimacy and codified in law. By bravely attempting to organize the unorganized and advocating the industrial union idea, the IWW provided inspiration and a model for the mass industrial union organizing drives led by the CIO during the 1930s. The radical reformers showed that large numbers of people could be mobilized around an explicitly radical program for social change without forming a third-party movement. In doing so, they provided some evidence that it was possible to effectively push for radical change within the two-party system.

In Montana, the Socialists in Butte established a new standard for municipal governance by combining the urge for urban reform with an explicit devotion to advancing the interests of the working class. The Wobblies in the mining city, though often given to flights of rhetorical excess, proved that the IWW could fight for the realization of the miners' immediate demands for a better wage, improvements in health and safety conditions, and union representation. Third, though their impact on changing public policy was minimal, the Farmer-Labor Alliance did save the state's open primary, providing an opportunity for further reform within the two-party system.

With no viable party of the left, the United States stands alone among the democracies. But even though the movement for socialism remained fully unrealized, the Socialists, the industrial unionists, and the farmer-labor nonpartisans made their permanent mark. They pushed the debate that would eventually lead to significant economic and institutional reforms that were first implemented during the New Deal, reforms that have forever changed the relations of citizens with each other and their relations with the governmental system.

Notes

Chapter 1: *The City and the Rebels*

1. The 1910 census reported the combined city and county population at slightly less than 57,000, 40,000 of whom lived in Butte. U.S. Department of Commerce, Bureau of the Census, *Thirteenth Census of the United States, vol. II: Population, 1910*, 1133, 1143. Population estimates by local boosters were higher, ranging from 60,000 to 100,000 in the city and county. See "Butte, Montana, At the Dawn of the Twentieth Century," *Western Resources*, no. 134 (June 1901), 3; *Irrepressible Butte: The Richest City in the World* (Butte: Butte Land and Investment Company, 1912), 27, 29; *Butte: Metropolis of Montana* (Butte: Chamber of Commerce, Merchants Association, and Rotary Club of Butte, 1915), 6.

2. Michael P. Malone, *The Battle for Butte: Mining and Politics on the Northern Frontier, 1864-1906* (Seattle: University of Washington Press, 1981), chapters 1-3.

3. Data derived from Y. S. Leong et al., *Technology, Employment and Output Per Man in Copper Mining* (Philadelphia: Works Projects Administration, 1940), 218-219.

4. *Thirteenth Census of the United States, vol. I: Population, 1910*, 179, 593. Among adult males of voting age, 55 per cent were immigrants. For details of the ethnic and social class characteristics of Butte, see Chapter 6.

5. *Thirteenth Census of the United States, vol. IV: Population, 1910*, 16; *Thirteenth Census of the United States, vol. XI: Mines and Quarries, 1910*, 111.

6. For the early development of labor unionism in Butte, see Richard Lingenfelter, *The Hardrock Miners: A History of the Mining Labor Movement in the American West, 1863-1893* (Berkeley: University of California Press, 1974), 182-185; Paul Frisch, "Gibraltar of Unionism: The Development of Butte's Labor Movement, 1878-1900," *The Speculator* 2 (Summer 1985): 12-20; Henry Grabenstein, "The History of Labor Unions in Butte," *The Labor Review*, no. 1 (1946), 27-28. The *Labor Review* was published by the Butte Building and Construction Trades Council. Local unions were listed in annual city directories published by R. L. Polk & Company.

7. Christopher C. Connelly, "The Labor Fuss in Butte," *Everybody's Magazine* 31 (August 1914): 206-207.

8. Gertrude Atherton, *Perch of the Devil* (New York: Frederick A. Stokes Company, 1914), 57.

9. Letter from J. A. Stromquist, (Chicago) *Industrial Union Bulletin*, March 24, 1908. The *IUB* was published by the radical Industrial Workers of the World.

10. *Butte Miner*, December 18, 1910. Butte's largest employer, the Anaconda Copper Mining Company, compiled accident statistics for 1910-1913 and 1915-1917. During those years, 275 ACM

workers were killed and 20,735 were injured, 1,611 of them seriously. Data derived from U.S. Senate, Commission on Industrial Relations, "Mining Conditions and Industrial Relations at Butte, Mont.," *Final Report and Testimony*, 64th Cong., 1st sess., 1916, S. Doc. 415 (Serial 6932), 3874-3879 ["Mining Conditions at Butte"]. A good overview is provided by Brian Shovers, "The Perils of Working in the Butte Underground: Industrial Fatalities in the Copper Mines, 1880-1920," *Montana the Magazine of Western History* 37 (Spring 1987): 26-39.

11. Daniel Harrington and A. J. Lanza, "Miners' Consumption in the Mines of Butte, Montana," U.S. Bureau of Mines Technical Paper No. 260 (1921), 7-9, 11-12. See also the testimony of Joseph Shannon, "Mining Conditions at Butte," 3857.

12. Lingenfelter, *Hardrock Miners*, 51-52; State of Montana, *Fourth Annual Report of the Bureau of Agriculture, Labor and Industry, 1895-1896*, 10-11; (Spokane) *Industrial Worker*, October 23, 1912. Data on benefits derived from the official proceedings of the annual conventions of the Western Federation of Miners.

13. *Butte Miner*, December 15, 1912; Malone, *Battle for Butte*, 149, 173-174; K. Ross Toole, *Twentieth-Century Montana: A State of Extremes* (Norman: University of Oklahoma Press, 1972), 101-104.

14. Malone, *Battle for Butte*, 210.

15. Eugene V. Debs, "The Outlook for Socialism in the United States," in *Writings and Speeches of Eugene V. Debs*, ed. Arthur M. Schlesinger, Jr. (New York: Hermitage Press, 1948), 38.

16. Testimony of William D. Haywood, U.S. Senate, Commission on Industrial Relations, "Labor and the Law," *Final Report and Testimony*, 64th Cong., 1st sess., 1916, S. Doc. 415 (Serial 6939), 10574 ["Labor and the Law"].

17. Quoted in Terrence McGlynn, "Socialist Organizers in Montana" (Montana State College of Mineral Science and Technology, Butte, n.d.).

18. Howard Quint, *The Forging of American Socialism: Origins of the Modern Movement* (Indianapolis: Bobbs-Merrill, 1964), 318-325; Ira Kipnis, *The American Socialist Movement, 1897-1912* (1952; reprint, Westport, Connecticut: Greenwood Press, 1968), chapters 4-6.

19. Jessie Wallace Hughan, *American Socialism of the Present Day* (New York: John Lane Company, 1911), chapters 11-12.

20. (Butte) *Labor World*, August 1, 1902.

21. (Helena) *Montana News*, September 3, 1908.

22. Carl D. Thompson, *Have the Socialists Made Good?* 1913, Pamphlet Collection, Socialist Party of America Papers, Perkins Library, Duke University, Durham, North Carolina [SPA Papers].

23. Hughan, *American Socialism*, 45-46; Kipnis, *American Socialist Movement*. 171-172.

24. For a critical evaluation of the development of the AFL, see Philip Foner, *From the Founding of the American Federation of Labor to the Emergence of American Imperialism*, vol. 2 of *History of the Labor Movement in the United States* (New York: International Publishers, 1955), 171-205, 345-368; Philip Foner, *The Policies and Practices of the A.F. of L., 1900-1909*, vol. 3 of *History of the Labor Movement in the United States* (New York: International Publishers, 1964), chapters 8-10. See also William M. Dick, *Labor and Socialism in America: The Gompers Era* (Port Washington, New York: Kennikat Press, 1972).

25. Nathan Fine, *Labor and Farmer Parties in the United States, 1828-1928* (1928; reprint, New York: Russell and Russell, 1961), 266; Dick, *Labor and Socialism*, 84-85.

26. Schlesinger, *Writings and Speeches of Eugene V. Debs*, 332.

27. Locally, however, close labor union-Socialist Party ties might occur. See, for example, Sally M. Miller, "Milwaukee: Of Ethnicity and Labor," in *Socialism and the Cities*, ed. Bruce M. Stave (Port Washington, New York: Kennikat Press, 1975), 44-45.

28. Foner, *Policies and Practices*, 393-438. See especially Melvyn Dubofsky, *We Shall Be All: A History of the Industrial Workers of the World* (Chicago: Quadrangle Books, 1969), 57-76.

29. Joyce L. Kornbluh, ed., *Rebel Voices: An I.W.W. Anthology* (Ann Arbor: University of Michigan Press, 1964), 1-13; Philip Foner, *The Industrial Workers of the World, 1905-1917*, vol. 4 of *History of the Labor Movement in the United States* (New York: International Publishers, 1965), 13-39.

30. Dubofsky, *We Shall Be All*, 146-170; Foner, *Industrial Workers of the World*, 133-146.

31. William D. Haywood and Frank Bohn, *Industrial Socialism* (Chicago: Charles H. Kerr, 1911), 54-59; "What Haywood Says on Political Action," *International Socialist Review* 13 (February 1913): 622.

32. Haywood and Bohn, *Industrial Socialism*, 47-48; testimony of Haywood, "Labor and the Law," 10574-10580.

33. Kornbluh, *Rebel Voices*, 12-13. For an analysis of IWW theory and practice, see Dubofsky, *We Shall Be All*, Chapter 7.

34. See Thomas A. Clinch, *Urban Populism and Free Silver in Montana* (Missoula: University of Montana Press, 1970).

35. The definitive history of the Nonpartisan League remains Robert L. Morlan, *Political Prairie Fire: The Nonpartisan League, 1915-1922* (Minneapolis: University of Minnesota Press, 1955).

Chapter 2: *The Birth of the Insurgent Era*

1. There is extensive literature on the war of the copper kings. The definitive account is Malone, *Battle for Butte*, chapters 5-6. See also C. B. Glasscock, *The War of the Copper Kings: Builders of Butte and Wolves of Wall Street* (New York: Bobbs-Merrill, 1935); Christopher Connelly, *The Devil Learns to Vote* (New York: Civici-Friede, 1938); Works Projects Administration Writers' Project, *Copper Camp: Stories of the World's Greatest Mining Camp* (New York: Hastings House, 1943); Joseph Kinsey Howard, *Montana: High, Wide and Handsome* (New Haven, Connecticut: Yale University Press, 1943), 58-72.

2. Robert A. Chadwick, "Montana's Silver Mining Era: Great Boom and Great Bust," *Montana the Magazine of Western History* 32 (Spring 1982): 16-31.

3. For a comprehensive analysis of the People's Party, see Lawrence Goodwyn, *Democratic Promise: The Populist Movement in America* (New York: Oxford University Press, 1976). For a history of the movement in Montana, see Clinch, *Urban Populism*. The urban character of Populism was not confined to Montana. See Robert W. Larson, *Populism in the Mountain West* (Albuquerque: University of New Mexico Press, 1986). Also relevant to the development of Populism in Montana is W. Thomas White, "Boycott: The Pullman Strike in Montana," *Montana the Magazine of Western History* 29 (Autumn 1979): 2-13; William L. Lang, "One Path to Populism: Will Kennedy and the People's Party in Montana," *Pacific Northwest Quarterly* 74 (April 1983): 77-87; Richard Roeder, "Crossing the Gender Line: Ella L. Knowles, Montana's First Woman Lawyer," *Montana the Magazine of Western History* 32 (Summer 1982): 64-75. Concerning Populist political successes, see Ellis Waldron, *An Atlas of Montana Elections Since 1864* (Missoula: Montana State University Press, 1958), 70, 82.

4. Clinch, *Urban Populism*, 6-7; *Anaconda Standard*, May 9, 1893, January 19, January 20, January 21, 1894, May 2, May 3, May 4, 1895; *Butte Bystander*, January 27, 1894, May 14, 1895; *Helena Independent*, May 4, 1895.

5. *Anaconda Standard*, November 19, 1895; *Butte Bystander*, November 5, November 12, November 25, 1895.

6. *Report of the Proceedings of the First Annual and Second Convention of the State Trades and Labor Council and the Butte Industrial Conference*, November 18-20, 1895, 32-33, 45-46.

7. *Butte Bystander*, December 3, 1895, November 29, 1896, November 20, 1897; Foner, *Policies and Practices of the A.F. of L.*, 413-418. The WLU would change its name to the American Labor Union in 1902.

8. Clinch, *Urban Populism*, 162-165.

9. Helen Sanders, *A History of Montana*, 3 vols. (Chicago: Lewis Publishing Company, 1913), 1:430.

10. *Anaconda Standard*, September 10, 1900; Waldron, *Atlas of Montana Elections*, 92, 94.

11. Malone, *Battle for Butte*, 140-147.

12. (Butte) *Reveille*, November 8, 1900.

13. Malone, *Battle for Butte*, 151.

14. Ibid., 151-152.

15. F. A. Heinze, *The Political Situation in Montana* (Butte: n.p., 1902), 61.

16. *Anaconda Standard*, November 13, 1900; *Reveille*, November 13, 1900; Malone, *Battle for Butte*, 159-161; State of Montana, *House Journal of the Seventh Session of the Legislative Assembly* (1901), 72.

17. Malone, *Battle for Butte*, 172-182.

18. *Anaconda Standard*, August 20, August 22, August 24, 1901.

19. *Anaconda Standard*, August 22, 1901.

20. *Livingston Post*, August 28, 1902.

21. Ibid.; *Butte Miner*, August 25, August 27, August 28, August 29, 1902; *Labor World*, August 29, 1902.

22. (Butte) *American Labor Union Journal*, October 30, 1902.

23. *Anaconda Standard*, August 29, 1902.

24. *Anaconda Standard*, October 6, 1902.

25. *Labor World*, August 8, September 19, September 26, 1902; *American Labor Union Journal*, October 30, 1902.

26. Quoted in *Labor World*, October 10, 1902.

27. *Anaconda Standard*, November 8, 1902; *American Labor Union Journal*, November 13, 1902; *Labor World*, November 14, 1902.

28. *Anaconda Standard*, September 18, September 25, October 25, November 1, November 8, 1902; *Labor World*, August 8, October 3, October 24, November 7, November 21, 1902.

29. *Anaconda Standard*, January 28, January 30, 1903; *American Labor Union Journal*, February 3, 1903; *Labor World*, February 6, 1903.

30. *Anaconda Standard*, March 13, March 17, April 2, 1903.

31. *Anaconda Standard*, March 19, March 21, March 26, 1903; *Labor World*, March 27, 1903; *Reveille*, March 27, 1903.

32. *Anaconda Labor-Socialist*, March 28, 1903. The *Labor-Socialist*, which began weekly publication in February 1903, was short-lived. The March 28 number, the only copy known to have survived, is in the collections of the Wisconsin State Historical Library, Madison. The municipal platform of the Anaconda Socialists was also printed in the *Anaconda Standard*, March 12, 1903.

33. *Anaconda Standard*, March 8, March 9, March 10, March 11, March 12, March 22, March 26, March 27, 1903.

34. *Anaconda Standard*, April 7, 1903; William Mailly to John Frinke, April 7, 1903, William Mailly Letterpress Copy Books, National Correspondence Files, SPA Papers. For a full description of the Socialist period in Anaconda, see Jerry W. Calvert, "The Rise and Fall of Socialism in a Company Town: Anaconda, Montana, 1902-1905," *Montana the Magazine of Western History* 36 (Autumn 1986): 2-13.

35. *Reveille*, March 13, 1903.

36. *Anaconda Standard*, April 7, 1903; *Labor World*, April 10, 1903. The Butte Socialists had expected total victory. See William Mailly to Adolph Holst, February 23, March 10, 1903, Mailly to Clarence Smith, April 7, 1903, Mailly Letterpress Copy Books, National Correspondence Files, SPA Papers.

37. *Reveille*, May 15, 1903; *Labor World*, June 5, 1903.

38. *Montana News*, October 21, 1909.

39. Percival J. Cooney to Louis Duncan, April 11, 1911, Duncan Correspondence Folder 82, Socialist Party of Montana Records, 1899-1950, Microfilm Collection 425, Montana Historical Society Archives, Helena [SPM Papers]. These papers are divided by topic into approximately one hundred folders. Approximately half of the folders contain routine correspondence from local party branches. There is also some correspondence by state secretaries, principally Louis Duncan in 1910-1911.

40. Although the Socialist Party did not endorse the *Labor World*, others did, including Eugene Debs, the Montana State Trades and Labor Council, and the Silver Bow Trades and Labor Assembly. *Labor World*, September 5, 1902.

41. *Reveille*, September 4, September 25, 1903.

42. WFM Executive Board Minutes, May 19, May 23, May 25, June 17, 1903, Archives of the Western Federation of Miners-International Union of Mine, Mill and Smelter Workers, Western History Collections, University of Colorado Library, Boulder.

43. WFM, *Proceedings of the Eleventh Annual Convention of the Western Federation of Miners* (1903), 184-194.

44. (Denver) *Miners Magazine*, September 17, October 22, 1903; *Reveille*, August 7, August 28, September 11, September 25, October 26, 1903; (Lewistown) *Judith Basin News*, June 17, 1903; *Montana News*, August 3, 1904.

45. *Message of Governor Joseph K. Toole to the Eighth Legislative Assembly, January 5, 1903*, 17-18.

46. *Anaconda Standard*, July 31, August 3, 1903; *Reveille*, June 26, July 31, August 7, 1903; William Mailly to Percival J. Cooney, July 26, 1903, Mailley Letterpress Copy Books, National Correspondence Files, Percival J. Cooney, "Taxation," a one-page typescript ca. 1903 in State and Local Files, SPA Papers.

47. *Anaconda Standard*, August 4, 1903.

48. *Anaconda Standard*, August 5, August 7, August 11, 1903; *Reveille*, August 14, 1903.

49. *Anaconda Standard*, February 26, 1904.

50. *Anaconda Standard*, April 3, April 5, 1904.

51. Malone, *Battle for Butte*, 173.

52. Ibid., 173-174.

53. Ibid., 174-179.

54. *American Labor Union Journal*, November 26, December 3, 1903; State of Montana, *House Journal of the Second Extraordinary Session of the Eighth Legislative Assembly: December 1-December 11, 1903*, 23, 25.

55. Malone, *Battle for Butte*, 173-179; Howard, *Montana*, 83.

56. Malone, *Battle for Butte*, 182-188.

57. *Montana News*, February 21, 1906.

Chapter 3: *A Time of Frustration*

1. *Anaconda Standard*, February 5, 1904.

2. *Anaconda Standard*, April 5, 1904.

3. *Red Lodge Picket*, April 10, 1903, March 24, April 7, April 14, 1904.

4. *Montana News*, September 20, November 8, 1905.

5. An early convert to the IWW, Walsh warmly endorsed its founding while he was still editor of the *News*. *Montana News*, July 19, 1905. For a description of Walsh's subsequent activities in the IWW, see Fred Thompson, *The IWW: Its First Fifty Years* (Chicago: Industrial Workers of the World, 1955), 47-50.

6. A biographical sketch of Graham appeared in *Montana News*, August 12, 1909.

7. *Montana News*, August 3, August 10, August 31, 1904, November 29, 1905; Mari Jo Buhle, *Women and American Socialism, 1870-1920* (Urbana: University of Illinois Press, 1981), 215, 241.

8. Waldron, *Atlas of Montana Elections*, 90, 106; *Presidential Elections Since 1789* (Washington, D.C.: Congressional Quarterly, 1975), 18.

9. *Anaconda Standard*, November 10, 1904; *Butte Miner*, November 10, 1904; *Montana News*, November 16, 1904; *Red Lodge Picket*, November 17, 1904.

10. *Anaconda Standard*, March 9, March 16, March 17, March 19, March 20, March 29, March 30, April 5, 1905.

11. *Anaconda Standard*, April 5, 1905; (Red Lodge) *Carbon County Gazette*, April 5, 1905; *Montana News*, April 12, 1906; *Anaconda Standard*, April 7, 1907.

12. *Anaconda Standard*, April 3, 1906; *Montana News*, March 14, March 21, 1906.

13. *Butte Miner*, November 6, 1906; *Montana News*, September 27, November 8, November 22, 1906.

14. *Anaconda Standard*, April 2, 1907, April 7, 1908; *Montana News*, March 5, March 15, March 21, March 18, April 4, 1907, March 5, March 12, March 26, 1908.

15. *Red Lodge Picket*, March 29, April 5, 1906; *Montana News*, March 28, April 4, 1906.

16. *Red Lodge Picket*, November 8, 1906; *Montana News*, November 15, 1906.

17. *Red Lodge Picket*, March 28, April 4, 1907; *Montana News*, April 11, 1907; (Red Lodge) *Republican Picket* (formerly *Red Lodge Picket*), April 7, 1908; *Montana News*, April 9, 1908.

18. *American Labor Union Journal*, September 3, 1903; *Anaconda Standard*, August 26, August 27, August 29, 1903; *Daily Missoulian*, August 25, August 26, August 27, August 28, August 29, 1903. Erler did not run for a second term.

19. *Anaconda Standard*, August 24, August 25, August 26, 1904; *Butte Evening News*, August 23, August 26, August 27, August 29, 1904; *Butte Miner*, August 25, August 26, 1904; *Great Falls Tribune*, August 26, August 27, 1904; (Hamilton) *Western News*, August 24, 1904.

20. Dubofsky, *We Shall Be All*, 76-87.

21. IWW, *Proceedings of the First Convention of the Industrial Workers of the World* (New York: New York Labor News Publishing Company, 1905), 305-306, 379-380, 425, 506-507.

22. *Great Falls Tribune*, August 25, August 26, 1905.

23. *Miners Magazine*, December 21, 1905, June 22, August 2, 1906; WFM, *Official Proceedings of the Fourteenth Annual Convention of the Western Federation of Miners, May 28-June 13, 1906*, 181-184, 293, 298, 301.

24. *Miners Magazine*, September 13, 1906; *Montana News*, December 13, 1906. The Butte Socialists had officially applauded the founding of the IWW, and they were not going to back away from that. See IWW, *Proceedings of the First Convention of the Industrial Workers of the World*, 265.

25. MFL, *Proceedings of the Thirteenth Annual Convention of the Montana Federation of Labor, August 20-24, 1906*, 18-19, 63; (Helena) *Montana Daily Record*, August 20, August 22, 1907; *Miners Magazine*, November 7, 1907; State of Montana, *Eleventh Annual Report of the Bureau of Agriculture, Labor and Industry, 1907-1908*, 167-168; *Miners Magazine*, September 3, September 17, 1908; *Anaconda Standard*, August 22, 1906.

26. MFL, *Proceedings of the Fifteenth Annual Convention of the Montana Federation of Labor, August 17-22, 1908*, 19-20; *Montana News*, October 7, 1909.

27. "Minutes: Butte Branch No. 1: September 1, 1907 to August 8, 1909," Folder 97, minutes of meetings, February 9, May 10, May 24, and July 5, 1908, SPM Papers [Local Butte Minute Book]. See also *Montana News*, May 28, 1908.

28. *Montana News*, September 3, September 17, October 15, 1908; Local Butte Minute Book, August 30, 1908, SPM Papers.

29. Local Butte Minute Book, August 30, October 4, October 18, November 29, December 20, 1908, January 17, March 7, March 18, 1909, SPM Papers; *Montana News*, January 9, 1909; Sanders, *A History of Montana*, 431.

30. Local Butte Minute Book, September 8, October 13, December 8, 1907, May 10, May 31, 1908, SPM Papers; *Anaconda Standard*, March 6, 1908; *Montana News*, March 12, 1908.

31. *Montana News*, December 13, 1906.

32. The bickering between Local Butte and Graham and Hazlett was often bitterly personal. For example, Louis Duncan characterized Hazlett as a "selfish, scheming woman" with an "unsavory character." Louis Duncan to the Socialist Party of Cook County, Illinois, Ward 21 Branch, April 25, 1911, Duncan to L. O. Bentell, State Secretary, Socialist Party of Illinois, October 4, 1910, "Graham-Hazlett Controversies," Folder 84, SPM Papers.

33. (Chicago) *Socialist Party Official Bulletin*, January 1909, January 1910; *Anaconda Standard*, April 6, 1909; *Montana News*, September 16, October 21, 1909.

34. Sanders, *History of Montana*, 3:1675; *Men of Affairs and Representative Institutions in Montana* (Butte: Butte Newspaper Writers Association, 1914).

35. J. Frank Mabie to Louis Duncan, October 7, 1910, Folder 82, SPM Papers.

36. Local Branches, Tabulated Reports, 1910-1912, Folder 105, SPM Papers; Waldron, *Atlas of Montana Elections*, 130.

37. *Anaconda Standard*, September 30, 1910; "Platforms," Folder 104, SPM Papers.

38. *Anaconda Standard*, November 16, 1910.

39. "Socialist Municipal Office Holders," *National Municipal Review* 1 (July 1912): 492-493; Victor L. Berger, "What Is the Matter with Milwaukee?" *Independent* 68 (April 21, 1910): 840-843; Miller, "Milwaukee," 46-47.

40. Louis J. Duncan, "Questions About Butte," Folder 82, SPM Papers; *Anaconda Standard*, March 9, 1911.

Chapter 4: *A Socialist Government*

1. Louis Duncan to F. E. Corwin, February 28, 1911, Duncan to A. W. Harrack, March 15, 1911, Folder 80, SPM Papers.

2. Berger, "What Is the Matter with Milwaukee?" 840-841; George Allen England, "Milwaukee's Socialist Government," *Review of Reviews* 42 (October 1910): 445-446.

3. The 1911 municipal platform of the Butte Socialists is printed in full in the *Anaconda Standard*, March 10, 1911.

4. Miller, "Milwaukee," 53.

5. Louis Duncan to Jackson H. Ralston, April 26, 1911, Folder 80, SPM Papers. The pro-working-class policies of Socialist municipal governments are well-documented. See Chad Gaffield, "Big Business, the Working-Class, and Socialism in Schenectady, 1911-1916," *Labor History* 19 (Summer 1978): 350-372; Frederick I. Olson, "The Socialist Party and the Unions in Milwaukee, 1900-1912," *Wisconsin Magazine of History* 44 (Winter 1960-1961): 110-116; David Paul Nord, "Minneapolis and the Pragmatic Socialism of Thomas Van Lear," *Minnesota History* 45 (Spring 1976): 2-10.

6. *Butte Socialist*, March 29, 1911; *Anaconda Standard*, March 9, 1911.

7. *Butte Miner*, April 4, 1911; Jack Keister, "Why the Socialists Won in Butte," *International Socialist Review* 11 (June 1911): 731-733.

8. Kelley Exhibit No. 8, "Mining Conditions at Butte," 3891.

9. Ibid., 3899.

10. Ibid., 3900.

11. State of Montana, *Second Biennial Report of the State Board of Health, December 1, 1902 to November 30, 1904*, 203-204; *Third Biennial Report of the State Board of Health, December 1, 1904 to November 30, 1906*, 96-97; *Fourth Biennial Report of the State Board of Health and First Biennial Report of the State Registrar of Births and Deaths, 1907 and 1908*, 64-75; *Fifth Biennial Report of the State Board of Health and Second Biennial Report of the State Registrar of Births and Deaths, 1909 and 1910*, 29, 69, 106-107.

12. Louis Duncan, "Questions About Butte," Folder 80, SPM Papers.

13. *Anaconda Standard*, March 31, 1911; (Butte) *Daily Inter Mountain*, March 31, 1911.

14. *Anaconda Standard*, April 4, 1911; *Butte Miner*, April 4, 1911.

15. Duncan, "Questions About Butte," SPM Papers; "The Victory in Butte," *The Coming Nation*, no. 33 (April 29, 1911), 10; *Butte Miner*, April 4, 1911.

16. See Chapter 6 for an analysis of the social classes supporting and opposing the Socialist Party.

17. Louis Duncan to Thurston Brown, April 12, 1911, Folder 82, SPM Papers.

18. *Anaconda Standard*, May 2, 1911.

19. Butte City Council Records, vol. 15, p. 3, Butte-Silver Bow Public Archives, Butte.

20. Ibid., 24, 33, 62-63, 65, 69-70, 129, 137-138; *Butte Miner*, June 18, 1911; *Anaconda Standard*, August 3, 1911, January 18, 1912.

21. Butte City Council Records, vol. 15, pp. 131, 137; *Revised Ordinances of the City of Butte, 1914*, 192-193, 372-377.

22. Louis Duncan, "Socialist Politics in Butte, Montana," *International Socialist Review* 12 (November 1911): 287-291.

23. *Socialist Campaign Book: City Election, April 1, 1912* (Butte: Socialist State Central Committee, 1912), 2-4, 8-9.

24. Ibid., 5.

25. *Anaconda Standard*, March 23, March 30, March 31, 1912; *Butte Miner*, March 21, March 22, March 31, 1912.

26. Butte City Council Records, vol. 15, p. 175. See Chapter 7 for a full discussion of this incident.

27. *Anaconda Standard*, April 2, 1912.

28. The turnout of registered voters was lower than it had been in 1911, but turnout is typically lower in off-year elections. Further, turnout was not noticeably lower in wards with the highest concentrations of miners compared to those wards with the lowest concentrations.

29. *Anaconda Standard*, May 7, 1912; *Butte Miner*, January 3, January 4, January 12, January 16, February 6, 1913; Butte City Council Records, vol. 15, pp. 315, 318, 322.

30. *Anaconda Standard*, July 9, 1912. The state party platform is found in Socialist Party Campaign Committee, *The Montana Campaign Issue*, October 8, 1912, State Historical Society of Wisconsin Library, Madison.

31. *Anaconda Standard*, August 31, 1912.

32. *Anaconda Standard*, September 27, 1912.

33. *Anaconda Standard*, October 6, October 7, 1912; *Butte Miner*, October 7, October 16, 1912.

34. *Anaconda Standard*, October 28, October 29, 1912; *Butte Miner*, October 17, October 18, October 27, 1912.

35. *Butte Miner*, October 30, October 31, November 2, 1912.

36. For a sample of editorial attacks against the Socialists, see *Anaconda Standard*, October 26, November 3, November 4, 1912; *Butte Miner*, October 23, October 25, October 26, October 27, October 28, October 31, November 1, November 2, November 5, 1912; *Daily Inter Mountain*, October 23, November 1, November 2, November 4, 1912.

37. *Butte Miner*, November 5, 1912.

38. *Anaconda Standard*, November 7, 1912; *Butte Miner*, November 13, 1912.

39. *Butte Miner*, November 7, 1912.

40. *Butte Miner*, December 3, December 17, December 20, 1912, January 9, 1913.

41. "Socialist Municipal Officeholders," 493-500; James Weinstein, *The Decline of Socialism in America, 1912-1925* (New York: Vintage Books, 1967), 116-118.

42. Robert F. Hoxie, "The Socialist Party and the November Elections," *Journal of Political Economy* 20 (March 1912): 218-219. See also Robert F. Hoxie, "The Rising Tide of Socialism: A Study," *Journal of Political Economy* 19 (October 1911): 621, 626-627. For a critical analysis of the reformist thrust of municipal socialism, see Richard W. Judd, "Socialist Cities: Explorations into the Grassroots of American Socialism" (Ph.D. diss., University of California-Irvine, 1979).

43. "Butte Socialist Administration Commendable," *National Municipal Review* 2 (January 1913): 134.

44. Keister, "Why the Socialists Won in Butte," 733; "Local Butte's Platform Amendment," *International Socialist Review* 13 (May 1912): 777-778; (Chicago) *Socialist Party Monthly Bulletin*, May, June, July 1912.

Chapter 5: *A Parting of the Ways*

1. Frank Bohn, "The Butte Socialists," *International Socialist Review* 13 (September 1912): 263.

2. (Butte) *Montana Socialist*, April 6, 1913. See also *Montana Socialist*, March 9, March 23, March 30, 1913.

3. *Anaconda Standard*, February 18, February 22, February 26, March 5, March 25, 1913; *Butte Miner*, February 19, February 21, February 22, February 28, 1913.

4. *Butte Miner*, March 6, 1913.

5. *Montana Socialist*, March 2, 1913.

6. *Anaconda Standard*, April 8, 1913; *Butte Miner*, April 8, 1913; *Montana Socialist*, April 13, 1913; "Socialist Victory in Butte," *International Socialist Review* 13 (May 1913): 829.

7. *Montana Socialist*, April 13, 1913.

8. Cited in *Montana Socialist*, April 20, 1913.

9. Kipnis, *American Socialist Movement*, 388-393; David Shannon, *The Socialist Party of America: A History* (Chicago: Quadrangle Books, 1967), 70-72; Fine, *Labor and Farmer Parties*, 272-273; "The National Socialist Convention of 1912," *International Socialist Review* 12 (June 1912): 825-826.

10. Fine, *Labor and Farmer Parties*, 273.

11. *Proceedings of the National Convention of the Socialist Party—1912* (Chicago: National Headquarters of the Socialist Party, 1912), 101, National Convention, Proceedings File, SPA Papers; *Socialist Party Monthly Bulletin* (September 1912).

12. There is no complete text of what Haywood said in December 1912. Portions of the speech that precipitated the recall move can be found in Mary Brown Sumner, "The Parting of the Ways in American Socialism," *Survey* 29 (February 1, 1913): 625; *Montana Socialist*, February 19, 1913.

13. Kipnis, *American Socialist Movement*, 412-417; Foner, *Industrial Workers of the World*, 408-410; *Montana Socialist*, March 9, 1913.

14. "From Montana," *International Socialist Review* 13 (February 1913): 623-624; *Montana Socialist*, February 19, 1913.

15. *Anaconda Standard*, April 17, April 18, April 21, April 25, April 29, 1913; *Montana Socialist*, April 20, May 11, 1913; Louis J. Duncan, "The Troubles in Butte: Mayor Duncan's Statement," State and Local Files, SPA Papers.

16. *Anaconda Standard*, September 27, 1912.

17. See Chapter 8.

18. *Butte Miner*, May 7, 1913; *Montana Socialist*, May 11, 1913; *Anaconda Standard*, May 22, 1913; Duncan, "The Troubles in Butte," SPA Papers.

19. *Anaconda Standard*, May 24, May 26, May 27, 1913; Duncan, "The Troubles in Butte," SPA Papers.

20. *Anaconda Standard*, June 16, June 17, 1913; *Butte Miner*, June 16, June 17, 1913.

21. *Anaconda Standard*, May 24, May 27, May 30, June 11, 1913; *Butte Miner*, May 30, June 12, 1913; "Plain Statement," State and Local Files, SPA Papers.

22. *Anaconda Standard*, June 13, June 14, June 16, 1913; *Butte Miner*, June 13, 1913; Duncan, "The Troubles in Butte," SPA Papers.

23. *Anaconda Standard*, June 14, June 16, 1913; *Butte Miner*, June 16, 1913; *Butte Daily Post*, June 16, 1913; Duncan, "The Troubles in Butte," SPA Papers; *Montana Socialist*, June 22, 1913.

24. *Anaconda Standard*, June 17, 1913; *Butte Miner*, June 17, 1913; *Montana Socialist*, June 22, 1913.

25. *Anaconda Standard*, June 19, 1913; *Butte Miner*, June 19, June 20, 1913.

26. *Anaconda Standard*, June 19, June 20, June 26, June 29, July 5, August 8, 1913; *Butte Miner*, June 19, June 20, June 21, June 27, July 5, 1913.

27. Frank Bohn, "Is the I.W.W. to Grow?" *International Socialist Review* 12 (July 1911): 42.

28. Debs quoted in William English Walling, *The Socialism of To-Day* (New York: Henry Holt and Company, 1916), 388. The text of Debs's letter to Walling on March 5, 1913, was undoubtedly used by the Duncan forces in the faction fight. It was leaked to the *Anaconda Standard* on May 26, 1913.

29. W. J. White, "Our Elected Servants," *International Socialist Review* 13 (June 1913): 868-870; Charles Edward Russell, "Socialism: Just Where It Stands Today," *Hampton's Magazine* 27 (January 1912): 756-759; Henry M. Hyde, "Socialists at Work," *Technical World Magazine* 16 (February 1912): 628-629.

30. Louis Duncan to Edward Moe, April 26, 1911, Folder 80, SPM Papers. The juridical basis for officeholder subordination to the Socialist Party's instructions is found in Article 8, Section 4, of the *Constitution of the Socialist Party of Montana, As Amended to March 1912*, which required that all party members nominated for elective office submit to the party local a signed and undated resignation for the office being sought. Folder 95, SPM Papers.

31. After the June 1913 purge, the constitution of Local Butte was redrafted to exclude any reference to the submission of signed and undated resignations. Under the new constitution, elected officeholders were to be under the "general supervision" of a "Parliamentary Committee" in which the same elected officeholders and party officials were the majority. In this way, any presumption that the local chapter might collectively instruct those officeholders was removed. *Constitution of Butte Local, Socialist Party of Montana, Adopted September 4, 1913*, 13-14, Folder 95, SPM.

32. "The Lesson of Lima, Ohio," *International Socialist Review* 14 (September 1913): 186; "Socialist Administration at Lima, Ohio," typescript, ca. November 1911, J. H. Andrew, Couer d'Alene, Idaho, to Carl D. Thompson, July 1, 1912, Walter Reece, Edmunds, Washington, to C.D.T., July 9, 1912, Julius Taylor, State Secretary of Spring Lake, Michigan, to C.D.T., May 10, 1913, W. E. Boynton, Ashtabula, Ohio, to C.D.T., September 12, 1913, National Correspondence Files, SPA Papers.

33. Among those union leaders lost as a result of the purge of June 1913 were George Curry, former president of the Butte Miners' Union, and Patrick Deloughery and Harry Lappin, both former presidents of the Butte Engineers' Union.

34. *Montana Socialist*, February 22, April 5, August 11, 1914.

35. *Montana Socialist*, August 3, 1913. In a similar vein, a national party organ reported: "The Socialist Administration of Butte, Mont., has issued a compiled statement showing that this year $300,000 of public work is being done, or is contracted for. Sidewalks are being built in the working class districts where before people traveled in the mud . . ." (Chicago) *Party Builder*, no. 43 (August 13, 1913).

36. *Montana Socialist*, November 2, 1913.

37. Butte City Council Records, vol. 16, pp. 34, 36, 45, 52, 54; *Revised Ordinances*, 443-444; *Butte Miner*, October 19, 1913; *Montana Socialist*, October 19, 1913.

38. Butte City Council Records, vol. 16, pp. 90-92, 103; *Montana Socialist*, December 28, 1913, January 11, February 1, 1914; *Butte Miner*, January 22, January 30, February 1, 1914.

39. *Montana Socialist*, November 2, 1913.

40. Butte City Council Records, vol. 16, p. 93; *Anaconda Standard*, December 23, December 27, 1913; *Montana Socialist*, April 5, 1914.

41. *Anaconda Standard*, October 15, October 16, November 30, 1913.

42. Butte City Council Records, vol. 16, pp. 105-106; *Montana Socialist*, February 1, February 8, 1914; *Butte Miner*, February 4, February 5, 1914.

43. *Montana Socialist*, March 8, 1914.

44. *Montana Socialist*, April 12, 1914.

45. Turnout of registered voters was lowest in the First, Third, and Fifth wards, which had the highest proportion of miners among the city's eight wards. See Chapter 6.

46. *Anaconda Standard*, April 7, 1914; *Butte Miner*, April 7, 1914; *Montana Socialist*, April 12, April 19, 1914.

Chapter 6: *Class and Community*

1. Weinstein, *The Decline of Socialism*, 84-118; "Socialist Municipal Office Holders," 492-500.

2. Morris Hillquit, *Socialism in Theory and Practice* (New York: Macmillan Company, 1913), 153-154.

3. Irish ethnic solidarity was reinforced by a common hatred of all things British, which contributed to tensions among the Irish and the immigrant population from Cornwall, who were Protestant, British, and Republican. See A. L. Rowse, *The Cousin Jacks: The Cornish in America* (New York: Charles Scribner's Sons, 1969), 351-354, 358-360; WPA Writers' Project, *Copper Camp*, 55-59; Glasscock, *War of the Copper Kings*, 132-136.

4. Richard K. O'Malley, *Mile High, Mile Deep* (Missoula: Mountain Press Publishing Company, 1971), 1-2.

5. *Anaconda Standard*, October 30, November 1, November 7, 1910.

6. *Anaconda Standard*, November 1, 1910.

7. *Butte Evening News*, July 24, 1910.

8. Quoted in Gerald Rosenblum, *Immigrant Workers: Their Impact on American Labor Radicalism* (New York: Basic Books, 1973), 146.

9. Jacob Ostberg, *Sketches of Old Butte* (Butte: n.p., 1972), 83.

10. Ibid., 23-24, 83-94. See also Helen Sanders, "Butte—The Heart of the Copper Country," *Overland Monthly* 48 (November 1906): 383.

11. *Thirteenth Census of the United States, vol. IV: Population, 1910*, 304-305; State of Montana, *First Biennial Report of the Department of Labor and Industry, 1913-1914*, 206.

12. Wayland D. Hand et al., "Songs of the Butte Miners," *Western Folklore* 9 (January 1950): 26.

13. *Butte Evening News*, July 24, 1910.

14. *Thirteenth Census of the United States, vol. IV: Population, 1910*, 305, 484. The nativity of shift bosses was derived by cross-referencing the 1912 *Butte City Directory* with the *Great Register of Butte City—1913*, Butte-Silver Bow Public Archives. The *Great Register* is a two-volume ledger that lists more than ten thousand voters and their occupations, nativities, and lengths of residence in Butte. Although only adult male citizens are listed, we can assume that the bulk of naturalized foreign-born males lived in the neighborhoods of their fellow countrymen. For example, the largest number of Finnish registrants were in Ward 3, the center of Finntown.

15. Data derived from the *Great Register of Butte City—1913*.

16. Lists of precinct delegates and alternates as well as candidates and central committee members are taken from the *Daily Inter Mountain*, August 24, September 2, 1912; *Anaconda Standard*, October 2, October 4, 1912; *Butte Miner*, November 4, 1912.

17. Membership Record of Butte Local No. 1, Socialist Party of Montana (ca. 1913-1915), Montana State College of Mineral Science and Technology, Butte. Socialist candidates and party leaders are listed in *Anaconda Standard*, September 28, 1912, and *Butte Miner*, November 4, 1912.

18. *Butte Miner*, February 4, 1914; *Montana Socialist*, February 8, 1914.

19. Marc Karson, *American Labor Unions and Politics, 1900-1920* (Carbondale: Southern Illinois University Press, 1958), 215-218.

20. Marc Karson and Philip Foner noted that many of the leaders of the American Federation of Labor were Catholics and argued that the AFL's political conservatism was reinforced by the con-

servatism of the Catholic church, especially the church's anti-Socialist stance. Karson, *American Labor Unions and Politics*, Chapter 9; Foner, *Policies and Practices of the American Federation of Labor*, Chapter 5. Henry J. Browne disagrees. See the exchange between Browne and Karson in John Laslett and Seymour Martin Lipset, eds., *Failure of a Dream: Essays in the History of American Socialism* (Garden City, New York: Anchor Press/Doubleday, 1974), 164-184.

21. *Anaconda Standard*, March 27, April 1, 1912.

22. *Butte Miner*, July 22, 1912, September 7, 1914.

23. Father W. J. Madden quoted in (Butte) *Montana Catholic*, September 1903.

24. *Butte Miner*, November 5, 1912.

25. *Montana Socialist*, June 1, September 28, 1913.

26. Louis Duncan, "Mayor Duncan of Butte Replies to Catholic Bishop," *International Socialist Review* 13 (October 1912): 327.

27. *Montana Socialist*, August 31, 1913.

28. Data derived from the *Great Register of Butte City – 1913*. No county registration records exist for the period covered, so no precise demographic analysis of the county precincts can be done. All county registration records prior to 1934 were destroyed as mandated by a law enacted by the state legislature. This analysis used demographic data from twenty-seven Butte precincts, which were correlated to the level of support the Socialist Party received in the 1912 general election. By examining each precinct's social environment some fairly precise generalizations can be made about the level and source of support enjoyed by the Socialists during the campaign.

29. The relationship between Irish voters and the Democratic Party in the 1912 election was also examined using a correlation coefficient, which measures the degree to which two or more variables associate with each other in either a positive or negative direction. The higher the value of the coefficient, the stronger is the association. Looking at twenty-seven Butte precincts and comparing the percentage of Irish voters with the percentage of the Democratic vote in 1912, the correlation between the vote for Wilson and the proportion of Irish voters was .73, a strong and statistically significant association. In comparison, the correlation between the vote for Debs and Irish nativity was small, at .18, while the correlation between the Republican vote (Taft) and Irish nationality was negative, at -.57. The correlation coefficients here simply reinforce the image drawn from the comparison of the three communities, especially the precincts in Northeast Butte.

Chapter 7: *Something Rotten in Gibraltar*

1. *Anaconda Standard*, June 14, 1913.

2. Lingenfelter, *Hardrock Miners*, 182-188, 193-195; Richard F. Peterson, *The Bonanza Kings: The Social Origins and Business Behavior of the Western Mining Entrepreneurs, 1870-1900* (Lincoln: University of Nebraska Press, 1977), 81-85; Vernon H. Jensen, *Heritage of Conflict: Labor Relations in the Nonferrous Metals Industry up to 1930* (Ithaca, New York: Cornell University Press, 1950), 289-292.

3. Jensen, *Heritage of Conflict*, 297; testimony of Clarence Smith, Dan D. Sullivan, and Joseph Shannon, "Mining Conditions in Butte," 3734, 3768-3771, 3854.

4. *Anaconda Standard*, August 20, 1901; *Great Falls Tribune*, August 26, 1904.

5. WFM, *Official Proceedings of the Thirteenth Annual Convention of the Western Federation of Miners, May 22-June 9, 1905*, 233-234, 344-345.

6. WFM, *Official Proceedings of the Fourteenth Annual Convention of the Western Federation of Miners, May 28-June 3, 1906*, 14, 30-31, 100-101, 127-128, 148, 158, 210-211, 213-214, 242, 285; *Miners Magazine*, June 14, June 28, July 26, 1906; Jensen, *Heritage of Conflict*, 298-302.

7. WFM, *Official Proceedings of the Fifteenth Annual Convention of the Western Federation of Miners, June 10-July 2, 1907*, 32, 153-154, 307-310, 314-318, 320-328, 330-331, 334-335, 352; *Miners Magazine*, August 1, August 15, 1907.

8. WFM, *Proceedings of the Fifteenth Annual Convention*, 372-391, 810-811.

9. See Dubofsky, *We Shall Be All*, 110-119.

10. WFM, *Official Proceedings of the Sixteenth Annual Convention of the Western Federation of Miners, July 13-July 29, 1908*, 18-19; WFM, *Official Proceedings of the Seventeenth Annual Convention of the Western Federation of Miners, July 12-August 3, 1909*, 20-21.

11. WFM, *Proceedings of the Fifteenth Annual Convention*, 252-253, 260-261, 486, 488, 700-701, 796-799. See also Jensen, *Heritage of Conflict*, 306-310.

12. WFM, *Proceedings of the Seventeenth Annual Convention*, 287-289, 419-422.

13. *Miners Magazine*, March 3, 1910.

14. WFM, *Official Proceedings of the Eighteenth Annual Convention of the Western Federation of Miners, July 18-August 1, 1910*, 296-303, 370; WFM, *Official Proceedings of the Nineteenth Annual Convention of the Western Federation of Miners, July 17-August 4, 1911*, 37-38; *Miners Magazine*, March 10, June 10, December 15, 1910, February 1, 1911.

15. *Miners Magazine*, September 7, 1911, May 30, 1912; WFM, *Proceedings of the Nineteenth Annual Convention*, 38-39, 229, 294, 297.

16. WFM, *Proceedings of the Nineteenth Annual Convention*, 39-40, 209-210, 241.

17. *Miners Magazine*, September 7, 1911, May 30, 1912; WFM, *Official Proceedings of the Twentieth Annual Convention of the Western Federation of Miners, July 15-26, 1912*, 12-14.

18. "Butte Miners' Union," *International Socialist Review* 12 (February 1912): 520.

19. "Butte Heard from Again," *International Socialist Review* 12 (October 1911): 250-251; Frank Bohn, "Butte," *International Socialist Review* 13 (August 1912): 127; testimony of Dennis Murphy and Joseph Shannon, "Mining Conditions at Butte," 3737-3738, 3856.

20. Testimony of Joseph Shannon, "Mining Conditions at Butte," 3854. For data on copper prices during this period, see Thomas R. Navin, *Copper Mining and Management* (Tucson: University of Arizona Press, 1978), 400.

21. Testimony of Clarence Smith and John D. Pope (general manager of the North Butte Mining Company), "Mining Conditions at Butte," 3717, 3726-3729, 3744, 3746-3747; *Työmies*, March 26, March 27, 1912. Published at Hancock, Michigan, *Työmies* was the daily newspaper of the Finnish Socialist Federation's central district. I would like to thank Timo Riippa of the University of Minnesota for his translations.

22. *Anaconda Standard*, March 23, March 26, 1912; *Butte Miner*, March 24, March 26, 1912; WFM, *Proceedings of the Twentieth Convention*, 221-223; testimony of Clarence Smith and Dan D. Sullivan, "Mining Conditions at Butte," 3730, 3765.

23. See the testimony of Jacob Oliver, "Mining Conditions at Butte," 3785-3786.

24. *Työmies*, April 7, 1912. See also statement of John Valimaki, WFM, *Proceedings of the Twentieth Annual Convention*, 251; testimony of Delegate Joyce, statement of Frank Aaltonen, WFM, *Proceedings of the Twenty-First Consecutive and First Biennial Convention of the Western Federation of Miners, July 20-August 3, 1914*, 151, 190, 191; report by A. O. Sarell, *Työmies*, April 24, 1912. Sarell was a reporter sent to Butte to investigate the conflict.

25. *Työmies*, April 4, 1912.

26. *Työmies*, April 3, April 4, April 7, 1912; *Anaconda Standard*, March 29, March 30, March 31, April 1, 1912.

27. In the miners' rejection of the strike call, the ethnic hostility of the older immigrant Cornish and Irish toward the Finns seems to have been a major factor. Testimony of Jacob Oliver, "Mining Conditions at Butte," 3785-3786; *Työmies*, April 7, April 16, 1912.

28. WFM, *Proceedings of the Twentieth Annual Convention*, 21-24, 258, 260, 335; *Industrial Worker*, April 18, 1912; "Smashing Us in Butte," *International Socialist Review* 12 (June 1912): 885; *Työmies*, April 16, April 24, 1912.

29. *Anaconda Standard*, May 15, June 3, June 5, June 8, 1912; *Butte Miner*, May 25, June 5, June 8, 1912; WFM, *Proceedings of the Twentieth Annual Convention*, 219-220.

30. WFM, *Proceedings of the Twentieth Annual Convention*, 11-12, 24, 216, 219, 221-229, 231-234, 249, 266, 315, 328-329, 330-331, 337, 341, 343-344, 359-360.

31. Kelley Exhibit No. 7, "Mining Conditions at Butte," 3880-3882; testimony of Con Kelley and Joseph Shannon, "Mining Conditions at Butte," 3896-3897, 3857; *Anaconda Standard*, June 26, June 27, June 29, June 30, 1912, December 20, 1914.

32. Paul F. Brissenden, "The Butte Miners and the Rustling Card," *American Economic Review* 10 (December 1920): 761-763.

33. *Anaconda Standard*, December 7, 1912; *Butte Miner*, December 7, 1912; *Solidarity*, December 28, 1912; George Tompkins, *The Truth About Butte* (Butte: n.p., 1917), 8-13.

34. *Butte Miner*, December 11, December 20, December 21, December 22, 1912; *Anaconda Standard*, December 20, 1912; testimony of Dan D. Sullivan, "Mining Conditions at Butte," 3767; *Industrial Worker*, January 13, 1913.

35. *Butte Miner*, June 4, June 8, June 11, 1913.

36. *Industrial Worker*, June 19, 1913.

Chapter 8: *The Destruction of the Butte Miners' Union*

1. *Anaconda Standard*, May 13, May 27, 1914; testimony of Daniel Shovlin and Jacob Oliver, "Mining Conditions at Butte," 3774-3775, 3783-3784.

2. Testimony of Jacob Oliver, "Mining Conditions at Butte," 3782.

3. *Anaconda Standard*, June 3, 1914.

4. *Anaconda Standard*, May 27, May 28, 1914.

5. *Anaconda Standard*, June 3, 1914; Daniel O'Regan, "The Situation at Butte, Montana," October 7, 1914, Reports to the U.S. Commission on Industrial Relations, Papers of the U.S. Commission on Industrial Relations, Wisconsin State Historical Society Library, Madison.

6. O'Regan, "The Situation at Butte," 4; Tompkins, *The Truth About Butte*, 13; *Anaconda Standard*, June 13, 1914; *Butte Miner*, June 14, 1914; *Butte Daily Post*, June 14, 1914.

7. O'Regan, "The Situation at Butte," 3; Tompkins, *The Truth About Butte*, 13-14; *Anaconda Standard*, June 13, 1914; *Butte Miner*, June 13, 1914; *Daily Missoulian*, June 14, 1914. In the 1913-1914 fiscal year, the Butte Miners' Union had been assessed $138,825.60, a large portion of which was earmarked for support of the WFM strike in Michigan. The BMU's share of the total WFM assessments was 35 per cent, an amount substantially in excess of the union's claimed membership in relation to the total membership of the WFM. WFM, "Report of the Secretary-Treasurer of the Western Federation of Miners for the Fiscal Year Ending June 30, 1914," in WFM, *Proceedings of the Twenty-First Consecutive Convention and First Biennial Convention*, 63. For an analysis of Butte and the Michigan strike, see Arthur W. Thurner, "The Western Federation of Miners in Two Copper Camps: The Impact of the Michigan Copper Miners' Strike on Butte's Local No. 1," *Montana the Magazine of Western History* 33 (Spring 1983): 34-45.

8. O'Regan, "The Situation at Butte," 6-9; Tompkins, *The Truth About Butte*, 14-15; *Anaconda Standard*, June 14, 1914; *Butte Miner*, June 14, 1914; *Butte Daily Post*, June 13, 1914; *Solidarity*, June 27, 1914; WPA Writers' Project, *Copper Camp*, 60-64; Jensen, *Heritage of Conflict*, 328-329; State of Montana, *First Biennial Report of the Department of Labor and Industry*, 26-27.

9. Sheriff Tim Driscoll to Governor Samuel V. Stewart, June 14, 1914, Stewart to Major McGuiness, Stewart to President Woodrow Wilson, June 14, June 15, June 17, 1914, MC 35, Box 180, "Report of the Adjutant General of the State of Montana, December 1, 1912 to November 30, 1914," MC 35, Box 239, Montana Governors' Papers, Montana Historical Society Archives, Helena [MHSA]; *Anaconda Standard*, June 15, June 16, June 17, 1914; *Butte Miner*, June 15, 1914.

10. *Anaconda Standard*, June 15, 1914; testimony of Daniel Shovlin and Jacob Oliver, "Mining Conditions at Butte," 3773-3776, 3781-3782; *Butte Miner*, July 1, 1914; *Montana Socialist*, June 21, 1914. See also *Milwaukee Leader*, June 16, 1914; *Daily Missoulian*, June 15, 1914.

11. Testimony of Daniel Shovlin and Jacob Oliver, "Mining Conditions at Butte," 3774-3776, 3784-3785; O'Regan, "The Situation at Butte," 2; WFM, *Proceedings of the Twenty-First Consecutive and First Biennial Convention*, 144-145. See also Frank Bohn, "Butte Number One," *The Masses* 5 (August 1914): 9-11; William Z. Foster, "The Miners' Revolt at Butte," *Mother Earth* 9 (September 1914): 216-217.

12. M. Rhea, "The Revolt in Butte," *The New Review* 2 (September 1914): 542. Further evidence concerning the union's inattention to miners' grievances can be found in the testimony of John Gillie, the ACM Company's manager of mines, and Dennis Murphy, conservative president of the Butte Miners' Union in 1912-1913. See "Mining Conditions at Butte," 3707-3708, 3740. See also the testimony of John Vickers and Joseph Guelfi, both progressive officers in the union in 1911, in Kelley Exhibit No. 12, "Mining Conditions at Butte," 3924-3925, 3933-3935.

13. *Milwaukee Leader*, June 18, 1914.

14. *Miners Magazine*, June 25, 1914.

15. *Butte Miner*, October 2, 1914; *Anaconda Standard*, November 24, 1914.

16. *Anaconda Standard*, June 20, June 21, 1914; WFM, *Proceedings of the Twenty-First Consecutive and First Biennial Convention*, 50-51.

17. *Anaconda Standard*, June 14, June 18, June 19, June 22, 1914; *Butte Miner*, June 18, June 23, 1914.

18. *Miners Magazine*, June 25, 1914.

19. *Montana Socialist*, July 12, 1914; testimony of Daniel Shovlin and Jacob Oliver, "Mining Conditions at Butte," 3776-3777, 3785.

20. Statements made by BMU leaders can be found in the *Butte Miner*, June 15, June 23, July 1, 1914, and the *Daily Missoulian*, June 16, 1914.

21. *Anaconda Standard*, June 21, June 23, 1914; *Montana Socialist*, June 28, 1914.

22. *Anaconda Standard*, June 24, 1914; *Butte Miner*, June 24, 1914; *Daily Missoulian*, June 24, 1914.

23. *Daily Missoulian*, June 24, 1914; Tompkins, *The Truth About Butte*, 15-16; *Butte Daily Post*, June 24, 1914; *Engineering and Mining Journal*, July 4, 1914; *Montana Socialist*, June 28, 1914; State of Montana, *First Biennial Report of the Department of Labor and Industry*, 27-28; O'Regan, "The Situation at Butte," 10.

24. Duncan is quoted in the *Anaconda Standard*, September 25, 1914. See also *Montana Socialist*, June 28, 1914.

25. *Montana Socialist*, September 26, 1914; Stewart to President Woodrow Wilson, June 23, 1914, Stewart to Senator Henry L. Myers, June 23, 1914, Box 180, Montana Governors' Papers, MHSA.

26. *Miners Magazine*, June 25, July 9, 1914; WFM, *Twenty-First Consecutive and First Biennial Convention*, 64-65, 106-108, 114, 123-126, 146, 192.

27. *Montana Socialist*, July 5, 1914. See Clarence Smith's reply in the *Miners Magazine*, July 30, 1914.

28. *Anaconda Standard*, July 3, July 4, 1914; *Butte Miner*, July 3, July 4, July 7, 1914; Stewart to Senator Thomas J. Walsh, July 13, 1914, Box 180, Montana Governors' Papers, MHSA.

29. *Anaconda Standard*, July 5, July 20, August 11, 1914; *Butte Miner*, July 4, July 9, July 20, August 10, 1914; *Miners Magazine*, July 16, 1914.

30. *Anaconda Standard*, August 1, 1914; testimony of Con Kelley, "Mining Conditions at Butte," 3692; *Engineering and Mining Journal*, August 8, August 29, 1914.

31. *Anaconda Standard*, August 25, August 27, August 29, 1914; *Butte Miner*, August 27, August 28, August 29, 1914; *Butte Daily Post*, August 26, August 27, August 28, 1914; *Engineering and Mining Journal*, September 5, September 12, 1914; State of Montana, *First Biennial Report of the Department of Labor and Industry*, 29-31; O'Regan, "The Situation at Butte," 18-20; Tompkins, *The Truth About Butte*, 15.

32. William D. Haywood, "The Battle of Butte," *International Socialist Review* 15 (October 1914): 223-224; *Anaconda Standard*, August 27, 1914; State of Montana, *First Biennial Report of the Department of Labor and Industry*, 30-31.

33. Regarding the hiring of additional guards by the ACM Company, see *Engineering and Mining Journal*, July 11, 1914; O'Regan to Dr. Charles McCarthy, October 10, 1914, Reports to the U.S. Commission on Industrial Relations, Papers of the U.S. Commission on Industrial Relations. The Company's decision to shut down its mines rather than recognize the new union was reported in the *Daily Missoulian*, August 27, August 28, 1914.

34. *Daily Missoulian*, August 28, 1914; *Helena Independent*, August 30, 1914; James H. Rowe to Stewart, August 28, 1914, Stewart to Driscoll, August 29, 1914, Stewart to Duncan, August 29, 1914, Driscoll to Stewart, August 29, 1914, Duncan to Stewart, August 29, 1914, Box 180, Montana Governors' Papers, MHSA.

35. Stewart to Major Dan Donohue, August 28, 1914, Stewart to Myers, August 27, 1914, Stewart to Walsh, telegram, August 28, 1914, Box 180, Montana Governors' Papers, MHSA.

36. *Anaconda Standard*, August 30, August 31, 1914; *Butte Miner*, August 30, 1914; Stewart to Brigadier General Phil Greenan, August 30, 1914, Box 239, 12-15, Montana Governors' Papers, MHSA.

37. Duncan to Stewart, September 1, 1914, Albert Meisser to Stewart, August 31, 1914, John Niva to Stewart, August 31, 1914, Box 180, Montana Governors' Papers, MHSA.

38. *Anaconda Standard*, September 2, September 3, September 10, 1914; *Butte Miner*, September 2, September 3, September 4, 1914; "Report of the Adjutant General," Box 239, 15-16, Montana Governors' Papers, MHSA; Stewart to Walsh, September 4, 1914, Box 191, Papers of Senator Thomas J. Walsh, Library of Congress, Washington, D.C. [Walsh Papers]; State of Montana, *First Biennial Report of the Department of Labor and Industry*, 33; Haywood, "The Battle of Butte," 25; *Solidarity*, September 12, September 19, 1914.

39. *Butte Mine Workers' Union Bulletin*, September 5, 1914. See also the *Butte Socialist*, September 5, 1914; *Montana Socialist*, September 19, October 3, 1914; (Chicago) *The American Socialist*, September 12, 1914; Tompkins, *The Truth About Butte*, 22-23.

40. *Anaconda Standard*, September 2, September 3, September 5, September 9, 1914; *Butte Miner*, September 3, September 4, September 11, 1914.

41. *Anaconda Standard*, September 6, September 9, September 23, September 25, September 30, October 2, 1914; *Butte Miner*, September 9, September 11, 1914; *Butte Socialist*, October 10, 1914.

42. William Tuohy to Stewart, September 11, 1914, Charles Austin to Stewart, September 20, 1914, Box 180, Montana Governors' Papers, MHSA; John D. Ryan to Walsh, September 17, 1914, Box 191, Walsh Papers.

43. Frank Jones, Hotel and Restaurant Employees International Alliance, Local 101, to Stewart, September 10, 1914, Claude Bartlett, Secretary, Miles City Trades and Labor Council, to Stewart, September 11, 1914, Stewart to William Bole, September 19, 1914, Box 180, Montana Governors' Papers, MHSA.

44. Walsh to Stewart, September 3, 1914, Box 191, Walsh Papers.

45. O'Regan to McCarthy, Papers of the U.S. Commission of Industrial Relations, 1-2, 9-10.

46. Ibid., 3-5; *Anaconda Standard*, September 9, September 10, September 21, October 4, October 6, 1914; *Butte Miner*, September 10, September 14, September 20, September 22, September 27, October 14, 1914; *Solidarity*, October 10, 1914; Maury to Walsh, September 11, 1914, Box 191, Walsh Papers.

47. *Butte Socialist*, October 10, 1914; *Helena Independent*, October 9, 1914.

48. *Anaconda Standard*, January 15, 1915.

49. *Anaconda Standard*, January 16, January 18, 1915; *Butte Miner*, January 18, 1915.

50. *Solidarity*, January 30, 1915.

51. *Montana Socialist*, December 19, 1914, February 13, 1915; *Anaconda Standard*, January 15, January 16, January 20, 1915; George Tompkins to Walsh, January 23, 1915, Walsh to Tompkins, February 1, 1915, Box 191, Walsh Papers.

52. *Anaconda Standard*, November 18, November 19, November 20, November 21, November 22, 1914; *Solidarity*, December 5, 1914.

53. *Bozeman Daily Chronicle*, December 8, December 9, 1914; *Anaconda Standard*, November 15, 1914.

54. *Anaconda Standard*, September 7, September 11, October 2, October 23, 1914; *Butte Miner*, September 7, September 25, October 2, October 21, October 22, 1914; Jensen, *Heritage of Conflict*, 350, 379, 402, 412. Corporate espionage directed against labor unionism was a common practice, and both the Socialists and the insurgent union leaders believed that private detectives had infiltrated the union. See *Montana Socialist*, September 15, 1914, March 13, 1915; *Solidarity*, September 26, 1914.

55. Jensen, *Heritage of Conflict*, 338, 346-347.

56. The Bradley letters were quoted in the *Butte Miner*, October 6, 1914, and the *Butte Daily Post*, October 16, 1914.

57. *Butte Miner*, June 14, 1911.

Chapter 9: *Vindication and Defeat*

1. *Montana Socialist*, January 2, 1915.

2. The Socialists opposed the commission form of city government and the attendant at-large election of commissioners and the nonpartisan ballot. Such devices, the Socialists argued, were designed to ensure the hegemony of business in metropolitan politics and to dilute that of the working class and working-class parties. See "The Socialists and the Commission Form of Government," *National Municipal Review* 2 (January 1913): 132-133; Samuel P. Hays, "Reform in Municipal

Government," *Pacific Northwest Quarterly* 55 (October 1964): 288-306; Weinstein, *The Decline of Socialism in America*, 113-114; James Weinstein, *The Corporate Ideal in the Liberal State* (Boston: Beacon Press, 1968), 107-113; Michael Ebner, "Socialism and Progressive Political Reform: The 1911 Change-of-Government in Passaic," in Stave, *Socialism and the Cities*, 116-140.

3. *Montana Socialist*, April 12, 1914; *Daily Missoulian*, March 24, April 7, 1914. The *Montana Socialist* was published by the Butte Socialist Publishing Company.

4. "Platform of the Socialist Party of Montana—1914," State and Local Files, SPA Papers; *Daily Missoulian*, September 15, 1914.

5. See *Anaconda Standard*, November 2, November 4, 1914; *Butte Miner*, October 26, October 27, October 28, October 29, October 30, October 31, November 1, November 2, 1914.

6. *Butte American*, October 23, 1914; Louis Duncan to Carl D. Thompson, National Correspondence Files, SPA Papers.

7. *Montana Socialist*, September 26, 1914.

8. Ibid.

9. *Anaconda Standard*, November 7, 1914; *Montana Socialist*, November 7, 1914.

10. Ellis Waldron and Paul Wilson, *Atlas of Montana Elections, 1889-1976* (Missoula: University of Montana Publications in History, 1978), 54-55.

11. *Anaconda Standard*, November 1, 1914; *Butte Miner*, October 31, November 2, 1914.

12. *Montana Socialist*, November 7, 1914.

13. "Letter from a Butte Miner," *International Socialist Review* 15 (January 1915): 436, 438.

14. *Anaconda Standard*, December 14, 1914, January 11, 1915; *Butte Miner*, December 29, 1914; Butte City Council Records, vol. 16, pp. 278-281.

15. *Anaconda Standard*, December 4, 1914, January 2, January 8, 1915.

16. *Anaconda Standard*, January 21, February 22, February 25, February 28, 1915; *Butte Miner*, January 22, February 22, February 26, 1915; *Montana Socialist*, March 6, 1915.

17. *Montana Socialist*, December 14, 1914, March 13, 1915. See P. George Hummasti, "The Workingman's Daily Bread: Finnish-American Working Class Newspapers, 1900-1921," in *For the Common Good: Finnish Immigrants and the Radical Response to Industrial America*, ed. Michael Karni (Superior, Wisconsin: The Työmies Society, 1977), 167-194; Douglas J. Ollila, Jr., *The Emergence of Radical Industrial Unionism in the Finnish Socialist Movement* (Turku, Finland: Institute of General History of the University of Turku, 1975), 36-49.

18. See T. E. Latimer, "Executive Committee Rule," *International Socialist Review* 15 (February 1915): 481-485.

19. *Montana Socialist*, March 6, March 13, 1915; *Anaconda Standard*, March 3, 1915; *Butte Miner*, March 3, 1915.

20. *Anaconda Standard*, February 28, March 2, March 4, March 15, March 19, 1915; *Butte Miner*, March 2, March 4, March 10, 1915.

21. *Anaconda Standard*, March 23, March 24, 1915.

22. Butte City Council Records, vol. 16, pp. 295, 297, 315, 321; *Anaconda Standard*, January 21, January 28, February 4, February 28, 1915.

23. *Montana Socialist*, March 27, 1915.

24. *Anaconda Standard*, March 23, March 26, 1915; *Butte Miner*, March 27, 1915.

25. *Anaconda Standard*, March 25, 1915; *Butte Miner*, April 3, 1915.

26. *Butte Socialist*, April 1, 1915.

27. *Montana Socialist*, March 27, 1915.

28. *Montana Socialist*, March 6, March 27, 1915; *Butte Socialist*, April 4, 1915.

29. *Butte Miner*, March 31, 1915; *Anaconda Standard*, April 4, 1915.

30. *Anaconda Standard*, April 6, 1915.

31. *Montana Socialist*, April 10, 1915.

32. Ibid.; *Anaconda Standard*, April 8, 1913, April 6, 1915; *Montana Socialist*, April 10, 1915. More research needs to be done on the amount of electoral support that women voters gave the Socialist Party. In a Chicago aldermanic race in 1918 and in the Milwaukee school trustee elections in 1917 and 1918, for example, Socialist candidates were apparently defeated by a negative women's vote. But a national Socialist Party survey concluded that there was "no discernible pattern" in the women's vote. See Weinstein, *The Decline of Socialism in America*, 62; John D. Buenker, "The Politics

of Mutual Frustration: Socialists and Suffragists in New York and Wisconsin," in *Flawed Liberation: Socialism and Feminism*, ed. Sally M. Miller (Westport, Connecticut: Greenwood Press, 1981), 113-144. The survey is cited in Buhle, *Women and American Socialism*, 238-239.

33. *Montana Socialist*, March 4, 1916; Waldron and Wilson, *Atlas of Montana Elections*, 62, 65.

34. *Montana Socialist*, June 12, July 10, August 7, September 4, 1915.

35. *Montana Socialist*, December 18, 1915.

36. *Butte Miner*, April 4, 1916, April 3, 1917; *Montana Socialist*, February 19, 1916, March 17, 1917.

37. This was a continuing problem for local Socialist officeholders. Claude Vose (Davis, Illinois) to J. M. Barnes, July 5, 1912, C. H. Lockwood (Kalamazoo, Michigan) to Carl D. Thompson, March 13, 1913, W. A. Davis (Naticoke, Pennsylvania) to Thompson, September 8, 1913, H. L. Larson (Crookston, Minnesota) to Thompson, September 10, 1913, Samuel M. Gaylord (Cuyahoga Falls, Ohio) to Thompson, September 14, 1913, National Correspondence Files, SPA Papers. See also Frank Bohn, "The Socialist Party and the Government of Cities," *International Socialist Review* 12 (November 1911): 275-278; James R. Simmons, "The Socialist Party in Indiana, 1900-1925," in *Socialism in the Heartland: The Midwestern Experience, 1900-1925*, ed. Donald T. Critchlow (South Bend, Indiana: University of Notre Dame Press, 1986), 58.

38. H. L. Maury, "What's the Matter with Butte, Montana?" *International Socialist Review* 15 (May 1915): 684-685.

39. The Socialist Party destroyed itself in Missoula in a faction fight over patronage appointments made by the two Socialist city commissioners and the Socialist county sheriff. *Daily Missoulian*, January 18, January 24, January 27, January 28, January 29, February 2, February 4, February 7, February 8, February 15, February 16, February 18, February 22, March 9, 1915.

40. A recent re-examination of Socialism in Milwaukee came to the same conclusion. Douglas E. Booth, "Municipal Socialism and City Government Reform: The Milwaukee Experience, 1910-1940," *Journal of Urban History* 12 (November 1985): 51-74.

41. Socialist policy toward strikes is succinctly described by M. E. Kirkpatrick, "What a Socialist Administration Should Do in Time of Strike," *Party Builder*, no. 51 (October 25, 1913). For an example of Socialist behavior, see Errol W. Stevens, "Labor and Socialism in an Indiana Mill Town, 1905-1921," *Labor History* 12 (November 1985): 374.

Chapter 10: *STRIKE!*

1. *Anaconda Standard*, December 12, 1915; *Solidarity*, November 5, 1915.

2. *Cost Reports of the U.S. Federal Trade Commission: Copper*, June 30, 1919, 21; *Anaconda Standard*, June 8, 1917.

3. State of Montana, *Third Biennial Report of the Department of Labor and Industry, 1917-1918*, 105-112; Tompkins, *The Truth About Butte*, 34; Abraham Glasser, "The Butte Miners' Strikes, 1917-1920," 10-14, RG 60, Records of the Department of Justice, National Archives, Washington, D.C. [Glasser File]. A typescript of Glasser's manuscript and supporting documents are also found in Microfilm Collection 439, K. Ross Toole Archives, Mansfield Library, University of Montana, Missoula. Abraham Glasser prepared this manuscript and collected the documents (which include letters, telegrams, and reports) for the Department of Justice during the late 1930s and early 1940s as a case study to illustrate how the military had been used to suppress dissent during World War I. sent during World War I.

4. State of Montana, *Second Biennial Report of the Department of Labor and Industry, 1915-1916*, 10-11.

5. *Montana Socialist*, October 23, 1915.

6. *Anaconda Standard*, June 1, June 4, June 6, 1917; *Butte Miner*, June 4, June 5, June 6, 1917.

7. *Anaconda Standard*, June 6, June 7, June 8, 1917; *Butte Miner*, June 6, June 7, June 8, 1917; Burton K. Wheeler to Attorney General, June 7, 1917, DJ 186233-61-1, Glasser File.

8. State of Montana, *Third Biennial Report of the Department of Labor and Industry*, 17, 21-22; Arnon Gutfeld, "The Speculator Disaster in 1917: Labor Resurgence at Butte, Montana," *Arizona and the West* 11 (Spring 1969): 27-30.

9. Gutfeld, "The Speculator Disaster," 31-32; State of Montana, *Third Biennial Report of the Department of Labor and Industry*, 18-19.

10. William Stoddard et al. to Secretary of Labor William B. Wilson, June 23, 1917, DL 33-493, Glasser File; *Anaconda Standard*, June 13, 1917; *Montana Socialist*, June 16, 1917; *Solidarity*, June 30, 1917. All of the men who signed the new union's list of demands, except Tom Campbell, had been leaders of the ill-fated Butte Mine Workers' Union of 1914; Campbell had led the progressive insurgency against Moyer and his leadership of the Western Federation of Miners in 1912. Since the June 1914 riots, which had destroyed the Butte Miners' Union, the WFM's (now the International Union of Mine, Mill and Smelter Workers) only affiliate in Butte had been the Butte Engineers' Union. The miners had been without a union for three years. The leaders of the Metal Mine Workers' Union hoped to fill that need.

11. *Anaconda Standard*, June 13, 1917.

12. *Anaconda Standard*, June 15, June 16, June 17, June 18, 1917.

13. *Anaconda Standard*, June 13, 1917; *Montana Socialist*, July 7, 1917.

14. Gutfeld, "The Speculator Disaster," 34-35; *Anaconda Standard*, June 16, June 17, June 20, 1917; "The Butte Miners' Strikes, 1917-1920," 34-35, Glasser File; State of Montana, *Third Biennial Report of the Department of Labor and Industry*, 19.

15. Arnon Gutfeld, *Montana's Agony: Years of War and Hysteria, 1917-1920* (Gainesville: University of Florida Social Science Monographs, 1979), 19-20; *Anaconda Standard*, June 16, June 17, June 18, June 20, June 23, June 24, June 25, 1917; *Montana Socialist*, June 30, 1917; *Miners and Electrical Workers' Joint Strike Bulletin*, July 4, 1917 [*Miners' Strike Bulletin*]. The *Strike Bulletin* appeared under various titles from its inception in mid-June 1917 until the end of the strike in December of that year. In December, the bulletin became a regular weekly labor paper, the *Butte Weekly Bulletin*. In August 1918, the *Butte Weekly Bulletin* became a daily newspaper, the *Butte Daily Bulletin*.

16. *Anaconda Standard*, June 15, 1917; John Doran et. al. to Congresswoman Jeannette Rankin, June 20, 1917, MC 147, Box 1, Jeannette Rankin Papers, MHSA [Rankin Papers].

17. *Anaconda Standard*, June 20, June 21, June 25, June 27, June 28, July 6, July 8, 1917.

18. *Anaconda Standard*, July 8, July 9, July 10, July 11, July 12, 1917; *Miners' Strike Bulletin*, July 12, 1917; *Montana Socialist*, July 14, 1917; State of Montana, *Third Biennial Report of the Department of Labor and Industry*, 20.

19. *Anaconda Standard*, July 4, 1917; *Montana Socialist*, July 7, 1917; "Resolution Adopted by the Miners of Butte, July 3, 1917," Rankin Papers.

20. *Miners' Strike Bulletin*, July 4, 1917.

21. Malone and Roeder, *Montana*, 215.

22. Gutfeld, *Montana's Agony*, 50-52. Rankin's speech is quoted in the *Industrial Worker*, September 19, 1917.

23. Mary O'Neill to Rankin, July 26, 1917, Rankin to O'Neill, July 27, 1917, O'Neill to Rankin, July 28, 1917, Rankin Papers.

24. Con Kelley to Rankin, August 12, 1917, Rankin Papers.

25. Gutfeld, *Montana's Agony*, 20-22; *Anaconda Standard*, July 15, 1917; *Miners' Strike Bulletin*, July 18, 1917.

26. *Anaconda Standard*, July 14, July 15, 1917; "The Butte Miners' Strikes, 1917-1920," 35-37, Glasser File.

27. "The Butte Miners' Strikes, 1917-1920," 34-35, 37, 42, Glasser File; *Miners' Strike Bulletin*, July 18, July 31, 1917.

28. *Miners' Strike Bulletin*, July 18, August 2, 1917.

29. *Miners' Strike Bulletin*, July 18, 1917; telegram, Edward Bassett to Rankin, July 13, 1917, Rankin Papers.

30. Rankin to President Wilson, July 14, 1917, J. P. Tummulty to Rankin, July 16, 1917, Rankin to Bassett, July 17, 1917, O'Neill to Rankin, July 30, 1917, Rankin Papers.

31. *Miners' Strike Bulletin*, August 6, August 25, 1917; *Solidarity*, July 21, 1917.

32. Arnon Gutfeld, "The Murder of Frank Little: Labor Agitation in Butte, Montana, 1917," *Labor History* 10 (Spring 1969): 183-186.

33. *Anaconda Standard*, July 21, 1917.

34. Ibid.

35. Burton K. Wheeler, *Yankee from the West* (Garden City, New York: Doubleday and Company, 1962), 139-140. The Espionage Act is described in Robert K. Murray, *Red Scare: A Study of National Hysteria, 1919-1920* (New York: McGraw-Hill, 1964), 13-14.

36. Gutfeld, "The Murder of Frank Little," 177-178, 187.

37. *Miners' Strike Bulletin*, August 2, 1917.

38. Wheeler, *Yankee from the West*, 184; *Butte Bulletin*, July 20, 1923.

39. "The Butte Miners' Strikes, 1917-1920," 48, Glasser File; Gutfeld, "The Murder of Frank Little," 188; Tompkins, *The Truth About Butte*, 140; *Miners' Strike Bulletin*, August 6, 1917; *Montana Socialist*, August 11, 1917; "The Man Who Was Hung," *International Socialist Review* 18 (September 1917): 135-138.

40. Wheeler to Attorney General, August 21, 1917, DJ 186701-27, Glasser File; *Miners' Strike Bulletin*, August 4, August 25, 1917. A few years later, the *Butte Bulletin* published the recollections of "Jim Browne," who had acted as an undercover operative during the war. "Browne" remembered that both Campbell and Shannon had come close to being murdered themselves. *Butte Bulletin*, August 25, September 1, 1922.

41. *Miners' Strike Bulletin*, August 6, August 11, August 23, September 15, September 17, September 21, 1917; *Montana Socialist*, August 25, 1917; O'Neill to Rankin, Rankin Papers; "The Butte Miners' Strikes, 1917-1920," 68-69, Glasser File; State of Montana, *Third Biennial Report of the Department of Labor and Industry*, 21.

42. *Miners' Strike Bulletin*, September 6, 1917; O'Neill to Rankin, September 6, 1917, Rankin Papers.

43. Secretary of Labor Wilson to Rankin, August 14, 1917, Rankin to Wilson, November 23, November 27, 1917, William G. Sullivan to Rankin, December 8, 1917, Rankin to Secretary of Labor Wilson, December 10, 1917, Rankin Papers.

44. Tompkins to Rankin, October 22, 1917, Rankin Papers.

45. *Industrial Worker*, December 29, 1917.

46. Gutfeld, *Montana's Agony*, 81-84; Governor Stewart to Attorney General A. Mitchell Palmer, April 20, 1910, MC 35, Box 24, Stewart Correspondence, Montana Governors' Papers, MHSA [Stewart Correspondence]. This motto is quoted from *Butte Bulletin*, January 1, 1920.

47. *Industrial Worker*, February 16, 1918. For Embree's career, see Stanley I. Phipps, "A. S. Embree: Labor Leader and Prisoner of Conscience," *The Speculator* 2 (Summer 1985): 35-41.

48. Concerning the ethnic composition of the work force in the Butte mines during the war, see DL 18233-61-30, Exhibits E, F, and G, Glasser File. See also *Solidarity*, June 16, 1917.

49. J. H. Rowe to John H. Smith, Chief Naturalization Examiner at Seattle, January 31, 1918, DJ 186233-61-19, Glasser File. Alley is quoted in a report filed by Thomas Barker, a special representative of the Department of Labor. Barker's report is contained in the U.S. Bureau of Investigation file OG 29156, U.S. Bureau of Investigation Investigative Records, RG 65, National Archives, Washington, D.C. [BI Records]. The investigative records filed by local agents of the Bureau of Investigation (later named the FBI) during the 1917-1920 period are an invaluable source on radical activities in Butte.

50. Gutfeld, *Montana's Agony*, 42-43, 61-62; *Report of the Montana Council of Defense, January 28, 1919*, RS 19, Box 4, Records of the Montana Council of Defense, MHSA [Montana Council of Defense Records].

51. *Statutes at Large of the United States, vol 40: April 1917 to March 1919* (Washington, D.C.: Government Printing Office, 1919), 217-231, 531-532, 545, 553-554, 884; Dubofsky, *We Shall Be All*, 450-451; Gutfeld, *Montana's Agony*, 46-48; William Preston, Jr., *Aliens and Dissenters: Federal Suppression of Radicals, 1903-1933* (New York: Harper and Row, 1966), 182-183.

52. Report of Special Agent Charles L. Tyman, July 13, 1918, OG 187254, BI Records. For an analysis of the origin and development of the BI's political surveillance activities, see David Williams, "The Bureau of Investigation and Its Critics, 1919-1921: The Origins of Federal Political Surveillance," *Journal of American History* 68 (December 1981): 560-579.

53. "The Butte Miners' Strikes, 1917-1920," 49-51, 55-56, 58-59, 66, Glasser File.

54. Gutfeld, *Montana's Agony*, 37-41, 44-46, 57-59; Wheeler, *Yankee from the West*, 138-139, 152, 156-164.

55. *Anaconda Standard*, March 15, March 18, 1918; *Industrial Worker*, March 23, March 30, April 6, 1918; "The Butte Miners' Strikes, 1917-1920," 80-82, 88, Glasser File.

56. "The Butte Miners' Strikes, 1917-1920," 91, Glasser File. On the growing tensions between the two unions, see *Industrial Worker*, April 27, 1918; testimony of Bill Dunne, in the *Testimony at Hearings Held at the State Capital, Helena, Montana, May 31, June 1-2, 1918, by the Montana Council of*

Defense, in Connection with the Arrest of Von Waldru, Alias Charles Store, and also in Connection with the Charges Against Oscar Rohn, p. 1363, RS 19, Box 6, Montana Council of Defense Records.

Chapter 11: *To the Anaconda Road*

1. Ralph Chaplin, "The Picket Line of Blood: Another Red Chapter of Labor History from Butte, Mont.," *One Big Union Monthly* 2 (June 1920): 9.

2. Dubofsky, *We Shall Be All*, 427-438, 450-452.

3. Special Agent Charles L. Tyman to Spokane BI office, August 23, 1918, Agent-in-Charge F. W. Byrn to the Spokane BI office, September 4, 1918, OG 45728, BI Records.

4. Byrn to A. Bruce Bielaski, Chief of the Bureau of Investigation, October 1, 1918, OG 291596, BI Records.

5. Ibid.; *Anaconda Standard*, September 10, September 14, 1918; *Butte Bulletin*, September 10, 1918.

6. Byrn to Bielaski, October 1, 1918, OG 291596, BI Records; "The Butte Miners' Strikes, 1917-1920," 180-181, Glasser File.

7. *Butte Bulletin*, September 13, September 16, 1918; *Anaconda Standard*, September 14, 1918; State of Montana, *Third Biennial Report of the Department of Labor and Industry*, 23; "The Butte Miners' Strikes, 1917-1920," 173, Glasser File; Byrn to Bielaski, October 1, 1918, OG 291596, BI Records; Burton K. Wheeler to the U.S. Attorney General, October 4, 1918, AG 370.6, Glasser File.

8. Byrn to Bielaski, September 16, 1918, OG 45728, Byrn to Bielaski, October 1, 1918, OG 291596, BI Records; Wheeler to the U.S. Attorney General, October 4, 1918, AG 370.6, Glasser File.

9. "The Butte Miners' Strikes, 1917-1920," 140-142, Glasser File; *Butte Bulletin*, September 16, September 17, September 18, September 19, 1918; *Anaconda Standard*, September 18, September 21, 1918; Report of Special Agent D. H. Dickason for September 18, 1918, OG 291596, BI Records. Gillis was tried several months later. The jury could not agree on a verdict, and he was released.

10. Stewart to Crowder, September 22, 1918, Crowder to Stewart, September 22, 1918, Crowder to Stewart, September 25, 1918, MC 35, Box 18, Montana Governors' Papers, MHSA.

11. *Anaconda Standard*, September 22, September 27, 1918; *Butte Bulletin*, September 20, September 21, 1918; Wheeler, *Yankee from the West*, 161.

12. *Butte Bulletin*, September 21, September 23, 1918.

13. Wheeler, *Yankee from the West*, 161-162; *Butte Miner*, September 29, 1918; *Butte Bulletin*, September 28, 1918; report of Agent-in-Charge Byrn for September 28, 1918, OG 291596, BI Records.

14. *Butte Bulletin*, September 30, 1918.

15. Both Thorpe and Shirley were known to Military Intelligence and the Bureau of Investigation. Shirley was an operative of the Thiel Detective Agency, and Thorpe was a Pinkerton employee. Both apparently supplied information to MI as well as the ACM Company and were identified as agents "C-371" and "C-758" in the MI records. See the report of Byrn for September 28, 1918, OG 291596, BI Records; "The I.W.W. Strike in the Northwest," War Department report, January 24, 1918, G-2 10110-753, Watkins of Butte MI to MI Branch, October 7, 1918, DW 10110-890, Captain J. H. Dengel, Spokane district MI to Director of MI, November 8, November 18, 1918, DW 10110-753, Glasser File.

16. *Butte Bulletin*, December 27, 1918, January 7, 1919; State of Montana, *Fourth Biennial Report of the Department of Labor and Industry, 1919-1920*, 11.

17. *Butte Bulletin*, December 27, 1918.

18. Stewart to Major General J. F. Morrison, December 7, 1918, Morrison to Stewart, December 9, 1918, MC 35, Box 18, Montana Governors' Papers, MHSA.

19. *Butte Bulletin*, January 3, 1919; *Anaconda Standard*, February 8, February 9, 1919; "The Butte Miners' Strikes, 1917-1920," 222, 237, Glasser File.

20. Reports of Special Agent Dickason for January 6, January 18, January 20, January 22, 1919, OG 291596, BI Records.

21. *Butte Bulletin*, December 10, 1918, January 15, January 23, 1919.

22. *Butte Bulletin*, January 23, February 6, February 7, 1919; *Anaconda Standard*, February 7, 1919.

23. *Butte Bulletin*, February 7, February 8, 1919; *Anaconda Standard*, February 8, February 9, 1919; *Butte Miner*, February 8, February 9, 1919; *Solidarity*, February 22, 1919; State of Montana, *Fourth Biennial Report of the Department of Labor and Industry*, 11-12. The BI office in Butte reported that the strike was disorganized because the IWW, the Metal Mine Workers' Union, and the Workers' Council seemed unable "to form a coherent strike organization to represent the miners as a class." Report of Byrn for February 11, 1919, OG 291596, BI Records.

24. Stewart to Morrison, February 8, 1919, Morrison to Stewart, February 8, 1919, MC 35, Box 18, Montana Governors' Papers, MHSA; *Anaconda Standard*, February 9, February 10, 1919; *Butte Miner*, February 11, 1919; *Butte Bulletin*, February 10, 1919; *Solidarity*, February 22, 1919.

25. *Anaconda Standard*, February 10, February 13, 1919; *Butte Miner*, February 12, February 13, 1919; *Butte Bulletin*, February 10, February 11, February 12, February 13, 1919; *Solidarity*, February 22, 1919; Harold Lord Varney, "Butte in the Hands of the I.W.W.," *One Big Union Monthly* 1 (March 1919): 36-37; State of Montana, *Fourth Biennial Report of the Department of Labor and Industry*, 12.

26. *Butte Bulletin*, February 12, February 13, February 15, 1919; *Anaconda Standard*, February 13, 1919; *Butte Miner*, February 12, February 13, 1919; *Solidarity*, February 22, 1919; Stewart to Major A. M. Jones, February 12, 1919, Mayor W. H. Maloney to Stewart, February 14, 1919, MC 35, Box 18, Montana Governors' Papers, MHSA.

27. *Butte Bulletin*, February 17, 1919; *Anaconda Standard*, February 16, February 18, 1919; *Solidarity*, March 1, 1919; State of Montana, *Fourth Biennial Report of the Department of Labor and Industry*, 13-14; Harold Lord Varney, "Was Butte a Defeat?" *One Big Union Monthly* 1 (March 1919): 27-28.

28. *Anaconda Standard*, February 11, 1919; *Butte Miner*, February 13, 1919; *Butte Bulletin*, February 17, 1919; State of Montana, *Fourth Biennial Report of the Department of Labor and Industry*, 12-13.

29. *Butte Bulletin*, July 15, July 24, 1919; State of Montana, *Fourth Biennial Report of the Department of Labor and Industry*, 16-17.

30. Morrison to Stewart, March 29, 1919, Stewart to Morrison, April 12, 1919, MC 35, Box 18, Montana Governors' Papers. MHSA.

31. *Butte Bulletin*, June 5, July 4, July 7, July 12, 1919; State of Montana, *Fourth Biennial Report of the Department of Labor and Industry*, 19.

32. *Butte Bulletin*, July 5, July 7, July 8, 1919.

33. State of Montana, *Fourth Biennial Report of the Department of Labor and Industry*, 17-19; *Butte Bulletin*, July 25, August 5, August 12, August 13, August 14, August 20, October 4, October 8, October 15, 1919; *Solidarity*, August 16, August 23, September 13, September 27, 1919.

34. Nick Verbanec to Joe Oates, March 22, 1920, Mike C. Sullivan to Oates, April 16, 1920, OG 45396, BI Records.

35. Report of Special Agent J. L. Webb for April 20, 1920, OG 291596, BI Records; *Butte Bulletin*, April 19, 1920; *Solidarity*, April 24, 1920; State of Montana, *Fourth Biennial Report of the Department of Labor and Industry*, 40-41.

36. Stewart to Liggett, telegram, April 19, 1920, Liggett to Stewart, telegram, April 20, 1920, Stewart to Liggett, telegram, April 20, 1920, Liggett to Stewart, telegram, April 20, 1920, Stewart to General Morrison, telegram, April 21, 1920, Morrison to Stewart, telegram, April 21, 1920, John Gillie to Stewart, telegram, April 21, 1920, Stewart to Gillie, telegram, April 21, 1920, MC 35, Box 24, Montana Governors' Papers, MHSA.

37. Roy Alley to Stewart, April 7, 1919, MC 35, Box 18, Montana Governors' Papers, MHSA.

38. *Butte Bulletin*, April 20, 1920.

39. *Butte Bulletin*, April 20, April 21, 1920; *Solidarity*, May 1, 1920; Chaplin, "The Picket Line of Blood," 10; State of Montana, *Fourth Biennial Report of the Department of Labor and Industry*, 42.

40. *Butte Bulletin*, April 22, April 23, April 24, April 26, 1920; *Solidarity*, May 1, 1920; State of Montana, *Fourth Biennial Report of the Department of Labor and Industry*, 42; Chaplin, "The Picket Line of Blood," 11-12.

41. State of Montana, *Fourth Biennial Report of the Department of Labor and Industry*, 42; *Butte Bulletin*, April 29, April 30, May 1, May 4, May 5, May 7, May 8, May 11, May 12, May 13, 1920.

42. Report of Special Agent Wehh for April 22, 1920, OG 291596, BI Records.

43. Bolling's testimony is quoted in the *Butte Bulletin*, January 22, 1922.

44. State of Montana, *Fourth Biennial Report of the Department of Labor and Industry*, 42; *Butte Bulletin*, April 23, April 24, May 15, 1920; Pete Petaja to Joe Oates, June 15, 1920, OG 45396, BI Records.

45. *Butte Bulletin*, May 13, 1920; *Solidarity*, May 22, 1920.

46. *Butte Bulletin*, May 11, May 13, 1920; *Solidarity*, May 29, 1920; State of Montana, *Fourth Biennial Report of the Department of Labor and Industry*, 44.

47. Report of Special Agent W. D. Bolling for May 12-13, 1920, BI Records.

48. Report of Special Agent Thomas F. Price for May 12, 1920, report of Special Agent F. W. Kelly for July 8, 1920, OG 381694, BI Records.

49. Reports of Special Agent Kelly for September 11, October 19, 1920, OG 291596, BI Records.

50. Report of Special Agent Kelly for October 25, 1920, OG 381694, report of Special Agent Kelly for November 4, 1920, BS 195397, BI Records.

51. *Butte Bulletin*, January 22, 1922.

52. Needless to say, the opponents of the IWW often stressed its real or imagined "foreign" character as justification for the sometimes harsh treatment of Butte's Wobblies. See Thomas Chope, Commissioner of Labor for the ACM Company, to Felix Frankfurter, September 18, 1918, DL 20-473, Governor Stewart to Colonel W. E. Ellis, December 18, 1917, DJ 195391-1, Lieutenant Will Germer to Captain J. C. Fisher, February 17, 1919, G-2 10110-903, Glasser File.

53. See Robert L. Morlan, *Political Prairie Fire: The Nonpartisan League, 1915-1922* (Minneapolis: University of Minnesota Press, 1955).

54. *Butte Bulletin*, August 20, 1918.

Chapter 12: *The Nonpartisan Challenge*

1. *Anaconda Standard*, August 26, August 27, 1918.

2. *Butte Miner*, August 24, 1918.

3. Biographical information on Dunne can be found in the *Butte Bulletin*, March 21, 1919, and Gutfeld, *Montana's Agony*, 81-83. It was Roy Alley who characterized Dunne as "one of the cleverest agitators" in Butte. Alley is quoted in the report of Special Agent Tyman for July 18, 1918, OG 187254, BI Records.

4. *Anaconda Standard*, August 29, 1918; *Butte Bulletin*, August 29, 1919; "Official Election Returns for Silver Bow County for the August 27, 1918 Primary Election," Office of the Secretary of State, Helena. State-wide totals are reported in Waldron and Wilson, *Atlas of Montana Elections*, 70.

5. *Butte Bulletin*, August 21, August 29, November 2, 1918; *Nonpartisan Leader*, August 12, September 30, 1918.

6. Eugene Carroll, President, Silver Bow County Council of Defense, to C. D. Greenfield, Secretary, Montana Council of Defense, August 7, 1918, RS 19, Box 2, Records of the Montana Council of Defense, MHSA; *Report of the Montana Council of Defense, January 28, 1919*, 22; Gutfeld, *Montana's Agony*, 85-86.

7. Gutfeld, *Montana's Agony*, 86-88. *Butte Bulletin*, May 3, 1920; *State v. Smith, State v. Dunne, Montana Reports*, vol. 57 (1920), 563-592. The Council's order insofar as it applied to the publication of the *Butte Bulletin* as a daily was clearly contrary to War Industries Board policy. Responding to an inquiry made by the Montana Council of Defense, Thomas Donnelley of the Pulp and Paper Section of the Board responded: "If a paper has spent a material amount of money in machinery, etc., to publish, before the date of our order of August fifth, papers are allowed to publish." Because the *Bulletin* had advertised and had planned to publish a daily for months, the August 5 order did not apply. Donnelley to Greenfield, September 10, 1918, RS 19, Box 5, Records of the Montana Council of Defense, MHSA. As to the legality of Council orders that had been challenged by the *Butte Bulletin*, it is important to note that Montana Attorney General Sam Ford told the Montana Council of Defense on November 25, 1918, that he had only given a verbal opinion concerning the legality of the Council and that he had not consulted the legal authorities. Ford to the Montana Council of Defense, November 25, 1918, RS 76, Box 17, Records of the Attorney General, MHSA.

8. *Butte Bulletin*, October 25, 1918.

9. *Butte Bulletin*, October 24, 1918.

10. "Official Election Returns from Silver Bow County for the November 5, 1918 General Election," Office of the Secretary of State, Helena. So strong was Rankin's support in working-class neighborhoods in Butte and in the county that she beat Walsh in Dublin Gulch, previously the most solid Democratic precinct in the county.

11. *Butte Bulletin*, November 6, November 7, November 9, 1918; *Nonpartisan Leader*, November 25, 1918; *Montana Nonpartisan*, November 30, 1918. The state senators elected were J. W. Anderson (R-Richland) and J. F. McKay (D-Sanders); the new representatives were James Griffin (R-Blaine), E. M. Naylor (R-Dawson), J. H. McAfee (R-Flathead), H. S. Buell and M. W. Penwell (R-Gallatin), Jasper Haaland (R-Hill), James Hunter (R-Musselshell), Dudley Jones (R-Phillips), J. Earl Jones (R-Richland), J. S. Nyquist (R-Sheridan), Roland C. Arnold and D. M. Sketman (D-Valley), and E. T. Eaton (R-Yellowstone).

12. *Butte Bulletin*, January 16, 1919.

13. Quoted in Kurt Wetzel, "The Defeat of Bill Dunne: An Episode in the Montana Red Scare," *Pacific Northwest Quarterly* 64 (January 1973): 14-15.

14. Ibid., 14; *Montana Nonpartisan*, February 22, 1919; *House Journal of the Sixteenth Legislative Assembly: January 6, 1919 – March 6, 1919*, 213, 389-390, 440, 453, 459, 504, 539, 605, 654-655.

15. *Butte Bulletin*, February 18, February 21, February 25, March 7, 1919.

16. *Butte Bulletin*, March 7, March 10, March 13, 1919.

17. *Butte Bulletin*, March 13, March 21, 1919.

18. *Butte Bulletin*, March 13, 1919. Dunne dropped the "e" from his last name while living in Butte.

19. *Butte Bulletin*, March 21, 1919.

20. *Anaconda Standard*, March 5, March 17, March 19, March 20, March 21, March 23, 1919; *Butte Miner*, March 24, 1919.

21. *Anaconda Standard*, March 22, March 27, 1919; *Butte Bulletin*, March 25, March 26, 1919.

22. *Anaconda Standard*, March 27, 1919; *Butte Bulletin*, March 27, 1919.

23. *Anaconda Standard*, March 27, March 30, April 3, April 4, 1919; *Butte Bulletin*, March 28, March 29, April 2, April 3, 1919.

24. *Butte Miner*, March 26, 1919.

25. *Butte Bulletin*, March 25, 1919; *Anaconda Standard*, March 25, 1919.

26. *Anaconda Standard*, March 30, April 4, April 5, April 6, 1919; *Butte Bulletin*, March 27, April 2, April 4, 1919; *State ex. rel. Dunn v. Treacy, State ex. rel. McCarthy v. Treacy, Montana Reports*, vol. 55 (1919), 620.

27. *Butte Bulletin*, April 7, 1919; *Butte Miner*, April 8, 1919.

28. *Butte Miner*, April 8, 1919; *Butte Bulletin*, April 8, April 9, 1919.

Chapter 13: *The Final Battle*

1. *Montana Nonpartisan*, February 8, 1919; *Anaconda Standard*, March 3, 1919; *House Journal of the Sixteenth Legislative Assembly, January 6, 1919-March 6, 1919*, 648; *Senate Journal of the Sixteenth Legislative Assembly, January 6, 1919-March 6, 1919*, 328; Waldron and Wilson, *Atlas of Montana Elections*, 78. Opponents' attempts to modify or abolish the direct primary in response to the political threat posed by the Nonpartisan League were not unique to Montana. See Morlan, *Political Prairie Fire*, 239.

2. *Montana Nonpartisan*, April 19, June 7, June 21, July 12, 1919; *Butte Bulletin*, May 19, June 14, July 4, 1919.

3. *Montana Nonpartisan*, August 2, 1919; *Butte Bulletin*, July 9, July 15, 1919; Waldron and Wilson, *Atlas of Montana Elections*, 78.

4. *House and Senate Journals of the Extraordinary Session of the Sixteenth Legislative Assembly, July 29, 1919-August 11, 1919*, 32; Waldron and Wilson, *Atlas of Montana Elections*, 78; *Montana Nonpartisan*, August 16, 1919; *Butte Bulletin*, August 8, August 11, 1919. Romney is quoted in the *Butte Bulletin*, August 18, 1919.

5. Waldron and Wilson, *Atlas of Montana Elections*, 78; *State ex. rel. Goodman v. Stewart, Montana Reports*, vol. 57 (1920), 166, 171, 174; *Butte Bulletin*, September 3, 1919, January 8, January 30, 1920.

6. *Butte Bulletin*, July 28, August 28, December 31, 1919.

7. *Butte Bulletin*, January 1, 1920.

8. *Montana Nonpartisan*, May 31, September 13, September 27, 1919; *Butte Bulletin*, October 18, 1919.

9. *Butte Bulletin*, February 25, February 27, 1920.

10. *Butte Bulletin*, February 26, February 27, 1920; *Great Falls Tribune*, February 23, February 27, 1920.

11. *Butte Bulletin*, March 10, June 11, July 2, 1920.

12. *Butte Bulletin*, June 18, June 22, June 23, June 24, July 30, 1920; *Great Falls Tribune*, June 23, June 24, 1920; Wheeler, *Yankee from the West*, 171-173.

13. *Butte Bulletin*, August 17, 1920.

14. *Butte Bulletin*, July 31, 1920.

15. Wheeler, *Yankee from the West*, 173-175.

16. Ibid., 176-177.

17. *Butte Bulletin*, July 3, July 13, July 14, July 27, 1920; *Anaconda Standard*, July 3, 1919; *Helena Independent*, July 3, July 27, 1920; *State ex. rel. Ely v. Stewart, Montana Reports*, vol. 58 (1920), 701.

18. *Butte Bulletin*, July 30, August 13, 1920.

19. *Anaconda Standard*, August 15, August 20, August 21, August 22, August 23, 1920; *Butte Miner*, August 20, August 21, August 23, 1920.

20. Bureau of Investigation surveillance of farmer-labor political activity (as well as BI fears of being spied on by the radicals) can be found in OG 87254, OG 291596, OG 381694, and OG 389857, BI Records.

21. *Butte Bulletin*, August 24, 1920; Report of Special Agent Kelly for August 30, 1920, OG 291596, BI Records; *Anaconda Standard*, August 24, 1920.

22. *Butte Bulletin*, August 24, August 25, August 26, 1920; *Anaconda Standard*, August 25, August 26, 1920; Waldron and Wilson, *Atlas of Montana Elections*, 76; report of Special Agent Costello for October 5, 1920, OG 291596, BI Records.

23. *Nonpartisan Leader*, September 6, September 20, 1920; *Butte Bulletin*, August 25, 1920.

24. Gutfeld, *Montana's Agony*, 102-115, 131-134; Jules A. Karlin, *Governor Versus the Anaconda, 1917-1934*, vol. 2 of *Joseph M. Dixon of Montana* (Missoula: University of Montana Publications in History, 1974), 45-61; Malone and Roeder, *Montana*, 219-220.

25. *Butte Miner*, October 27, 1920; Karlin, *Governor Versus the Anaconda*, 47-57; Wheeler, *Yankee from the West*, 179-180.

26. Karlin, *Governor Versus the Anaconda*, 52-53; *Butte Bulletin*, September 12, September 24, October 3, October 6, 1920.

27. Toole, *Twentieth-Century Montana*, 247; Wheeler, *Yankee from the West*, 182.

28. *Anaconda Standard*, October 27, October 28, 1920. Wheeler is quoted in the *Butte Miner*, October 26, 1920.

29. Special Agent Kelly to J. Edgar Hoover, September 23, 1920, OG 291596, report of Special Agent Costello for October 1, 1920, OG 187254, BI Records.

30. *Butte Miner*, October 21, October 29, 1920; Wheeler, *Yankee from the West*, 182-183.

31. Malone and Roeder, *Montana*, 217-218; *Engineering and Mining Journal*, December 11, 1920, January 22, 1921.

32. Waldron and Wilson, *Atlas of Montana Elections*, 81-82; *Nonpartisan Leader*, November 29, 1920.

33. *Anaconda Standard*, November 3, 1920; *Butte Bulletin*, November 4, 1920; report of Special Agent Kelly for November 8, 1920, OG 291596, BI Records.

34. Waldron and Wilson, *Atlas of Montana Elections*, 83-84.

35. *Butte Bulletin*, November 4, 1920.

Afterword

1. Wetzel, "The Defeat of Bill Dunne," 20.

2. Wheeler, *Yankee from the West*, 188-196; Waldron and Wilson, *Atlas of Montana Elections*, 90, 92.

3. Malone and Roeder, *Montana*, 221-222; Karlin, *Governor Versus the Anaconda*, 62-83, 142-208.

4. The Montana Farmer-Labor Party was founded in convention in the city of Great Falls in October 1923. Present at the convention were Dunne, Charles Gildea, and John Driscoll of Butte. Shortly thereafter, a local branch of the party was founded in Butte. *Butte Bulletin*, October 26, November 9, 1923; (Plentywood, Montana) *Producers News*, October 5, October 26, 1923. Election returns for November 1924 were reported in the *Butte Miner*, November 7, 1924, and Waldron and Wilson, *Atlas of Montana Elections*, 198.

5. This is not to say that the Farmer-Labor Party was without significance in Montana. In Sheridan County in the northeast corner of the state, former Socialists and Nonpartisans organized a Farmer-Labor Party political machine whose newspaper was the *Producers News*, edited by Charles "Red Flag" Taylor. Taylor was also elected a state senator on the Farmer-Labor ticket. Eventually, both the party and the paper became part of the abortive effort by the Communist Party to organize American farmers. See Lowell K. Dyson, *Red Harvest: The Communist Party and American Farmers* (Lincoln: University of Nebraska Press, 1982), Chapter 1.

6. *Butte Bulletin*, March 24, 1919.

7. Adam Przworski and John Sprague, *Paper Stones: A History of Electoral Socialism* (Chicago: University of Chicago Press, 1986), 1.

8. Ibid., 30-40.

9. *Historical Statistics of the United States*, Part 1 (Washington, D.C.: Government Printing Office, 1975), 137-140.

10. For a summary of explanations, see Leonard B. Rosenberg, "The 'Failure' of the Socialist Party in America," *Review of Politics* 31 (July 1969): 329-352. See also Irving Howe, *Socialism and America* (New York: Harcourt, Brace Jovanovich, 1985), 105-144.

11. Selig Perlman, *A Theory of the Labor Movement* (New York: Macmillan, 1928), 167-168.

12. Przworski and Sprague, *Paper Stones*, 35-36. Dieter Nohlan, "Changes and Choices in Electoral Systems," in *Choosing an Electoral System: Issues and Alternatives*, ed. Arend Lijphart and Bernard Grofman (New York: Praeger, 1984), 219-221.

13. Thomas Mackie and Richard Rose, eds., *The International Almanac of Electoral History* (New York: The Free Press, 1974), 341-353.

14. Erik W. Austin, ed., *Political Facts of the United States Since 1789* (New York: Columbia University Press, 1986), 244-257; *Congressional Quarterly's Guide to U.S. Elections*, 2d ed. (Washington, D.C.: Congressional Quarterly, 1985), 873-879.

15. *Socialist Campaign Book—1912* (Chicago: The Socialist Party, 1912), 5; Hillquit, *Socialism in Theory and Practice*, 274-277.

16. Leon Epstein, *Political Parties in Western Democracies* (New York: Praeger, 1967), 146.

17. Dick, *Labor and Socialism in America*, 120-133; Philip Foner, *The AFL in the Progressive Era, 1910-1913*, vol. 5 of *History of the Labor Movement in the United States* (New York: International Publishers, 1979), chapters 4 and 5.

18. John D. Stephens, *The Transition from Capitalism to Socialism* (London: Macmillan, 1979), 103-128.

19. See Benjamin Page, *Who Gets What from Government* (Berkeley: University of California Press, 1983); Jonathan Turner and Charles Starnes, *Inequality: Privilege and Poverty in America* (Pacific Palisades, California: Goodyear Publishing Company, 1976); Lars Ostberg, *Economic Inequality in the United States* (Armonk, New York: M. E. Sharpe, 1984).

20. Bingham Powell, "American Voter Turnout in Comparative Perspective," *American Political Science Review* 80 (March 1986): 35.

21. Walter Dean Burnham, *The Current Crisis in American Politics* (New York: Oxford University Press, 1982), 123-125.

22. A comprehensive and careful examination of participation and organizational mobilization is developed in Sidney Verba and Norman Nie, *Participation in America: Political Democracy and Social Equality* (New York: Harper and Row, 1972), 334-341; Sidney Verba et al., *Participation and Political Equality: A Seven Nation Comparison* (Cambridge, England: Cambridge University Press, 1978), 307-309.

23. Paul Kleppner, *Who Voted? The Dynamics of Electoral Turnout, 1870-1980* (New York: Praeger, 1982), 149.

Bibliography

An important source of information on the history of the working-class insurgency in Butte was the labor and radical newspapers of the period. The *Butte Bystander* (1892-1897) helps document the insurgency as it emerged under the Populist banner; Butte's *Labor World* (1902-1903) and the *Montana News* (1904-1909) tell of the early years of the Socialist Party of Montana in the mining city. The years of Socialist government in Butte are detailed in the weekly *Montana Socialist* (1913-1917) and in the few surviving copies of the *Butte Socialist* (1910-1915), Local Butte's campaign newspaper. The Nonpartisan period finds expression in the surviving numbers of the *Montana Nonpartisan* (1918-1919) and in the *Butte Bulletin* (1918-1921). Information contained in the labor and radical press was supplemented by a critical reading of Butte's daily press, particularly the *Anaconda Standard* and the *Butte Miner*. Of the two, the *Standard* was the more creditable, especially during the Socialist Party's formative years (1900-1903).

Research into the relevant documentary records was both rewarding and frustrating. The Socialist Party of Montana Papers provide only a partial record of the party's role in state and local politics. There is almost nothing in the papers before 1910, and there is little of substance about Butte after 1911. The party's papers are primarily useful in documenting the successful reorganization of the party under Louis Duncan and Frank Mabie and in indicating Socialist thinking when the party achieved political victory in Butte. There are no surviving records of the Montana branch of the Nonpartisan League, and the National Nonpartisan League Papers at the University of Minnesota contain virtually no correspondence from or about Montana.

More rewarding was the rich lode of government documents housed in the library of the Montana Historical Society in Helena. Especially important are the papers of Governor Samuel V. Stewart (1912-1920) that deal with the destruction of the Butte Miners' Union and the 1917-1920 miners' strikes. The Jeannette Rankin papers reveal the depth of emotion and the issues that precipitated the 1917 miners' strike.

The National Archives in Washington, D.C., contain important information about labor unrest in Butte during 1917-1920. Especially important is the Abraham Glasser File in the Department of Justice records and the investigative records of the Bureau of Investiga-

177

tion. The BI records for Butte reveal a consistent pattern of the government's surveillance of political dissidents and radical labor unionists and open a window on the local IWW during 1918-1920.

The social terrain in which the insurgents and their opponents lived was made evident by the statistics and testimony collected by federal and state agencies. The world of work in the Butte mines is detailed in the reports of the Montana Inspector of Mines and in later investigations and reports of the U.S. Bureau of Mines. Particularly revealing about conditions in the mines and also ACM Company employment practices is the testimony offered by the insurgents and their opponents before the U.S. Commission on Industrial Relations in early August 1914.

The evidence concerning the quality of life in Butte is relatively thin, but a State Board of Health study entitled "Report on the Sanitary Conditions in the Mines and Community, Silver Bow County, December, 1908-April, 1912" described the difficult conditions in which many of Butte's workers and their families found themselves when the Socialists assumed power.

The people and their settlement patterns emerge in an analysis of Butte's voter registration records, in the recollections of Jacob Ostberg, *Sketches of Old Butte* (1972), and in Richard O'Malley's autobiographical novel, *Mile High, Mile Deep* (1971). Transcripts of the 1910 census enumeration were closed to the public under federal law until April 1982. Information in the census records could expand our view of Butte and Silver Bow County, but they became available too late for this study.

Examination of the primary sources was complemented and inspired by several published works. The Populist period in Montana was nicely sketched by Thomas A. Clinch in *Urban Populism and Free Silver in Montana* (1970). The war of the copper kings, which preceded and followed the Populist movement, has been one of the most written about episodes in Montana's history, with Michael Malone's *The Battle for Butte* (1981) being the definitive treatment.

There are no published accounts of the formative years of labor unionism in Montana, nor are there any published works on the Socialist Party and the Nonpartisan League in the state. Readers interested in the general development of labor unionism among miners should consult Richard Lingenfelter's *The Hardrock Miners* (1974) and Mark Wyman's *Hard Rock Epic* (1979). There are also several general and specialized works on the Socialist Party in America. James Weinstein's *The Decline of Socialism in America, 1912-1925* (1967) is an excellent overview of the party's place in American political history. Much less has been written about the Nonpartisan League. The only recent treatment is the now somewhat dated *Political Prairie Fire* (1955) by Robert Morlan.

Finally, a great deal has been written recently about the Industrial Workers of the World. By far the best treatments of the IWW are Melvyn Dubofsky's *We Shall Be All* (1969) and Joyce Kornbluh's *Rebel Voices: An IWW Anthology* (1964).

Archival Collections

Butte-Silver Bow Public Archives, Butte, Montana: Butte City Council Records; *Great Register of Butte City, 1913*

California State University-Fullerton, Special Collections: Socialist Party of America Papers (microfilm copy of collection held at the Perkins Library, Duke University, Durham, North Carolina)

Library of Congress, Washington, D.C.: Papers of Senator Thomas J. Walsh

Montana Historical Society Archives, Helena: Montana Adjutant General's Records, 1912-1915, RS 86; Montana Attorney General's Office Records, ca. 1890-1910, RS 76; Montana Council of Defense Records, 1916-1921, RS 19; Montana Governors' Papers, MC 35; Montana Mine Inspectors' Reports, MC 35; Jeannette Rankin Papers, MC 147; Socialist Party of Montana Records, 1899-1950, Microfilm Collection 425

Montana State College of Mineral Science and Technology, Butte: Membership Record of Butte Local Number 1, Socialist Party of Montana

National Archives, Washington, D.C.: U.S. Bureau of Investigation Investigative Records, 1908-1922, RG 65; Abraham Glasser File, RG 60; Records of the Department of Justice (Microfilm copy held at the Mansfield Library, University of Montana, Missoula)

State of Montana, Secretary of State Archives, Helena: Official Election Returns for Silver Bow County

University of Colorado, Boulder, Western History Collections: Western Federation of Miners—International Union of Mine, Mill and Smelter Workers Papers

Wisconsin State Historical Society Library, Madison: Papers of the U.S. Commission on Industrial Relations

Government Documents and Publications

Butte, Montana. *Revised Ordinances of the City of Butte, 1914.*

State of Montana. *Biennial Reports of the State Board of Health of Montana,* 1902-1904, 1909-1910, 1911-1912.

_____. *Biennial Reports of the Bureau of Agriculture, Labor and Industry,* 1895-1896, 1899-1900, 1907-1908, 1909-1910.

_____. *Biennial Reports of the Department of Labor and Industry,* 1913-1914, 1915-1916, 1917-1918, 1919-1920.

_____. *House Journal of the Extraordinary Session of the Sixteenth Legislative Assembly, July 29, 1919-August 11, 1919.*

_____. *Senate Journal of the Extraordinary Session of the Sixteenth Legislative Assembly, July 29, 1919-August 11, 1919.*

_____. *House Journal of the Second Extraordinary Session of the Eighth Legislative Assembly, December 1-December 11, 1903.*

_____. *House Journal of the Sixteenth Legislative Assembly, January 6-March 6, 1919.*

_____. *House Journal of the Twelfth Session of the Legislative Assembly, January 2-March 2, 1911.*

_____. *Annual Reports of the State Inspector of Mines,* 1900, 1902.

_____. *Biennial Reports of the State Inspector of Mines,* 1905-1906, 1907-1908, 1909-1910.

_____. *Message of Governor Joseph K. Toole to the Eighth Legislative Assembly, January 5, 1903.*

_____. *Senate Journal of the Sixteenth Legislative Assembly, January 6, 1919-March 6, 1919.*

_____. *Session Laws of the Twelfth Montana Legislative Assembly, January 2, 1911-March 2, 1911.*

U.S. Bureau of Labor Statistics. *Bulletin* 157 (1915).

U.S. Bureau of Mines. *Bulletin* 69 (1913); 75 (1915); 115 (1916); 257 (1925).

_____. Technical Papers 40 (1913); 48 (1913); 61 (1913); 94 (1914); 129 (1916); 168 (1917); 202 (1918); 224 (1919); 229 (1920); 260 (1921).

U.S. Bureau of the Census. *11th Census of the United States (1890),* Vol. 1: *Population.*

_____. *12th Census of the United State (1900),* Vols. 1 and 2: *Population.*

U.S. Department of Commerce, Bureau of the Census, *Thirteenth Census of the United States, Vol. I: Population, 1910; Vol. II: Population; Vol. IV: Population; Vol. XI: Mines and Quarries.*

_____. *14th Census of the United States,* Vol. 2: *Population.*

_____. *Historical Statistics of the United States, Part 1* (1975).

U.S. Federal Trade Commission. *Cost Reports of the U.S. Federal Trade Commission: Copper* (1919).

U.S. Government, *Statutes at Large, April 1917-March 1919* (1919).

U.S. Immigration Commission. *Immigrants in Industry, Part 17: Copper Mining and Smelting* (1911).

U.S. Senate, Commission on Industrial Relations. "Mining Conditions and Industrial Relations at Butte, Mont.," *Final Report and Testimony,* 64th Cong., 1st sess., 1916, S. Doc. 415 (Serial 6932), 3681-4095.

_____. Commission on Industrial Relations. "Labor and the Law." *Final Report and Testimony,* 64th Cong., 1st sess., 1916, S. Doc. 415 (Serial 6939), 10451-10928.

Newspapers and Periodicals

American Labor Union Journal (Butte)
American Socialist (Chicago)
Anaconda Labor-Socialist
Anaconda Standard
Bozeman Daily Chronicle
Butte American
Butte Daily Bulletin
Butte Bystander
Butte Daily Post
Butte Evening News
Butte Mine Workers' Union Bulletin
Butte Miner
Butte Socialist
Butte Weekly Bulletin
Carbon County Gazette (Red Lodge)
Daily Inter Mountain (Butte)
Daily Missoulian
Great Falls Tribune
Helena Independent
Industrial Union Bulletin (Chicago)
Industrial Worker (Spokane)
Judith Basin News (Lewistown)
Labor Review (Butte)
Labor World (Butte)
Livingston Post
Milwaukee Leader
Miners' and Electrical Workers' Joint Strike Bulletin (Butte)
Miners Magazine (Denver)
Montana Catholic (Butte)
Montana Daily Record (Helena)
Montana News (Helena)
Montana Nonpartisan (Great Falls)
Montana Socialist (Butte)
Nonpartisan Leader (Fargo, North Dakota)
Party Builder (Chicago)
Producers News (Plentywood, Montana)
Republican Picket (Red Lodge, Montana)
Reveille (Butte)
Red Lodge Picket
Socialist Party Monthly Bulletin (Chicago)
Socialist Party Official Bulletin (Chicago)
Solidarity (Chicago)
Työmies (Hancock, Michigan)
Western News (Hamilton, Montana)

Books and Pamphlets

Atherton, Gertrude. *Perch of the Devil*. New York: Frederick A. Stokes Company, 1914.

Austin, Erik W., ed. *Political Facts of the United States Since 1789*. New York: Columbia University Press, 1986.

Bercuson, David J. *Fools and Wise Men: The Rise and Fall of the One Big Union*. Toronto: McGraw-Hill-Ryerson, 1978.

Brissenden, Paul F. *The I.W.W.: A Study of American Syndicalism*. New York: Columbia University Press, 1920.

Brown, Ronald C. *Hard-Rock Miners: The Intermountain West, 1860-1920*. College Station: Texas A & M University Press, 1979.

Buhle, Mari Jo. *Women and American Socialism, 1870-1920*. Urbana: University of Illinois Press, 1981.

Burnham, Walter Dean. *The Current Crisis in American Politics*. New York: Oxford University Press, 1982.

Butte: Metropolis of Montana. Butte: Chamber of Commerce, Merchants Association, and Rotary Club of Butte, 1915.

Clinch, Thomas A. *Urban Populism and Free Silver in Montana*. Missoula: University of Montana Press, 1970.

Conlin, Joseph R. *Big Bill Haywood and the Radical Union Movement*. Syracuse: Syracuse University Press, 1969.

Connelly, Christopher. *The Devil Learns to Vote*. New York: Civici-Friede, 1938.

Critchlow, Donald T., ed. *Socialism in the Heartland: The Midwestern Experience, 1900-1925*. South Bend, Indiana: University of Notre Dame Press, 1986.

Dick, William M. *Labor and Socialism in America: The Gompers Era*. Port Washington, New York: Kennikat Press, 1972.

Dubofsky, Melvyn. *We Shall Be All: A History of the Industrial Workers of the World*. Chicago: Quadrangle Books, 1969.

Draper, Theodore. *The Roots of American Communism*. New York: Viking Press, 1957.

Dyson, Lowell K. *Red Harvest: The Communist Party and American Farmers*. Lincoln: University of Nebraska Press, 1982.

Epstein, Lem. *Political Parties in Western Democracies*. New York: Praeger, 1967.

Fine, Nathan. *Labor and Farmer Parties in the United States, 1828-1928*. 1928; reprint, New York: Russell and Russell, 1961.

Foner, Philip. *From the Founding of the American Federation of Labor to the Emergence of American Imperialism*. Vol. 2 of *History of the Labor Movement in the United States*. New York: International Publishers, 1955.

_____. *The Policies and Practices of the A.F. of L., 1900-1909*. Vol. 3 of *History of the Labor Movement in the United States*. New York: International Publishers, 1964.

_____. *The Industrial Workers of the World, 1905-1917*. Vol. 4 of *History of the Labor Movement in the United States*. New York: International Publishers, 1965

_____. *The AFL in the Progressive Era, 1910-1913*. Vol. 5 of *History of the Labor Movement in the United States*. New York: International Publishers, 1979.

Glasscock, C. B. *The War of the Copper Kings: Builders of Butte and Wolves of Wall Street*. New York: Bobbs-Merrill, 1935.

Goodwyn, Lawrence. *Democratic Promise: The Populist Movement in America*. New York: Oxford University Press, 1976.

Guide to U.S. Elections. 2d ed. Washington, D.C.: Congressional Quarterly, 1985.

Gutfeld, Arnon. *Montana's Agony: Years of War and Hysteria, 1917-1920*. Gainesville: University of Florida Social Science Monographs, 1979.

Haywood, William D. and Frank Bohn. *Industrial Socialism*. Chicago: Charles H. Kerr, 1911.

Heinze, F. A. *The Political Situation in Montana*. Butte: n. p., 1902.

Herfindahl, Orris C. *Copper Costs and Prices, 1870-1957*. Baltimore: Johns Hopkins University Press, 1959.

Hillquit, Morris. *Socialism in Theory and Practice*. New York: Macmillan, 1913.

Holliday, Walt "Rags." *Mining Camp Melodies*. Butte: Gates and Roberts, 1924.

Howard, Joseph Kinsey. *Montana: High, Wide and Handsome*. New Haven, Connecticut: Yale University Press, 1943.

Howe, Irving. *Socialism and America*. New York: Harcourt, Brace Jovanovich, 1985.

Hughan, Jessie Wallace. *American Socialism of the Present Day*. New York: John Lane Company, 1911.

Industrial Workers of the World. *Proceedings of the First Convention of the Industrial Workers of the World*. New York: New York Labor News Publishing Company, 1905.

Irrepressible Butte: The Richest City in the World. Butte: Butte Land and Investment Company, 1912.

Jensen, Vernon H. *Heritage of Conflict: Labor Relations in the Nonferrous Metals Industry Up to 1930*. Ithaca, New York: Cornell University Press, 1950.

Karlin, Jules A. *Governor Versus the Anaconda, 1917-1934*. Vol. 2 of *Joseph M. Dixon of Montana*. Missoula: University of Montana Publications in History, 1974.

Karni, Michael, ed. *For the Common Good: Finnish Immigrants and the Radical Response to Industrial America*. Superior, Wisconsin: The Työmies Society, 1977.

Karson, Marc. *American Labor Unions and Politics, 1900-1920*. Carbondale: Southern Illinois University Press, 1958.

Kipnis, Ira. *The American Socialist Movement, 1897-1912*. 1952; reprint, Westport, Connecticut: Greenwood Press, 1968.

Kleppner, Paul. *Who Voted? The Dynamics of Electoral Turnout, 1870-1980*. New York: Praeger, 1982.

Kolehmaninen, John I. *The Finns in America: A Guide to Localized History*. New York: Teachers College Press, 1968.

Kornbluh, Joyce L., ed. *Rebel Voices: An I.W.W. Anthology*. Ann Arbor: University of Michigan Press, 1964.

Larson, Robert W. *Populism in the Mountain West*. Albuquerque: University of New Mexico Press, 1986.

Laslett, John. *Labor and the Left*. New York: Basic Books, 1970.

————— and Seymour Martin Lipset, eds. *Failure of a Dream: Essays in the History of American Socialism*. Garden City, New York: Anchor Press/Doubleday, 1974.

Leong, Y. S. et al. *Technology, Employment and Output Per Man in Copper Mining*. Philadelphia: Works Projects Administration, 1940.

Lijphart, Arend and Bernard Grofman, eds. *Choosing an Electoral System: Issues and Alternatives*. New York: Praeger, 1984.

Lingenfelter, Richard. *The Hardrock Miners: A History of the Mining Labor Movement in the American West, 1863-1893*. Berkeley: University of California Press, 1974.

Mackie, Thomas and Richard Rose, eds. *The International Almanac of Electoral History*. New York: The Free Press, 1974.

Malone, Michael P. *The Battle for Butte: Mining and Politics on the Northern Frontier, 1864-1906*. Seattle: University of Washington Press, 1981.

————— and Richard B. Roeder. *Montana: A History of Two Centuries*. Seattle: University of Washington Press, 1976.

Marcosson, Isaac. *Anaconda*. New York: Dodd, Mead, and Company, 1957.

Men of Affairs and Representative Institutions in Montana. Butte: Butte Newspaper Writers Association, 1914.

Montana Federation of Labor. *Convention Proceedings*. Butte: Butte Bystander, 1895.

—————. *Convention Proceedings*. Helena: Montana News, 1906.

—————. *Convention Proceedings*. Helena: Thurber Printers, 1908.

Morlan, Robert L. *Political Prairie Fire: The Nonpartisan League, 1915-1922*. 1955; reprint, Westport, Connecticut: Greenwood Press, 1974.

Murphy, Jerre C. *The Comical History of Montana: A Serious History for a Free People*. San Diego: E. L. Scofield, 1912.

Murray, Robert K. *Red Scare: A Study of National Hysteria, 1919-1920*. New York: McGraw-Hill, 1964.

Navin, Thomas R. *Copper Mining and Management*. Tucson: University of Arizona Press, 1978.

Ollila, Douglas J., Jr. *The Emergence of Radical Industrial Unionism in the Finnish Socialist Movement*. Turku, Finland: Institute of General History of the University of Turku, 1975.

O'Malley, Richard K. *Mile High, Mile Deep*. Missoula: Mountain Press Publishing Company, 1971.

Ostberg, Jacob. *Sketches of Old Butte*. Butte: n.p., 1972.

Osterberg, Lars. *Economic Inequality in the United States*. Armonk: M. E. Sharpe, 1984.

Page, Benjamin. *Who Gets What from Government*. Berkeley: University of California Press, 1983.

Perlman, Selig. *A Theory of the Labor Movement*. New York: Macmillan, 1928.

————— and Phillip Taft. *Labor Movements*. Vol. 4 of *History of the Labor Movement in the United States*. New York: Macmillan Company, 1935.

Peterson, Richard F. *The Bonanza Kings: The Social Origins and Business Behavior of the Western Mining Entrepreneurs, 1870-1900*. Lincoln: University of Nebraska Press, 1977.

Presidential Elections Since 1789. Washington, D.C.: Congressional Quarterly, 1975.

Preston, William, Jr. *Aliens and Dissenters: Federal Suppression of Radicals, 1903-1933*. New York: Harper and Row, 1966.

Przworski, Adam and John Sprague. *Paper Stones: A History of Electoral Socialism*. Chicago: University of Chicago Press, 1986.

Quint, Howard. *The Forging of American Socialism: Origins of the Modern Movement*. Indianapolis: Bobbs-Merrill, 1964.

Rosenblum, Gerald. *Immigrant Workers: Their Impact on American Labor Radicalism*. New York: Basic Books, 1973.

Ross, Carl. *The Finn Factor in American Labor, Culture and Society*. New York: Parta Printers, 1977.

Rowe, John. *The Hard-Rock Men: Cornish Immigrants and the North American Mining Frontier*. New York: Barnes and Noble, 1974.

Rowse, A. L. *The Cousin Jacks: The Cornish in America*. New York: Charles Scribner's Sons, 1969.

Sanders, Helen. *A History of Montana*. 3 vols. Chicago: Lewis Publishing Company, 1913.

Schlesinger, Arthur M., Jr., ed. *Writings and Speeches of Eugene V. Debs*. New York: Hermitage Press, 1948.

Shannon, David. *The Socialist Party of America: A History*. Chicago: Quadrangle Books, 1967.

Socialist Campaign Book: City Election, April 1, 1912. Butte: Socialist State Central Committee, 1912.

Socialist Campaign Book – 1912. Chicago: The Socialist Party, 1912.

Stave, Bruce M., ed. *Socialism and the Cities*. Port Washington, New York: Kennikat Press, 1975.

Stephens, John D. *The Transition from Capitalism to Socialism*. London: Macmillan, 1979.

Thompson, Fred. *The IWW: Its First Fifty Years*. Chicago: Industrial Workers of the World, 1955.

Tompkins, George. *The Truth About Butte*. Butte: n.p., 1917.

Toole, K. Ross. *Twentieth-Century Montana: A State of Extremes*. Norman: University of Oklahoma Press, 1972.

Turner, Jonathan and Charles Starnes. *Inequality: Privilege and Poverty in America*. Pacific Palisades, California: Goodyear Publishing Company, 1976.

Verba, Sidney and Norman Nie. *Participation in America: Political Democracy and Social Equality*. New York: Harper and Row, 1972.

Verba, Sidney et al. *Participation and Political Equality: A Seven Nation Comparison*. Cambridge, England: Cambridge University Press, 1978.

Waldron, Ellis. *An Atlas of Montana Elections Since 1864*. Missoula: Montana State University Press, 1958.

_____ and Paul Wilson. *Atlas of Montana Elections, 1889-1976*. Missoula: University of Montana Publications in History, 1978.

Walling, William English. *The Socialism of To-Day*. New York: Henry Holt and Company, 1916.

Weinstein, James. *The Decline of Socialism in America, 1912-1925*. New York: Vintage Books, 1967.

Western Federation of Miners. Convention Proceedings. Denver, 1903, 1905, 1906, 1907, 1908, 1909, 1910, 1911, 1912, 1913-1914.

Wheeler, Burton K. *Yankee from the West*. Garden City, New York: Doubleday, 1962.

Works Projects Administration Writers' Project. *Copper Camp: Stories of the World's Greatest Mining Camp*. New York: Hastings House, 1943.

Wyman, Mark. *Hard Rock Epic: Western Miners and the Industrial Revolution, 1860-1910*. Berkeley: University of California Press, 1979.

Articles

"An Appeal to Stupid Prejudice." *International Socialist Review* 12 (June 1912): 874-875.

Baker, Ray Stannard. "Butte City, Greatest of the Copper Camps." *Century Magazine* 65 (April 1903): 870-879.

Berger, Victor L. "What Is the Matter with Milwaukee?" *Independent* 68 (April 21, 1910): 840-843.

Bohn, Frank. "Butte." *International Socialist Review* 13 (August 1912): 123-128.

_____. "Butte Number One." *The Masses* 5 (August 1914): 9-11.

_____. "Is the I.W.W. to Grow?" *International Socialist Review* 12 (July 1911): 42-44.

_____. "Some Definitions." *International Socialist Review* 12 (May 1912): 747-749.

_____. "The Butte Socialists." *International Socialist Review* 13 (September 1912): 263-264.

_____. "The Socialist Party and the Government of Cities." *International Socialist Review* 12 (November 1911): 275-278.

Booth, Douglas E. "Municipal Socialism and City Government Reform: The Milwaukee Experience, 1910-1940." *Journal of Urban History* 12 (November 1985): 51-74.

Brissenden, Paul F. "The Butte Miners and the Rustling Card." *American Economic Review* 10 (December 1920): 755-775.

Brown, Ira Cross. "Socialism in California Municipalities." *National Municipal Review* 1 (July 1912): 611-619.

"Butte Heard from Again." *International Socialist Review* 12 (October 1911): 250-251.

"Butte Miners' Union." *International Socialist Review* 12 (February 1912): 520.

"Butte, Montana, At the Dawn of the Twentieth Century." *Western Resources*, no. 134 (June 1901), 1-50.

"Butte Socialist Administration Commendable." *National Municipal Review* 2 (January 1913): 134.

Callender, Harold. "The Truth About the I.W.W." *International Socialist Review* 17 (January 1918): 332-342.

Calvert, Jerry W. "The Rise and Fall of Socialism in a Company Town: Anaconda, Montana, 1902-1905." *Montana the Magazine of Western History* 36 (Autumn 1986): 2-13.

Chadwick, Robert A. "Montana's Silver Mining Era: Great Boom and Great Bust." *Montana the Magazine of Western History* 32 (Spring 1982): 16-31.

Chaplin, Ralph. "The Picket Line of Blood: Another Red Chapter of Labor History From Butte, Mont." *One Big Union Monthly* 2 (June 1920): 9-13.

Conlin, Joseph R. "The I.W.W. and the Socialist Party." *Science and Society* 31 (Winter 1967): 22-36.

_____. "Wobblies and Syndicalists." *Studies on the Left* 6 (March-April 1966): 81-91.

Connolly, Christopher C. "The Labor Fuss in Butte." *Everybody's Magazine* 31 (August 1914): 205-208.

Debs, Eugene V. "Danger Ahead." *International Socialist Review* 11 (January 1911): 413-415.

Duncan, Louis J. "Mayor Duncan of Butte Replies to Catholic Bishop." *International Socialist Review* 13 (October 1912): 321-327.

_____. "Socialist Politics in Butte, Montana." *International Socialist Review* 12 (November 1911): 287-291.

England, George Allen. "Milwaukee's Socialist Government." *Review of Reviews* 42 (October 1910): 445-455.

Fitch, John A. "A Union Paradise at Close Range." *Survey* 23 (August 24, 1914): 538-539.

Foster, William Z. "The Miners' Revolt in Butte." *Mother Earth* 9 (September 1914): 216-220.

Frisch, Paul. "Gibraltar of Unionism: The Development of Butte's Labor Movement, 1878-1900." *The Speculator* 2 (Summer 1985): 12-20.

"From Montana." *International Socialist Review* 13 (February 1913): 623-624.

Gaffield, Chad. "Big Business, the Working-Class, and Socialism in Schenectady, 1911-1916." *Labor History* 19 (Summer 1978): 350-372.

Grabenstein, Henry. "The History of Labor Unions in Butte." *The Labor Review*, no. 1 (1946), 27-28.

Griffin, Henry F. "The Rising Tide of Socialism." *Outlook* 100 (February 24, 1912): 438-448.

Gutfeld, Arnon. "The Murder of Frank Little: Labor Agitation in Butte Montana, 1917." *Labor History* 10 (Spring 1969): 177-192.

_____. "The Speculator Disaster in 1917: Labor Resurgence at Butte, Montana." *Arizona and the West* 11 (Spring 1969): 27-38.

Haggerty, M. P. "Recollections of Socialist Beginnings in Montana." *International Socialist Review* 12 (August 1911): 104-106.

Hand, Wayland D. et al. "Songs of the Butte Miners." *Western Folklore* 9 (January 1950): 1-49.

Haywood, William D. "Butte Better." *International Socialist Review* 15 (February 1915): 473-475.

_____. "Socialism the Hope of the Working Class." *International Socialist Review* 12 (February 1912): 461-471.

_____. "The Battle of Butte." *International Socialist Review* 15 (October 1914): 223-226.

_____. "The Revolt at Butte." *International Socialist Review* 15 (August 1914): 89-95.

Hoxie, Robert F. "The Rising Tide of Socialism: A Study." Journal of Political Economy 19 (October 1911): 609-631.

_____. "The Socialist Party and the November Elections." *Journal of Political Economy* 20 (March 1912): 205-223.

Hyde, Henry M. "Socialists at Work." *Technical World Magazine* 16 (February 1912): 621-629.

Keister, Jack. "Why the Socialists Won in Butte." *International Socialist Review* 11 (June 1911): 731-733.

Lang, William L. "One Path to Populism: Will Kennedy and the People's Party in Montana." *Pacific Northwest Quarterly* 74 (April 1983): 77-87.

Latimer, T. E. "Executive Committee Rule." *International Socialist Review* 15 (February 1915): 481-485.

"Letter from a Butte Miner." *International Socialist Review* 15 (October 1914): 227-228.

"Letter from a Butte Miner." *International Socialist Review* 15 (January 1915): 436, 438.

"Local Butte's Platform Amendment." *International Socialist Review* 13 (May 1912): 777-778.

Marcy, Mary. "A Month of Lawlessness." *International Socialist Review* 18 (September 1917): 154-157.

Maury, H. L. "What's the Matter with Butte, Montana?" *International Socialist Review* 15 (May 1915): 684-685.

Moore, Ed. "What We Can Do by Political Action." *International Socialist Review* 12 (October 1911): 234-235.

Nord, David Paul. "Minneapolis and the Pragmatic Socialism of Thomas Van Lear." *Minnesota History* 45 (Spring 1976): 2-10.

O'Connell, Tom. "Be Your Own Government." *International Socialist Review* 12 (October 1911): 243.

Olson, Frederick I. "The Socialist Party and the Unions in Milwaukee, 1900-1912." *Wisconsin Magazine of History* 44 (Winter 1960-1961): 110-116.

Phipps, Stanley I. "A. S. Embree: Labor Leader and Prisoner of Conscience." *The Speculator* 2 (Summer 1985): 35-41.

Powell, Bingham. "American Voter Turnout in Comparative Perspective." *American Political Science Review* 80 (March 1986): 17-43.

Rhea, M. "The Revolt in Butte." *The New Review* 2 (September 1914): 538-542.

Roeder, Richard. "Crossing the Gender Line: Ella L. Knowles, Montana's First Woman Lawyer." *Montana the Magazine of Western History* 32 (Summer 1982): 64-75.

Rosenberg, Leonard B. "The 'Failure' of the Socialist Party in America." *Review of Politics* 31 (July 1969): 329-352.

Russell, Charles Edward. "Socialism: Just Where It Stands Today." *Hampton's Magazine* 27 (January 1912): 752-762.

Sanders, Helen. "Butte–The Heart of the Copper Country." *Overland Monthly* 48 (November 1906): 367-384.

Shovers, Brian. "The Perils of Working in the Butte Underground: Industrial Fatalities in the Copper Mines, 1880-1920." *Montana the Magazine of Western History* 37 (Spring 1987): 26-39.

"Smashing Us in Butte." *International Socialist Review* 12 (June 1912): 885.

Smith, Clarence. "Miners' Union Day in Butte." *International Socialist Review* 12 (July 1911): 5-6.

"Socialist Municipal Office Holders." *National Municipal Review* 1 (July 1912): 492-500.

"Socialist Victory in Butte." *International Socialist Review* 13 (May 1913): 829.

Stegner, S. Page. "Protest Songs of the Butte Miners." *Western Folklore* 26 (July 1967): 157-167.

Stevens, Errol W. "Labor and Socialism in an Indiana Mill Town, 1905-1921." *Labor History* 12 (November 1985): 353-383.

Sumner, Mary Brown. "The Parting of the Ways in American Socialism." *Survey* 29 (February 1, 1913): 623-630.

"The Lesson of Lima, Ohio." *International Socialist Review* 14 (September 1913): 186.

"The Man Who Was Hung." *International Socialist Review* 18 (September 1917): 135-138.

"The National Socialist Convention of 1912." *International Socialist Review* 12 (June 1912): 806-828.

"The Victory in Butte." *The Coming Nation*, no. 33 (April 29, 1911), 10.

Thurner, Arthur W. "The Western Federation of Miners in Two Copper Camps: The Impact of the Michigan Copper Miners' Strike on Butte's Local No. 1." *Montana the Magazine of Western History* 33 (Spring 1983): 30-45.

Varney, Harold Lord. "Butte in the Hands of the I.W.W." *One Big Union Monthly* 1 (March 1919): 36-37.

_____. "Was Butte a Defeat?" *One Big Union Monthly* 1 (March 1919): 27, 39.

Walker, John T. "Socialism in Dayton, Ohio, 1912-1915: Its Membership, Organization, and Demise." *Labor History* 26 (Summer 1985): 384-404.

Wetzel, Kurt. "The Defeat of Bill Dunne: An Episode in the Montana Red Scare." *Pacific Northwest Quarterly* 64 (January 1973): 12-20.

"What Haywood Says on Political Action." *International Socialist Review* 13 (February 1913): 622-623.

White, W. J. "Our Elected Servants." *International Socialist Review* 13 (June 1913): 868-870.

White, W. Thomas. "Boycott: The Pullman Strike in Montana." *Montana the Magazine of Western History* 29 (Autumn 1979): 2-13.

Williams, David. "The Bureau of Investigation and Its Critics, 1919-1921: The Origins of Federal Political Surveillance." *Journal of American History* 68 (December 1981): 560-579.

Wiprud, Theodore. "Butte, A Troubled Labor Paradise." *Montana the Magazine of Western History* 21 (October 1971): 31-38.

Unpublished Papers

Frisch, Paul A. " 'Gibralter of Unionism': The Development of Butte's Labor Movement, 1878-1900." Paper presented at the conference "Butte: The Urban Frontier," Butte Historical Society, September 24-26, 1982, in Butte.

Judd, Richard W. "Socialist Cities: Explorations into the Grassroots of American Socialism," Ph.D. diss., University of California-Irvine, 1979.

Leeper, Joseph S. "The Changing Urban Landscape of Butte, Montana." Ph.D. diss., University of Oregon, Eugene, 1974.

McGlynn, Terrence. "Louis J. Duncan: Butte's Socialist Mayor." Paper presented at the conference "Butte: The Urban Frontier," Butte Historical Society, September 24-26, 1982, in Butte.

_____. "Socialist Organizers in Montana." Ms., Montana State College of Mineral Science and Technology, Butte, n. d.

Phipps, Stan. "A. S. Embree and the Butte I.W.W." Paper presented at the conference "Butte: The Urban Frontier," Butte Historical Society, September 24-26, 1982, in Butte.

Smith, Norma. "The Rise and Fall of the Butte Miners' Union, 1878-1914." M.A. thesis, Montana State University, Bozeman, 1961.

Thurner, Arthur W. "The Western Federation of Miners in Two Copper Camps: The Impact of the Michigan Copper Miners' Strike on Butte Local No. 1." Ms., DePaul University, Chicago, 1982.

Toole, K. Ross. "A History of the Anaconda Copper Mining Company: A Study of the Relationships Between a State and its People and a Corporation, 1880-1950." Ph.D. diss., University of California-Los Angeles, 1954.

Index

187

About the Author

Jerry W. Calvert is Associate Professor and Head of the Department of Political Science at Montana State University. He has been awarded grants from the American Council of Learned Societies, the Montana Committee for the Humanities, and Montana State University. Professor Calvert has researched and published articles on environmental politics and policy, representative government, and labor history. He is currently an associate editor of the *Western Political Quarterly* and is doing research on the democratic implications of the direct initiative and the influence that political party rules and state laws have in determining the nomination of American presidential candidates.

SPECULATOR

HIGH ORE

COMP'R PLANT

BREWING CO